WordPress Complete

Sixth Edition

A comprehensive guide to WordPress development
from scratch

Karol Król

BIRMINGHAM - MUMBAI

WordPress Complete

Sixth Edition

First published: November 2006

Second edition: June 2009

Third edition: January 2011

Fourth edition: November 2013

Fifth edition: April 2015

Sixth edition: August 2017

Production reference: 2241017

Published by Packt Publishing Ltd.
Livery Place
35 Livery Street
Birmingham
B3 2PB, UK.
ISBN 978-1-78728-570-5

www.packtpub.com

Credits

Author
Karol Król

Copy Editors
Charlotte Carneiro
Sameen Siddiqui

Reviewer
Olivier Pons

Project Coordinator
Sheejal Shah

Commissioning Editor
Amarabha Banarjee

Proofreader
Safis Editing

Acquisition Editor
Nitin Dasan

Indexer
Rekha Nair

Content Development Editor
Jason Pereira

Production Coordinator
Melwyn D'sa

Technical Editors
Prajakta Mhatre
Rutuja Vaze

About the Author

Karol Król is a WordPress developer, PHP programmer, professional blogger, and writer. He has been building expertise in WordPress ever since his early years at the Silesian University of Technology (Poland), where he graduated with a master's degree in computer science. Early in his career, he worked as a freelance website developer for several years. Later on, he decided to shift his interest towards popularizing WordPress as the perfect solution for all web-based projects and devoted his time to growing his writing career.

About the Reviewer

Olivier Pons is a project manager, highly-skilled developer, and teacher, who's been building websites for many years. He's a teacher in France at the IUT (University of Sciences) of Aix-en-Provence, CESI (Centre d'Études Supérieures en Informatique), ISEN (Institut Supérieur de l'Électronique et du Numérique), G4 Marseille, and École d'Ingénieurs des Mines de Gardanne, where he teaches state of the art web techniques such as Django/Python, NodeJS, big data/NoSQL, MVC fundamentals, PHP for experts, WordPress for experts, Symfony, jQuery, Apache, nginx and Apache advanced configuration, Linux basics, and advanced VIM techniques. He has already done some technical reviews, including the Packt books *Learning Ext JS*, *Building Modern JavaScript Applications*, *jQuery Hotshots*, *jQuery Mobile Web Development Essentials*, and *Meteor JS* among others.

In 2011, he left a full-time job as a Delphi developer and PHP expert to concentrate on his own company, HQF Development. He currently runs a number of websites and his own web development blog. He's currently making a Unity mcq mobile application, which works together with a Django website. He sometimes helps CTOs of big companies in making the best choice for their web projects.

www.PacktPub.com

For support files and downloads related to your book, please visit `www.PacktPub.com`. Did you know that Packt offers eBook versions of every book published, with PDF and ePub files available? You can upgrade to the eBook version at `www.PacktPub.com` and as a print book customer, you are entitled to a discount on the eBook copy. Get in touch with us at `service@packtpub.com` for more details.

At `www.PacktPub.com`, you can also read a collection of free technical articles, sign up for a range of free newsletters and receive exclusive discounts and offers on Packt books and eBooks.

`https://www.packtpub.com/mapt`

Get the most in-demand software skills with Mapt. Mapt gives you full access to all Packt books and video courses, as well as industry-leading tools to help you plan your personal development and advance your career.

Why subscribe?

- Fully searchable across every book published by Packt
- Copy and paste, print, and bookmark content
- On demand and accessible via a web browser

Customer Feedback

Thanks for purchasing this Packt book. At Packt, quality is at the heart of our editorial process. To help us improve, please leave us an honest review on this book's Amazon page at https://www.amazon.com/dp/1787285707.

If you'd like to join our team of regular reviewers, you can e-mail us at customerreviews@packtpub.com. We award our regular reviewers with free eBooks and videos in exchange for their valuable feedback. Help us be relentless in improving our products!

Table of Contents

Preface

WordPress Complete, Sixth Edition will take you through the complete process of building a fully-functional WordPress site from scratch. The journey goes all the way from teaching you how to install WordPress to the most advanced topics, such as creating your own themes, writing plugins, and even building non-blog websites. The best part is that you can do all of this without losing your shirt along the way. Moreover, once you get some practice, you will be able to launch new WordPress sites within minutes (not a metaphor, by the way; this is as true as it gets).

This book guides you along the way in a step-by-step manner to explain everything there is to know about WordPress. We'll start by downloading and installing the core of WordPress, where you will learn how to choose the correct settings in order to guarantee a smooth experience for yourself and your visitors. After that, this book will teach you all about content management functionalities for your site, from posts and pages to categories and tags, all the way to links, media, menus, images, galleries, administration, user profiles, and more. Next, you will find out what plugins and themes are and how to use them effectively. Finally, you'll learn how to create your own themes and plugins to enhance the overall functionality of your website. Once you're done with *WordPress Complete, Sixth Edition*, you'll have all the knowledge required to build a professional WordPress site from scratch.

What this book covers

Chapter 1, *Introducing WordPress*, explains what makes WordPress excellent software that can run your website (blog or not). WordPress is packed with world-class features and is so flexible that it can really do anything you want. It has a wealth of online resources. Additionally, it's super easy to use, and you need no special skills or prior experience to use it. Last but not least, it is free!

Chapter 2, *Getting Started with WordPress*, describes how to install WordPress on a remote server, change the basic default settings of your blog, write posts, and comment on those posts. This chapter also shows you how to work with sites hosted on WordPress.com, which is one of the branches of the WordPress world.

Chapter 3, *Creating Blog Content*, teaches everything you need to know in order to add content to your blog and then manage that content, be it posts, categories, and comments, or tags, spam, and excerpts.

Chapter 4, *Pages, Media, and Importing/Exporting Content*, explores all the other types of content that WordPress is capable of handling. You'll be able to create static pages that aren't a part of your ongoing blog, add various types of media to your posts, and create appealing image galleries to display photos and other images (working with the new media library).

Chapter 5, *Plugins - What They Are and Why You Need Them*, explains what plugins are, why to use them, how to use them, where to get them, and how to be up-to-date with any new and useful plugins that get released to the community.

Chapter 6, *Choosing and Installing Themes*, describes how to manage the basic look of your WordPress website. You also get to learn where to find themes, why they are useful, and how to implement new themes in your WordPress website.

Chapter 7, *Customizing Your Website Appearance/Design*, explores how to manage widgets, navigation menus and work with the basic layout customization features to further enhance the capabilities of your entire website. Also covers the WordPress Customizer--an easy to use interface that allows you to tweak how your current theme looks and performs.

Chapter 8, *Developing Your Own Theme*, explains how to create your own theme. With just the most basic HTML and CSS abilities, you can create a design and turn it into a fully-functional WordPress theme.

Chapter 9, *Social Media Integration, Podcasting, and HTTPS*, explores social media integration, podcasting, and HTTPS, which is all about making your website more secure by adding an additional level of encryption to the browser-website communication.

Chapter 10, *Developing Plugins, Widgets, and an Introduction to the REST API*, teaches everything you need to know about creating basic plugins and widgets: how to structure the PHP files, where to put your functions, and how to use hooks. This chapter also teaches you how to add management pages and build widgets that are run by a plugin.

Chapter 11, *Community Blogging*, explains how to manage a group of users working on a single blog, which is a community of users. Community blogging can play an important role in a user group or a news website. This chapter also explains how to manage the different levels of privileges for users in the community.

Chapter 12, *Creating a Non-Blog Website, Part One – The Basics*, explores the endless possibilities of WordPress when it comes to using it to launch various types of websites. This chapter presents the first batch of our non-blog websites and explains in detail how to build them on top of a standard WordPress installation.

Chapter 13, *Creating a Non-Blog Website Part Two - E-Commerce Websites and Custom Content Elements*, goes through some additional types of non-blog websites and also presents some technical aspects of building them (caution--code talk inside).

What you need for this book

- A computer
- A web browser
- A plain text editor
- FTP software

You may consider a text editor that highlights code (such as Coda, TextMate, HTMLKit, and so on), but a simple plain text editor is all that's required. You may like to run a local copy of WordPress on your computer, in which case you may need a server such as Apache and MySQL installed (though WAMP and MAMP can take care of all that for you). But even this is not necessary, as you could do the entire thing remotely.

Who this book is for

This book is a guide to WordPress for both beginners and those who have slightly more advanced knowledge of WordPress. If you are new to blogging and want to create your own blog or website in a simple and straightforward manner, then this book is for you. It is also for people who want to learn how to customize and expand the capabilities of a WordPress website. You do not require any detailed knowledge of programming or web development, and any IT-confident user will be able to use this book to produce an impressive website.

Conventions

In this book, you will find a number of text styles that distinguish between different kinds of information. Here are some examples of these styles and an explanation of their meaning. Code words in text, database table names, folder names, filenames, file extensions, pathnames, dummy URLs, user input, and Twitter handles are shown as follows: "The wp-config.php file allows us to set this."

A block of code is set as follows:

```
function doctype_styles_new_styles() {
    wp_register_style('doctypes_styles', plugins_url
```

```
    ('doctype_styles_new.css', __FILE__));
  wp_enqueue_style('doctypes_styles');
}
```

New terms and **important words** are shown in bold. Words that you see on the screen, for example, in menus or dialog boxes, appear in the text like this: "Click on **Save**, as you would with any widget."

Warnings or important notes appear like this.

Tips and tricks appear like this.

Reader feedback

Feedback from our readers is always welcome. Let us know what you think about this book-what you liked or disliked. Reader feedback is important for us as it helps us develop titles that you will really get the most out of. To send us general feedback, simply e-mail feedback@packtpub.com, and mention the book's title in the subject of your message. If there is a topic that you have expertise in and you are interested in either writing or contributing to a book, see our author guide at www.packtpub.com/authors.

Customer support

Now that you are the proud owner of a Packt book, we have a number of things to help you to get the most from your purchase.

Downloading the example code

You can download the example code files for this book from your account at http://www.packtpub.com. If you purchased this book elsewhere, you can visit http://www.packtpub.com/support and register to have the files e-mailed directly to you. You can download the code files by following these steps:

1. Log in or register to our website using your e-mail address and password.
2. Hover the mouse pointer on the **SUPPORT** tab at the top.

3. Click on **Code Downloads & Errata**.
4. Enter the name of the book in the **Search** box.
5. Select the book for which you're looking to download the code files
6. Choose from the drop-down menu where you purchased this book from.
7. Click on **Code Download**.

Once the file is downloaded, please make sure that you unzip or extract the folder using the latest version of:

- WinRAR / 7-Zip for Windows
- Zipeg / iZip / UnRarX for Mac
- 7-Zip / PeaZip for Linux

The code bundle for the book is also hosted on GitHub at `https://github.com/PacktPublishing/WordPress-Complete-Sixth-Edition`. We also have other code bundles from our rich catalog of books and videos available at `https://github.com/PacktPublishing/`. Check them out!

Errata

Although we have taken every care to ensure the accuracy of our content, mistakes do happen. If you find a mistake in one of our books-maybe a mistake in the text or the code-we would be grateful if you could report this to us. By doing so, you can save other readers from frustration and help us improve subsequent versions of this book. If you find any errata, please report them by visiting `http://www.packtpub.com/submit-errata`, selecting your book, clicking on the **Errata Submission Form** link, and entering the details of your errata. Once your errata are verified, your submission will be accepted and the errata will be uploaded to our website or added to any list of existing errata under the Errata section of that title.

To view the previously submitted errata, go to `https://www.packtpub.com/books/content/support` and enter the name of the book in the search field. The required information will appear under the **Errata** section.

Piracy

Piracy of copyrighted material on the Internet is an ongoing problem across all media. At Packt, we take the protection of our copyright and licenses very seriously. If you come across any illegal copies of our works in any form on the internet, please provide us with the location address or website name immediately so that we can pursue a remedy.

Please contact us at `copyright@packtpub.com` with a link to the suspected pirated material.

We appreciate your help in protecting our authors and our ability to bring you valuable content.

Questions

If you have a problem with any aspect of this book, you can contact us at `questions@packtpub.com`, and we will do our best to address the problem.

1
Introducing WordPress

So there she was, with her new business, the business that she left her job as a teacher for, and she needed a website urgently. *ASAP*, as they say.

At that point, I knew I needed to step in and help her out. After all, she's my mother, and it's hard to say *no* to your mom.

That was somewhere around 2008, I think, and it was my first real experience having to build a website *really quickly* and make sure that it is *top quality* at the same time.

A week later, the thing was online. Built on WordPress.

Back in the day, when you wanted to launch a new website, you either had to learn web programming yourself or hire a professional who would take care of the whole process for you. Those times are gone, and we can thank WordPress for that.

More than a quarter of the entire web runs on WordPress already, and that number is only expected to increase in the coming years. In simple terms, with WordPress, anyone can build a beautiful website with the least amount of effort possible and then make it available to the world in no time.

I feel I need to emphasize on this some more. With WordPress, you don't need to hire a team of developers and designers. You don't need to learn advanced PHP, and you can still end up with a high-quality website with almost unlimited extension possibilities.

Frankly, these days, everyone has a good reason to have a website. It's not just large companies anymore. Individuals, families, freelancers, or small/independent businesses can all benefit from a website. However, not everyone has the financial resources to hire a web development company or a freelance web developer to create a website for them. This is where WordPress comes into play. WordPress is free, easy to use, and packed with excellent features.

In short, WordPress is an open source web software application that you can use to create and maintain a modern website. Since WordPress is a web application, it does not need to be installed on your home PC or Mac, or any other machine under your control. It can live on a server (a kind of computer) that belongs to your website hosting company.

Originally, WordPress was an application meant to run a blog website. However, it has now evolved into a fully featured **Content Management System** (**CMS**). Actually, at the time of writing, WordPress powers nearly 30 percent of the entire internet. Impressive, isn't it?

In this chapter, we'll explore:

- The reasons that will make you choose WordPress to run your website
- The greatest advantages of WordPress
- Online resources for WordPress
- Some of the most useful features in the newest versions of WordPress

Getting into WordPress

WordPress is an open source content management system. **Open source** means that the source code of the system is made available with a license whereby the copyright holder provides the rights to study, change, and distribute the software to anyone and for any purpose (as Wikipedia defines it). **Content management system** means a software application that can run a website (for example, a blog) and allows you to publish, edit, and modify the content. It's a piece of software that lives on the web server (more on what a web server is later on) and makes it easy for you to add and edit posts, themes, comments, and all of your other content. The following is the logo of WordPress:

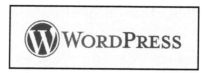

Even though WordPress was originally a blog engine, used primarily to run blogs, it's now being used by a number of big (by today's standards) online agencies to run their entire websites. Brands such as The New York Times, The Wall Street Journal, Forbes, Reuters, Wired.com, Sony, Toyota, plus some of the biggest artists (such as Beyonce or The Rolling Stones) all use WordPress as the base of their web platforms and outlets.

Undoubtedly, WordPress has evolved a lot over the years, and even though a large number of new functionalities have been introduced, WordPress remains one of the easiest to use web publishing platforms out there.

Originally, WordPress was a fork of an older piece of software named **b2/cafelog**. WordPress was developed by Matt Mullenweg and Mike Little, but is now maintained and developed by a team of developers that includes Mullenweg.

What WordPress is good for

There are generally three popular types of websites for which WordPress is meant to be used:

- A normal website with relatively static content, pages, subpages, and so on
- A blog website, chronologically organized and frequently updated, categorized, tagged, and archived
- An e-commerce website, a fully functional online store that allows people to buy goods or services, and the website owner to manage orders and fulfill them

However, as experience shows, these days WordPress is successfully used to run a wide variety of other sites as well, such as:

- Corporate business sites
- One-page profile sites
- Portfolio sites
- Membership sites
- Video blogs
- Photo blogs
- Product sites
- Education sites (e-courses) and more

For those of you unfamiliar with blog websites and blogging terminology, let's take a look at the basics.

Starting the journey – what is a blog?

Originally, the blog was short for weblog. According to Wikipedia, the term weblog was first used in 1997, and people started using blogs globally in 1999. The terms weblog, web blogging, and weblogger were added to the Oxford Dictionary in 2003, though these days most people leave off the *we* part.

Just to give you a more plain-English explanation, a blog is a website that usually contains regular entries made by an author. These entries can be of various types, such as commentary, descriptions of events, photos, videos, personal remarks, tutorials, case studies, long opinion pieces, political ideas, or whatever else you can imagine. They are usually displayed in a reverse chronological order, with the most recent additions at the top. Those entries can be organized in a variety of ways, by date, topic, subject, and so on.

One of the main characteristics of a blog is that it's meant to be updated regularly. Unlike a website where the content is static, a blog behaves more like an online diary, wherein the blogger posts regular updates. Hence, blogs are dynamic with ever-changing content. A blog can be updated with new content and the old content can be changed or deleted at any time (although deleting content is not a common practice).

Most blogs focus their content on a particular subject, for example, current events, hobbies, niche topics, and technical expertise. This doesn't mean that blogs are meant to be published only by individuals sharing their personal opinions on given matters. On the contrary, these days, blogs have become a major part in the online presence for many businesses and even corporations. The modern practice of *content marketing* is now one of the most widely accepted web marketing methods, and its core is based on publishing quality content, often in the blog form.

Understanding the common terms

If you are new to the world of blogging (sometimes called *blogosphere*, which is a fairly popular expression these days), you may want to familiarize yourself with the following common terms.

Post

Each entry in the blog is called a **post**. Every post usually has a number of different parts. Of course, the two most obvious parts are title and content. The **content** is text, images, links, and so on. Posts can even contain multimedia (for example, videos and audio files). Every post also has a publication timestamp, and most have one or more categories and tags assigned to them. It is these posts, or entries, that are displayed in a reverse chronological order on the main page of the blog. By default, the latest post is displayed first, in order to give the viewer the latest news on the subject.

Categories and tags

Categories and **tags** are ways to organize and find posts within a blog and even across blogs. Categories are like topics, while tags are more like keywords. For example, for a blog about food and cooking, there might be a category called **Recipes**, but every post in that category might have different tags (for example, soup, baked, vegetarian, and dairy-free).

The purpose and correct usage of tags and categories are one of the widely discussed topics among bloggers. Although there are basic guidelines such as the ones presented here, every blogger develops their own approach after a while, and there are no *written in stone* rules.

Comments

Most blogs allow visitors to post comments on the posts. This gives readers the opportunity to interact with the author of the blog, thus making the whole experience interactive. Often, the author of the blog will respond to comments by posting additional comments with a single click on the reply button, which makes for a continuous public online conversation or dialog.

Comments are said to be one of the most important assets for a blog. The presence of a large number of comments shows how popular and authoritative the blog is.

Themes

The **theme** for a blog is the design and layout that you choose for your blog. On most blogs, the content (for example, posts) is separate from the visual layout. This means you can change the visual layout of your blog at any time without having to worry about the content being affected. One of the best things about themes is that it takes only minutes to install and start using a new one. Moreover, there are a number of very good free or low-cost themes available online.

That being said, you need to be careful when working with free themes from uncertain developers. Often, they contain encrypted parts and code that can hurt your site and its presence on Google. Always look for user reviews before choosing a theme. Most importantly, the safest bet is getting your free themes only from the official WordPress directory at `https://wordpress.org/themes/`. The themes there have been tested and checked for any suspicious code.

You can learn more about this whole issue at `http://newinternetorder.com/free-wordpress-themes-are-evil/`.

Plugins

WordPress plugins are relatively small pieces of web software that can be installed on a WordPress site. They extend the native functionality to do almost anything that the technology of today allows. Just like WordPress itself, the code within plugins is open source, which means that anyone can build a new plugin if they have the required skill set. Every WordPress website or blog can work with an unlimited number of plugins (although it is not a recommended approach). The most popular functionalities introduced through plugins include spam protection, **search engine optimization** (**SEO**), caching, social media integration, interactive contact forms, and backups.

Widgets

In short, **widgets** are a simplified version of plugins. The most common usage of widgets is to have them showcased within the sidebars on your site. Typically, your current theme will provide you with a number of widget areas where you can display widgets (as mentioned, many of these are located in the sidebar). Some of the common usages for widgets is to display content such as categories and tags, recent posts, popular posts, recent comments, links to archived posts, pages, links, search fields, or standard non-formatted text.

Menus

We need to talk some history to explain the meaning of menus in WordPress. Back in the day, WordPress didn't allow much customization in terms of tweaking navigation menus and hand-picking the links we wanted to display. This changed in version 3.0, whereby the new **Custom Menus** feature was introduced. In plain English, it allows us to create completely custom menus (featuring any links of our choice) and then display them in specific areas on our sites. To be honest, this feature, even though it sounds basic, is one of the main ones that have turned WordPress into a full-fledged web publishing platform from a simple blogging tool. I promise this will sound much clearer in the upcoming chapters.

Page

It's important to understand the difference between a page and a post. Unlike posts, pages do not depend on timestamps and are not displayed in a chronological order. Also, they do not have categories or tags. A **page** is a piece of content with only a title and content (an example would be *About Me* or *Contact Us*--the two most popular pages on almost any blog). It is likely that the number of pages on your blog remains relatively static, while new posts can be added every day or so.

Homepage

A **homepage** is simply the main page that visitors see when they visit your website by typing in your domain name or URL address. In the early days of WordPress' existence, a homepage wasn't something we used to talk about as a separate kind of page. Originally, a homepage was generated automatically from the newest posts, it was a listing of those posts in a reverse chronological order. Right now, however, WordPress allows us to build a completely custom homepage and display whatever content we wish to it.

Users

As mentioned earlier, WordPress is now a complete web publishing platform. One of its characteristics is that it is capable of working with multiple user accounts, not just a single account belonging to the owner (admin/main author) of the site. There are different types of user accounts available, and they have different credentials and access rights.

WordPress is clearly trying to resemble a traditional publishing house where there are *authors*, *editors*, and other *contributors* all working together. Even though the possibility to create an unlimited number of user accounts won't be that impressive for anyone planning to manage a site on their own, it can surely be a more than an essential feature for big, magazine-like websites.

Why choose WordPress?

WordPress is not the only publishing platform out there, but it has an awful lot to offer. In the following sections, I've called attention to WordPress' most outstanding features.

Main benefits of WordPress summarized:

- WordPress *gives you full control over your website*. You can change/adjust/modify/customize everything, and I mean everything, about your site.
- There are *thousands of themes and plugins* to choose from, hence giving you the possibility to make your website look and work however you wish. WordPress is extremely extendable. Basically, any additional functionality that you can dream of can be added by means of a plugin that you or your programmer friends can write.
- The day-to-day work with *the platform is very easy to grasp*. Tasks such as editing content, publishing new articles/posts, or interacting with the audience through comments have no learning curve.
- *WordPress is open source*. There's no price tag on the platform, you can get it for free. This also means that learning how the platform works under the hood and how to extend it even further doesn't require anyone's permission.

Who should use WordPress?

Basically, if you need a website, and you want to be able to build it yourself, then WordPress is the platform that will make it possible.

WordPress is the perfect tool, both for beginners just dipping their toes in website building for the first time and developers working on client websites professionally.

WordPress has been around for quite a while and was in development the whole time. Developers are working on WordPress constantly to keep it ahead of spammers and hackers, and to *evolve* the application on the basis of the *evolving* needs of its users.

WordPress' very first release, Version 0.70, was launched in May 2003. Since then, it has had more than two dozen major releases, with a number of minor ones in between. Each release came with more features and better security. Each major release comes with a codename honoring a great Jazz musician, and this has become a tradition in the WordPress world.

WordPress is not being developed by a lonely programmer in a dark basement room, by the way. On the contrary, there is a large community of people working on it collaboratively by developing, troubleshooting, making suggestions, and testing the application. With such a large group of people involved, the application is likely to continue to evolve and improve without pause.

Getting to know the WordPress family

WordPress as a platform and as a community of users has grown in two main areas. The first one is gathered around WordPress.org (`https://wordpress.org/`), the native, main website of the WordPress project. The other is WordPress.com (`https://wordpress.com/`), a platform providing free blogs for every user who wants one:

Essentially, WordPress.org is about developing the platform itself, sharing new plugins, discussing the technical aspects of WordPress, and being all *techie* in general. WordPress.com (the preceding screenshot) is a purely community-driven site where bloggers can meet with each other, and publish their content on free blogs under the wordpress.com subdomain (for example, something like `https://paleorecipeslog.wordpress.com/` is a subdomain). That being said, there are paid plans available at WordPress.com as well.

In `Chapter 2`, *Getting Started with WordPress*, we will discuss all of the differences between having your blog on WordPress.com and downloading the software from WordPress.org and hosting it yourself, but the basic difference is the level of control. If your blog is on WordPress.com, you have less control over plugins, themes, and other details of the blog because everything is managed and made worry-free by the WordPress.com service, which obviously has its pros and cons.

Digging into WordPress – the features

Here is a list of some of the features that WordPress has to offer (in no particular order):

- Compliance with the **World Wide Web Consortium** (**W3C**) standards, although it does depend on the theme you're using
- Unlimited posts and pages
- Unlimited categories and subcategories
- Unlimited tags
- Mobile friendly (depending on the design/theme you use)
- Flexible--create any type of website you want
- Scalable--can handle any size of website
- Automatic syndication (RSS and Atom)
- Ability to post via email and mobile devices (there are apps available for all major mobile platforms, including iOS and Android)
- Support for plugins and themes
- Import of data from other blogs (Moveable Type, Textpattern, Greymatter, b2evolution, Blogger, and others)
- Easy to administer and blog without any previous experience
- Convenient, fully functional, built-in search
- Multilingual capability
- Ability to password protect content
- Comments manager and spam protection

- Built-in workflow (write, draft, review, and publish)
- Intelligent text editing via a **What You See Is What You Get** (**WYSIWYG**) editor
- Multi-user and multi-author support for user accounts
- Feature-rich *Media Library* for managing photos and other non-text content through a visual and highly usable interface
- Social media integration capabilities
- Dynamic and scalable revision functionality with post (edit) locking
- Built-in embed functionality through shortcodes (compatible with services such as YouTube, Vimeo, Flickr, SoundCloud, Reddit Comments, and others)
- An admin panel that's accessible via all modern devices, operating systems, and web browsers
- Pre-made color schemes for the admin panel
- User-friendly image editing, plus a drag-and-drop image importing feature
- Advanced **Search Engine Optimization** (**SEO**) features through plugins and themes

Getting familiar with the new feature list since 4.1

Since the last edition of this book was published, quite a staggering number of new features have been added to the WordPress software. If you're new to WordPress, this list may not mean a whole lot to you, but if you're familiar with WordPress and have been using it for a long time, you'll find this list quite enlightening:

- New default theme--*Twenty Seventeen*
- New *Press This* feature--making it easier to take any content you've found on the web and share it onto your WordPress website
- Easier theme installation and switching--all within the WordPress *Customizer*
- Easier plugin update and install from the **Plugins** screen--done with just a couple of clicks
- Support for native Chinese, Japanese, and Korean characters, musical and mathematical symbols, hieroglyphs, and also a plethora of emojis (including all of the latest Unicode 9.0 emoji characters)
- Improvements to the way that passwords are chosen and changed
- Possibility to manage the site's favicon--both on desktop and mobile

- Improved customizer panels and Sections and new Customizer Media Controls
- Better display rules for matching images to different screen sizes and devices
- Integrated REST API infrastructure and the addition of API endpoints for WordPress content
- Extended custom header feature to introduce support for video headers
- Added user admin languages and locale switching
- Device previewer buttons added to the customizer to better visualize what the website looks like on desktop, tablet, and mobile
- Added inline link editing--enables adding links without switching to modal dialog
- Introduction of native device fonts for the WordPress admin panel
- Improvements to internationalization
- A lot of security improvements to protect your site from hacks and malicious scripts

Learning more

If you'd like to see detailed lists of all new features added since WordPress Version 4.1, take a look at the docs here:

- http://codex.wordpress.org/Version_4.2
- http://codex.wordpress.org/Version_4.3
- http://codex.wordpress.org/Version_4.4
- http://codex.wordpress.org/Version_4.5
- http://codex.wordpress.org/Version_4.6
- http://codex.wordpress.org/Version_4.7
- http://codex.wordpress.org/Version_4.8
- http://codex.wordpress.org/Version_4.9
- http://codex.wordpress.org/Version_5.0

Also, you can read a fully explained feature list at https://wordpress.org/about/features/.

Learning more with online WordPress resources

One very useful characteristic of WordPress is that it has a large, active online community. Everything you will ever need for your WordPress website can likely be found online, and probably for free. In addition to this, these days we can also find many paid resources and training programs that offer expert advice and training, revolving around many different possible usages of a WordPress site.

Staying updated with WordPress news

As WordPress is constantly being developed, it's important to keep yourself up to date with the software community's latest activities.

If you visit the dashboard of your own WordPress site regularly, you'll be able to stay up-to-date with WordPress news and software releases. There are widgets on the dashboard that display the latest news and announcements, and an alert always appears when there is a new version of WordPress available for download and installation.

If you prefer to visit the website, then the most important spot to visit or subscribe to is WordPress Releases. Whenever there is a new release, be it a major release, or an interim bug fix, or an upgrade, it will be at `https://wordpress.org/news/category/releases/`.

Also, be sure to stay tuned to the main WordPress blog at `https://wordpress.org/news/`.

Some additional resources worth mentioning are as follows:

- `https://wordpress.org/`: The absolute main hub for WordPress
- `https://wordpress.com/`: The main platform for free WordPress blogging
- `http://jobs.wordpress.net/`: Job listings for anyone searching for employment in various areas related to WordPress (or anyone searching for WordPress help)
- `http://wordpress.tv/`: A great source of top-notch WordPress tutorials, how-to advice, case studies, product demonstrations, and WordPress-related conference presentation recordings
- `https://central.wordcamp.org/`: WordCamp is a conference that focuses on everything WordPress; it takes place a number of times during the year in different locations around the world, and this site is the central point for the conference

Understanding the Codex

The WordPress **Codex** is the central repository of all the information that the official WordPress team has published to help people work with WordPress.

The Codex has some basic tutorials for getting started with WordPress, such as a detailed step-by-step discussion of the installation, and lists of every template tag and hook. Throughout this book, I'll be providing links to specific pages within the Codex, which will deliver more or advanced information on the topics in this book.

The Codex can be found at `https://codex.wordpress.org/Main_Page`. Refer to the following screenshot:

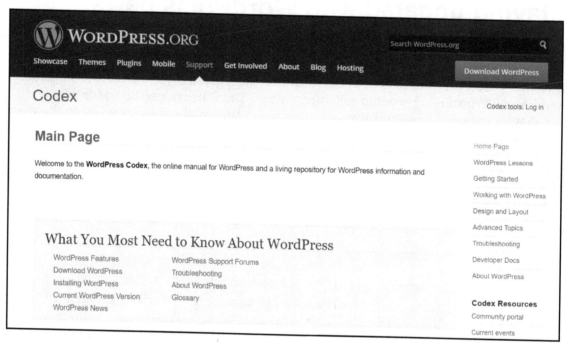

Apart from the Codex, there's also one more resource that will come in handy to new and experienced developers alike. It's called the WordPress **Code Reference**, and it can be found at `https://developer.wordpress.org/reference/`. It delivers a lot of docs on WordPress' functions, classes, methods, and hooks.

Getting support from other users

The online WordPress community asks questions and responds with solutions on the WordPress forum at `https://wordpress.org/support/`. It's an excellent place to go if you can't find the answer to a problem in the Codex. If you have a given question, then probably someone else has had it as well, and WordPress experts spend time in the forum answering them and giving solutions.

Using theme and plugin directories

There are official directories for themes and plugins on WordPress.org. Though not every theme and plugin is available here, the ones that are have been vetted by the community to some extent. Anything you download from these directories is likely to be relatively bug-free. Plugins and themes that you get from other sources can have malicious code, so be careful. You can also see what the community thinks of these downloads by looking at ratings, comments, and popularity.

Additionally, plugins in the **Plugin Directory** are automatically updatable from within your WordPress administration panel (wp-admin), while other plugins have to be updated manually. We'll cover this in detail in a later chapter.

You can find the **Theme Directory** at `https://wordpress.org/themes/` and the **Plugin Directory** at `https://wordpress.org/plugins/` as shown in the following screenshot:

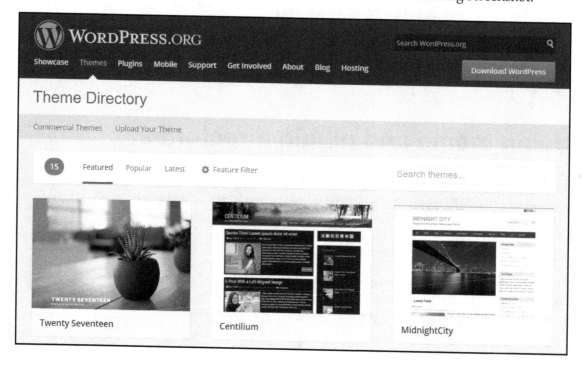

Summary

Having a website of your own is essential these days, no matter if you are an individual or a small business, and no matter if you are blogging regularly or want some accurate static content up on the internet. In this chapter, we reviewed basic information about WordPress, blogging, and common blog terms for those of you who are new to the concept.

WordPress is an excellent software application that can run your website (blog or not). It's packed with excellent features and is so flexible that it can really do anything you want, and it has a wealth of online resources. Additionally, it's easy to use, and you need no special skills or prior experience to work with it. Last but not least, it is 100% free!

In the next chapter, we will explore the choices and steps involved in installing WordPress and getting started.

2

Getting Started with WordPress

This chapter will guide you through the process of setting up WordPress and customizing its basic features. You can choose between a couple of options regarding where your WordPress website will live. WordPress is relatively small (less than 10 MB) as well as easy to install and administer.

WordPress is available in easily downloadable formats at `https://wordpress.org/download/`. WordPress is a free, open-source application and is released under GNU **General Public License (GPL)** - `https://en.wikipedia.org/wiki/GNU_General_Public_License`. This means that anyone who produces a modified version of the software released under the GPL is required to maintain the same freedom and that people buying or using the software can also modify and redistribute it. Thus, WordPress and other software released under the GPL are maintained as open source. In this chapter, you will learn how to:

- Create a free blog on WordPress.com
- Install WordPress manually on your web host
- Perform basic setup tasks in the WordPress admin panel (the wp-admin)
- Publish your first content

Building your WordPress website – start here

The first decision you have to make is where your blog is going to live. You have two basic options when creating your site:

- Do it at `https://wordpress.com`
- Install on a third-party web server (usually hosted by an external company)

Let's look at some of the advantages and disadvantages of each of these two options.

The advantage of using WordPress.com (`https://wordpress.com/`) is that they take care of all the technical details for you. The software has already been installed, and it will be upgraded for you whenever there is an upgrade available. You're not responsible for anything else but the management of your content. A major disadvantage is that you lose almost all of the theme and plugin control you'd have otherwise. The other advantages and disadvantages are as follows:

- WordPress.com will not let you upload or edit your own theme, though it will let you (for a fee) edit the CSS of the themes that are already there.
- WordPress.com will not let you upload or manage plugins at all. Some plugins are installed by default (most notably Akismet, for spam blocking, and also plugins supporting Google Sitemaps, caching, carousel slideshows, image galleries, polls, site stats, and some social media buttons), but you can neither uninstall them nor install others. Additional features are available for a fee.

In this chapter, you'll learn all the basics about working with WordPress.com (how to launch a website there and how to manage it). The subsequent chapters will all be about the self-hosted version of WordPress--the *main* version of WordPress, as many people would say, plus how to work with it.

A major advantage of installing WordPress on another server (which means either a server that belongs to the web host with which you signed up or a server you set up on your own computer) is that *you have control over everything*. You can add and edit themes, add and remove plugins, and even edit the WordPress application files yourself, if you wish to (however, don't do this unless you're confident about your WordPress skills). You'll have to keep your own WordPress software up to date, but that's relatively simple, and we'll cover it in this chapter. The only disadvantage is that you have to perform the installation and maintenance tasks on your own, which, as you'll see, shouldn't be too intimidating. Moreover, some web hosts provide a one-click or easy-to-use installer, which lets you skip over some of the nitty-gritty steps involved in the manual installation.

In this chapter, we'll discuss how to create a new blog on WordPress.com and how to start working with it on a daily basis. However, if you want to accomplish any of the more advanced tasks concerning the topics in this book, you will have to install WordPress on your own server as opposed to using WordPress.com.

The following table is a brief overview of the essential differences between using WordPress.com and downloading a package from WordPress.org and then installing it on your own server:

-	WordPress.com (online platform/service)	WordPress.org (open-source software)
Installation	**No need to install anything, just sign up.**	**Install WordPress yourself, either manually or via your host's control panel (if offered).**
Themes	Use any theme made available by WordPress.com.	Use any theme available anywhere, written by anyone (even by yourself).
Plugins	No ability to add third-party plugins.	Use any plugin available anywhere, written by anyone (even by yourself).
Upgrades	WordPress.com provides automatic upgrades.	You have to upgrade it yourself when upgrades are available.
Widgets	Widget availability depends on available themes.	You can widgetize any theme yourself.
Maintenance	You don't have to do any maintenance.	You're responsible for the maintenance of your site.
Advertising	No advertising of your own allowed. However, WordPress.com itself sometimes runs ads on your site.	You can advertise anything and in any amount you like.
Ownership	Even though the content belongs to you, WordPress.com can take down your blog at any moment if they consider it being inappropriate.	You have complete control over your site, and no one can force you to take it down.
Domain	Your site is available as a subdomain under .wordpress.com by default, but you can also upgrade to the Premium package (for a fee) and use your own, manually registered domain name.	You can use any manually registered internet domain name.

Using WordPress.com

WordPress.com (`https://wordpress.com`) is a free service provided by the WordPress developers, where you can register a blog or non-blog website quickly and easily with no hassle. However, because it is a hosted service, your control over some things will be more restricted than it would be if you hosted your own WordPress website. As mentioned earlier, WordPress.com will not let you edit or upload your own themes or plugins. Apart from this, WordPress.com is a great place to maintain your personal site if you don't need to do anything fancy with your theme or the source code of your site in general. To begin, go to `https://wordpress.com` and click the big **Get Started** button:

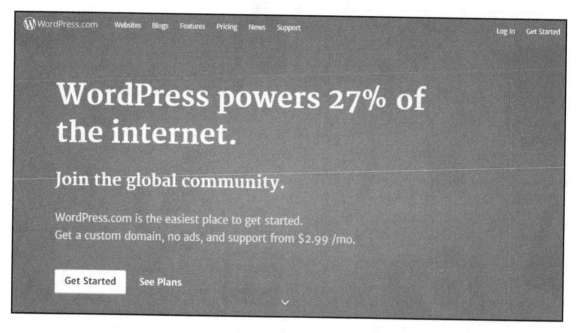

Right away, WordPress will take you through the step-by-step wizard that makes the setup process super easy. First, you get asked about the type of website that you want to build. There are four options here: a website layout based on *a list of latest posts, a grid of latest posts, a welcome page for the site, an online store*. The selection you make will impact the designs that WordPress.com suggests to you in the next step. Whatever design, theme, you pick in that next step will be installed on your site immediately.

The step after that is all about coming up with a name for your site and an address. You can enter any name that you wish and let WordPress suggest a specific domain name. You can see an example in the following screenshot:

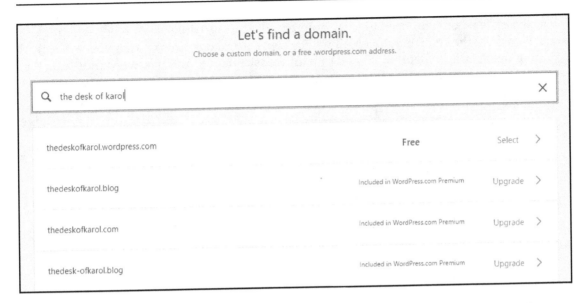

You'll notice that the subdomain--the one built like `SOMENAME.wordpress.com`--is always free. For all the other options, you'll have to pay extra by signing up to WordPress.com **Premium**. Speaking of Premium, the next step in the signup process is all about picking whether you want to stay with the free plan or upgrade to a paid one. You can read through the options on that page and make a decision based on what's available, but in most cases, you'll want to stick with Free. Take a look at the following screenshot:

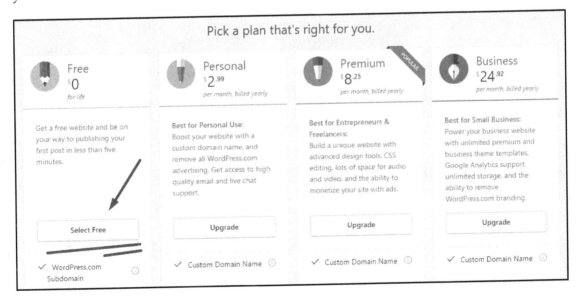

The next step is where you need to enter your email address (triple-check when entering yours; it's where the confirmation email will be sent), username (this is what you will sign in with in the future; by default, it is set to your website name), and password (note that the password measurement tool will notify you whether your password is strong or weak) as shown in the following screenshot:

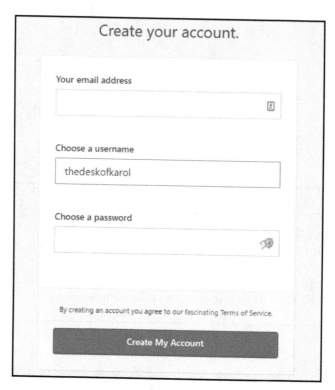

Congrats! You've just created a blank WordPress.com website. Just one caveat; you will also be prompted to visit your inbox and search for the activation email that has just been sent to you. The email itself is very clear and only requires you to click the big activation button or link.

Right now, your new WordPress.com site is fully installed and visible to the world, and you can begin to publish content and build your audience.

Publishing your first content on a WordPress.com blog

All you have to do in order to publish some content on your WordPress.com blog is click on the **Write** link in the top menu:

When you do so, you're presented with a handy online text editor window, where you can type in the contents of your post. Every post needs a title, the actual content, and some optional parameters such as tags and categories. You can add a photo for your publication also. Refer to the following screenshot:

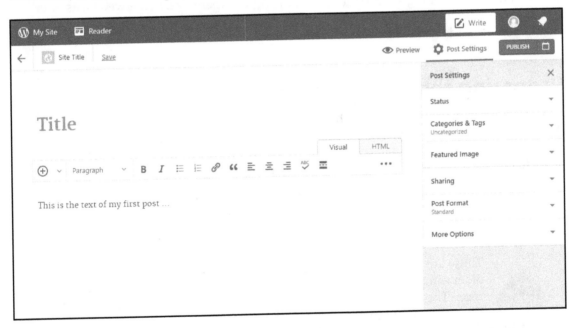

Once you have finished editing, you can either save the write up as a draft (for further modifications), preview what it's going to look like on the blog, or publish it straight away with the **Publish** button.

Essentially, a WordPress.com blog can be managed just like any other WordPress site (content-wise), so you do get access to the Dashboard (explained later in this chapter), where you can edit and publish your content, too. The interface described here is a specially designed panel that can't be found on any other type of blog. In other words, you won't get it with a regular WordPress site (a standalone site on your own domain and hosting). Therefore, if WordPress.com is your preferred way of launching a blog or website then you should skip the next section of this chapter, which is all about installing WordPress manually as a standalone site.

Installing WordPress manually

The WordPress application files can be downloaded for free if you want to perform a manual installation. If you've got a website host, this process is extremely easy and requires no previous programming skills or advanced blogging experience. Some web hosts offer automatic installation through the host's online control panel. One of these automatic installation methods is described later in this chapter.

Preparing the environment

A good first step is to make sure you have an environment setup that is ready for WordPress. This means you need to ensure that the server meets the minimum requirements and that your database is ready. For WordPress to work, your web host must provide you with a server that fulfills the following requirements:

- Support for PHP version 5 or greater (PHP 7 is recommended)
- Provision of a MySQL database (full access) of version 5.6 or greater (alternatively, MariaDB version 10.0 or greater)

Those are recommended parameters. WordPress will also work on slightly older setups, but opting for those may expose your website to security risks. The current absolute minimum requirements are PHP 5.2.4+ and MySQL 5.0+, but to quote the official information on WordPress.org: "[...] these versions have reached official End Of Life and as such may expose your site to security vulnerabilities."

Additionally, these minimum requirements tend to change occasionally. The most current requirements can always be found at https://wordpress.org/about/requirements/.

You can determine whether your host meets these two requirements by contacting the support team at your web host. If it does, you're ready to move on to the next step.

Downloading WordPress

Once you have checked your environment, you need to download WordPress from `https:/`
`/wordpress.org/download/`. There's a big blue download button there. Hard to miss. What you get once you click it is a `.zip` archive of the most recent version of the WordPress software. Extracting that archive onto your desktop will give you a folder called `wordpress`. In itself, that folder isn't very useful as a standalone thing. In order to make it work, you need to get it somehow onto your web server. This, we'll cover in the next sub-sections in this chapter.

We're going to focus mainly on the remote installation of WordPress here, as in, getting it installed somewhere else other than on your own computer. However, if you plan to develop themes or plugins, it is recommended that you install WordPress locally as well, on a local server. Testing and deploying themes and plugins directly to the remote server will be much more time-consuming than working locally. If you look at the screenshots depicting WordPress installation throughout the book, you'll notice that all these are examples of working locally.

Uploading the files

Now, we need to upload all the files of WordPress to our web server using any **File Transfer Protocol** (**FTP**) client (or simply put them in our local server directory on our local computer). There are several FTP clients available on the internet that are either freeware (no cost) or require a small fee. If you don't already have an FTP client, try one of the following:

- **Filezilla**: `https://filezilla-project.org/download.php?type=client` (for Mac, Windows, or Linux)
- **Fetch**: `https://fetchsoftworks.com/` (for Mac only)
- **SmartFTP**: `https://www.smartftp.com/` (for Windows only)

A note about security

Whenever possible, you should use **Secure FTP** (**sFTP**) rather than regular FTP. If you're using sFTP, all of the data sent and received is encrypted. With FTP, data is sent in plain text and can easily be nabbed by hackers. Check both your FTP software and your hosting options and select sFTP if it's available.

Using your FTP client, connect to the FTP server using the server address, username, and password provided to you by your host (if you're not sure what those are, you can always contact your web host support and ask a support agent for these details). Next, open the folder where you want WordPress to live. You may want to install WordPress in your root folder, which will mean that visitors will see your WordPress website's home page when they go to your main URL--for example, `http://yoursite.com`. Alternatively, you may want to install WordPress in a subfolder, for example, `http://yoursite.com/blog/`. Refer to the following screenshot:

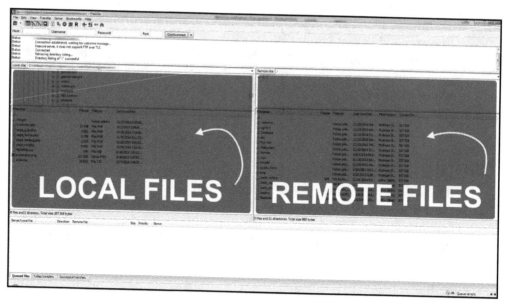

On the left side, you will see the files from your local folder, and on the right side, you will see your remote folder. (Note that the FTP client you are using may have a slightly different layout, but this is a general idea.)

Now select all of the WordPress files on your local machine from the left pane, and drag them onto the right pane. You can watch as your FTP client uploads the files one at a time and they appear on the right panel. This may take a few minutes, so be patient.

If you're installing WordPress on your local server, just be sure to place the WordPress files in the correct `webroot` directory on your computer.

Once all of the files have been uploaded, you're ready to proceed with the installation.

If you want to learn more about local WordPress installations, consider reading through these online tutorials (all of them step by step):
Installing WordPress locally on Windows with WAMP: `https://themeisle.com/blog/local-wordpress-testing-site-for-windows/`
Installing WordPress locally on Windows with XAMPP: `https://themeisle.com/blog/install-xampp-and-wordpress-locally/`
Installing WordPress locally on MAC: `https://themeisle.com/blog/local-by-flywheel-wordpress-on-mac/`

Installing WordPress

Now, it's time to proceed with the famous five-minute installation of WordPress (the fact that WordPress can be installed in five minutes or less is widely advertised on the official WordPress website). If you access your WordPress URL via your browser, you will see a short introduction message instructing you to choose the language that you want to perform the installation in:

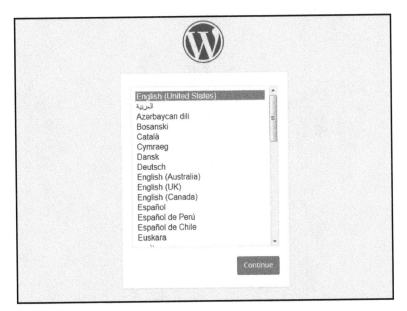

After this, you will be presented with another screen, informing you of all the required details that you'll need in order to complete the installation successfully. Currently, those details are the following:

- **Database name**: For example, this can be `wptestblog`.
- **Database username**: For example, this can be `localdbuser`.
- **Database password**: For example, `62dcx%^_0hnm` - the more complex the password, the better.
- **Database host**: This is the host address of your web server's database. If you're running the server locally, this will be `localhost`. If you're trying to run WordPress on a third-party web host, this is the address of the database server of that host.

The big question, therefore, is where to get all this information from. The answer is your web host. Most of the large web hosts offer you a way to create your own databases via an online control panel, with usernames and passwords of your choice. If you're not sure how to do this, just email or call your hosting provider for assistance. Professional support teams will be glad to help you with this.

Once you have those four parameters, you can press the **Let's go!** button and proceed to the next step of the installation. The following is a screenshot of the main setup form:

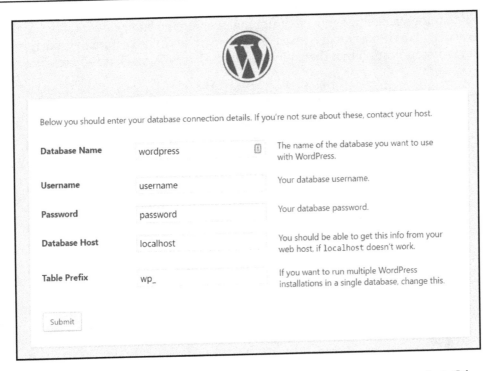

As you can see, the details are the same as those shown in an earlier screenshot. Of course, your details will be different. Also, another important point to note is that there's an additional field labeled **Table Prefix**. This is the default prefix that every table in your database will have before its name. The default value in that field is wp_. It is recommended that you change this to any two- or three-letter word of your choice and end it with an underscore (_), just as a safety precaution against standard database attacks on known WordPress tables.

After pressing the **Submit** button, you will be redirected to the final confirmation page. All you have to do here is click on the **Run the install** button.

At this point, things can either go well or not that well. In the latter case, proceed to the next section, *Installing WordPress through a hand-built configuration file*. Fortunately, such problems are rare. The best indication that the online installation is going well is the presence of the following screen:

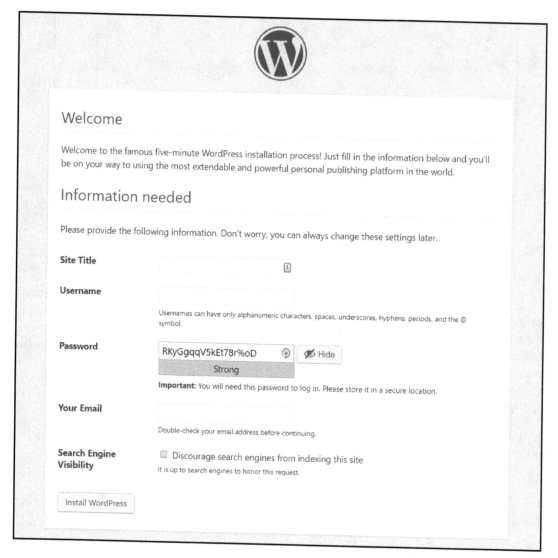

This is the final setup page. Here, you set up the core details of your new site. Now, fill out the installation form (you will be able to change all of these later, so don't be too worried about getting locked into your choices):

- **Site Title**: Fill in the name of your blog (it can be something simple, such as *Daily Cooking*).
- **Username**: It's in your best interest to choose a username that's not obvious. For instance, if you go with *admin*, it will be very easy to guess for someone who might want to hack into your blog. Also worth pointing out is the fact that this account is the administrator account, which has the most privileges and access rights to all areas of the site. Opt for something difficult to guess, such as *Site-Master-45* and don't worry, silly is good.
- **Password**: Choose a secure password, one that has both upper and lowercase letters, a number or two, and even a few punctuation marks. WordPress suggests some options for you here.
- **Your Email**: Double-check that this is correct. This is the email address WordPress will use to contact you about the blog, comments, and so on. If you do not get an email from your WordPress site shortly after installing it, check your spam folder.
- **Search Engine Visibility**: This is the final checkbox, yet possibly one of the most important settings on this list. If you leave it unchecked (recommended), your site is going to be accessible through Google and other search engines. Checking it means banning your site from the search engines.

Now, click on **Install WordPress**. You're done with the installation!

WordPress will now greet you with the main login page - this is where you can access the main admin panel of the website (also known as the wp-admin). Alternatively, you can also always enter the admin panel by pointing your browser to `http://yoursite.com/wp-admin`. If you're not already logged in, this URL will redirect you to the login page.

Installing WordPress through a hand-built configuration file

Now, in some cases, your web hosting account will prevent WordPress from creating a valid configuration file. This issue may be caused by access rights limitations. However, it's not a big obstacle because you can always create a configuration file manually. To do this, just open the `wordpress` folder and find the file named `wp-config-sample.php`. Make a copy of this file and rename it `wp-config.php`. We'll modify this file together.

You need not be a PHP programmer to do this. Just open this file with a simple editor such as Notepad. The following is the copied text from the original `wp-config.php` file. One thing to know about PHP is that any text that comes after a double slash (`//`), or between a slash-star and star-slash (`/*` and `*/`), is a comment. It's not actual PHP code. Its purpose is to inform you what that line or that section is about. With that said, note that most of the comments have been removed, so that we can focus on the items we need to change.

```php
<?php
/** The name of the database for WordPress */
define('DB_NAME', 'database_name_here');

/** MySQL database username */
define('DB_USER', 'username_here');

/** MySQL database password */
define('DB_PASSWORD', 'password_here');

/** MySQL hostname */
define('DB_HOST', 'localhost');

/** Database Charset to use in creating database tables. */
define('DB_CHARSET', 'utf8mb4');

/** The Database Collate type. Don't change this if in doubt. */
define('DB_COLLATE', '');

define('AUTH_KEY', 'put your unique phrase here');
define('SECURE_AUTH_KEY', 'put your unique phrase here');
define('LOGGED_IN_KEY', 'put your unique phrase here');
define('NONCE_KEY', 'put your unique phrase here');
define('AUTH_SALT', 'put your unique phrase here');
define('SECURE_AUTH_SALT', 'put your unique phrase here');
define('LOGGED_IN_SALT', 'put your unique phrase here');
define('NONCE_SALT', 'put your unique phrase here');

$table_prefix = 'wp_';
```

As you can see from the code, you can insert a number of settings here, but they do resemble the ones we were filling out in the online installer just a minute ago. Let's walk through the most important ones.

Just as in the online installation, we fetched the database information, but this time we put it in the `wp-config.php` file:

```
// ** MySQL settings ** //
define('DB_NAME', 'wptestblog');
define('DB_USER', 'localdbuser');
define('DB_PASSWORD', '62dcx%^_0hnm');
define('DB_HOST', 'localhost');
```

Next, for security purposes, you need to put some unique phrases into what's called the *WordPress salt keys*. These secret keys are used by WordPress to add random elements to your passwords and in some other situations. This will help to keep your WordPress installation uniquely protected. No one else is likely to choose the same unique keys that you chose, and therefore, breaking or hacking into your site will be more difficult. You can get some secret keys generated from `https://api.wordpress.org/secret-key/1.1/salt/` (the sample config file itself will remind you of this through the in-code PHP comments). Once you have finished, you will get the following code snippet, which you can paste directly into the default code in `wp-config.php`:

```
define('AUTH_KEY',         'uu|6#00Pc/3h?Pg5:Zc#:S=;<3mdw-ai');
define('SECURE_AUTH_KEY',  'vy1.@Nr@Zb^G|0Vfz-|TH5&W');
define('LOGGED_IN_KEY',    'sryMVd'jVpiMWWQqx~!v XE5@fJMTt2[Z');
define('NONCE_KEY',        'i,+UPpMR>Mj3o}(B**^<T:/md,YFF76d]Kf');
define('AUTH_SALT',        'n.8Li=9OjV+_p||}e5yN2k<s{!KJs|[S&Zh');
define('SECURE_AUTH_SALT', 'I#2vPT^u[5vLX|'MzPg/J*y]RTfr');
define('LOGGED_IN_SALT',   'gR%QP^c*jfFUy,iQ}-0g_%;%H)pNOB5');
define('NONCE_SALT',       '&L);.IH'v{]zYLO2:h_t#JOD-p)cvyc');
```

Important!
Don't ever get the salt keys from anywhere other than `https://api.wordpress.org/secret-key/1.1/salt/`. This is an important security mechanism that protects your browser session from being hijacked and then used for unauthorized access to your WordPress site.

Finally, we have the aforementioned table prefix. The `wp-config.php` file allows us to set this, too. Again, here's the prefix of our choice:

```
$table_prefix  = 'wp_';
```

The WordPress Codex has a long and detailed page that describes everything about editing your `wp-config.php` file: `https://codex.wordpress.org/Editing_wp-config.php`. Once you save the `wp-config.php` file and either upload it to your web host or place it on your local server, you can visit your site through your domain name (like `http://yoursite.com/`). You should be presented with the final setup page, the one visible in the earlier screenshot. All you have to do now is proceed according to the instructions described earlier in this chapter.

Learning more

If you'd like to see an even more detailed step-by-step guide for manual installation, take a look at this page in the WordPress Codex at `https://codex.wordpress.org/Installing_WordPress`.

Furthermore, if you visit `https://codex.wordpress.org/Getting_Started_with_WordPress#Installation`, you will find additional installation instructions as well as specifics on changing file permissions, using FTP and languages, importing from other blogging engines, and more.

Installing WordPress through an auto-installer script

Some web hosts provide their customers with access to a range of auto-installer scripts for various web platforms, including WordPress. Most of these auto-installers have quite similar functionalities, and the actual process of installing a new WordPress site is similar as well. Here, we're going to focus on one of these scripts, **Softaculous** (`https://www.softaculous.com/`).

This is yet another way of installing a WordPress site, and we're covering it here to make this book as complete as it can be. However, if you've already managed to install your site using the methods described earlier, then this section won't be of any use to you at this point.

Softaculous is the preferred method of WordPress installation for many professional developers and bloggers. In some cases, it's the fastest method when dealing with a completely new hosting account maintained by a new web host. Softaculous is provided on hosting accounts running on many management platforms, such as *cPanel*, *Plesk*, *DirectAdmin*, *InterWorx*, and *H-Sphere*. Most likely, your hosting account (a commercial hosting account you've bought from a respected provider) is certain to be using one of these platforms. The following screenshot shows cPanel, which is one of the platforms:

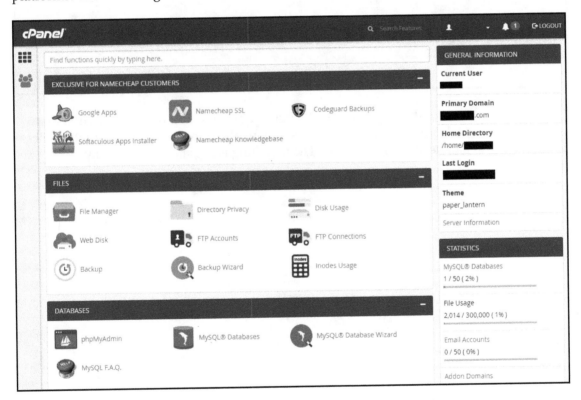

Although such platforms have different user interfaces, the core functionalities from a user's point of view remain mostly the same. To access Softaculous, just scroll down until you see the main section (or icon) labeled Softaculous. Once there, you can see the WordPress icon among the others:

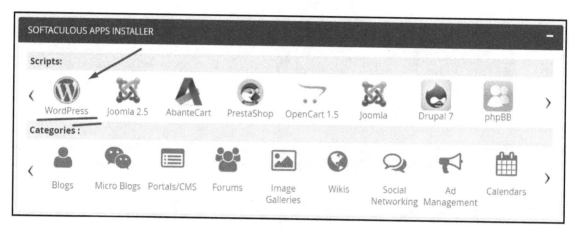

The whole idea of using this script is to make things quicker and more hassle-free so that you don't have to take care of creating databases manually or by setting configuration files. Softaculous will handle all of this for you. The following is the site creation form:

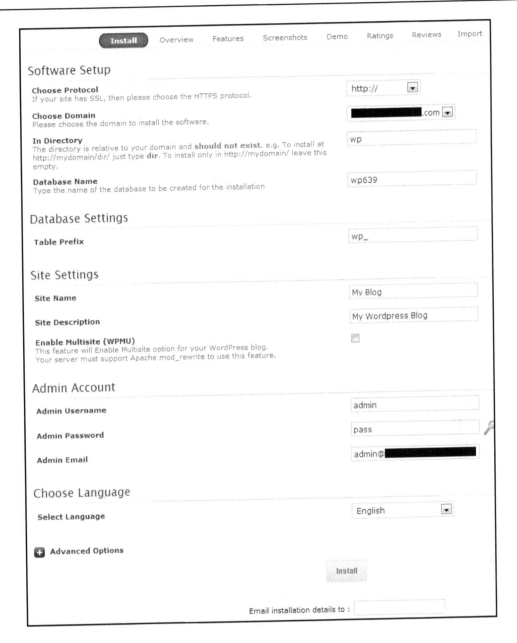

Keep in mind that these interfaces tend to change from time to time, so depending on when you read this book, your Softaculous panel may look different. Don't worry though, as it surely will be similarly understandable. Here's a breakdown of all the fields you can expect to see and what details to put in them:

- **Choose Protocol**: You can stick with the default value of `http://`.
- **Choose Domain**: If you have more than one domain assigned to your hosting account, then you get to choose which one you want to use here. For single-domain accounts (most likely the case), this drop-down field has only one option.
- **In Directory**: If you want to install your WordPress site under a subdirectory, then input its name here (just the name). If you want to install the site in the main directory (`http://yoursite.com/`), then make sure the field is blank.
- **Database Name**: You can confidently go with the default value.
- **Table Prefix**: As discussed earlier in this chapter, you can change this to something unique (in my case, it's `wp_`).
- **Site Name**: This is the name of your site (in the present case, `My Blog`).
- **Site Description**: This is the tagline (in the present case, **My WordPress Blog**).
- **Enable Multisite (WPMU)**: Leave this unchecked unless you're an advanced user planning to launch a multisite installation.
- **Admin Username**, **Admin Password**, and **Admin Email**: These are the details of your admin account, similar to the ones we had to provide during the manual WordPress installation.
- **Select Language**: WordPress has many localized versions of the platform, not only English, and you can choose one here.

Clicking on the **Install** button starts the installation process. The process itself requires no supervision, and you will be able to access your site as soon as it finishes after roughly one or two minutes. You can check whether the installation has been successful through the standard `http://yoursite.com/` and `http://yoursite.com/wp-admin/` URLs. In other words, this is the end of the installation process through Softaculous. As you can see, it's much simpler and quicker than manual installation. Furthermore, Softaculous always installs the most recent version of WordPress, so you don't have to worry about getting something out of date.

 You can also encounter other auto-installer scripts, which are similar to Softaculous, such as *Fantastico, Installatron, MOJO,* and *SimpleScripts.*

The wp-admin panel

WordPress installs a powerful and flexible administration area where you can manage all of your website content and do much more. Throughout the book, this will be referred to in shorthand as the **wp-admin** or **WP Admin**.

Now that you've successfully installed WordPress, it's time for our first look at the wp-admin. There are some immediate basic changes that are recommended to make sure your installation is set up properly.

You can always get to the wp-admin by visiting `http://yoursite.com/wp-admin/` (this URL is also the reason why we're calling it the wp-admin). If it's your first time there, you'll be re-directed to the login page. In the future, WordPress will check whether you're already logged in and if so, you'll skip the login page.

To log in, just enter the username and password you chose during the installation. Then, click on **Log In**.

Whenever you log in, you'll be taken directly to the **Dashboard** section of the wp-admin. The following is a screenshot of the wp-admin that you will see immediately after logging in:

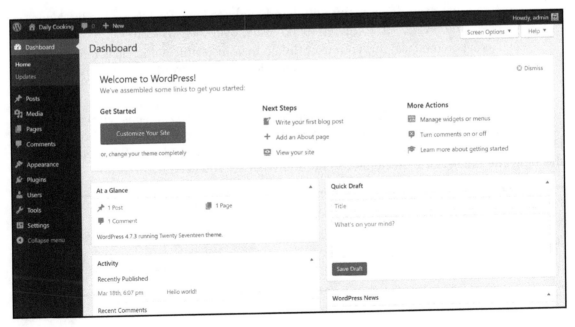

You'll see a lot of information and options here, which we will explore throughout this book. For now, we will focus on the items that we need to consider right after a successful installation. First, let's take a brief look at the top of the wp-admin and the **Dashboard** section.

The very top bar, referred to as the *top bar* or *admin bar*, is mostly dark gray and contains the following:

- A rollover drop-down menu, triggered by hovering over the WordPress logo in the top left corner, featuring a set of links to About WordPress (some details about the current installation of WordPress), WordPress.org, Documentation, Support Forums, and Feedback
- A link to the front page of your WordPress website (in this example, the title of the whole site is Daily Cooking), the clickable *house* icon
- An updates and activity section containing either links to the newest comments or to pending updates
- A rollover drop-down menu with handy links to New Post, New Media, New Page, and New User, triggered by hovering over the *plus* icon
- Lastly, on the far right, your user linked to your profile, which is yet another drop-down menu containing a link labeled Edit My Profile and, finally, the Log Out link

You'll also notice the **Screen Options** tab, which appears on many screens within the wp-admin. If you click on it, it will slide down a checklist of items on the page to show or hide. This will be different on each page. I encourage you to play around with this element by checking and unchecking the items, as you find whether you need them or not:

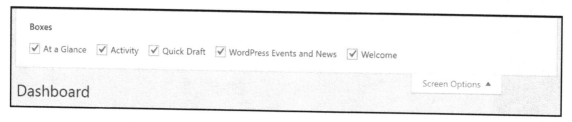

Right next to the **Screen Options** tab, you find the **Help** tab. Just like the **Screen Options** tab, this one appears on many screens within the wp-admin. Whenever you're in doubt regarding a specific screen, you can always check the **Help** tab for instructions. Accessing the **Help** tab is always quicker and, in most cases, more effective than searching for solutions online.

On the left side of the screen is the main menu:

You can click on any word in the main menu to be taken to the dedicated page for that section, or you can hover your cursor over a given link to see all of the possible subsections you can visit. For example, if you hover your cursor over **Settings**, you'll see the subpages for the **Settings** section, and at that point, you can click on either of the subpages or the main Settings link itself:

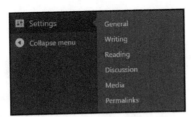

The top menu and the main menu exist on every page within the wp-admin. The main section on the right contains information for the current page you're on. In this case, we're in the **Dashboard** section. It contains boxes that have information about your blog, and about WordPress in general.

In the new versions of WordPress, when you log in for the first time, you're presented with a welcome message, similar to the one that follows:

In short, it's the welcome panel that allows you to access some of the crucial sections of the wp-admin with just one click. Once you click on the **Dismiss** link, the panel will no longer be displayed after login. In its current version, the panel allows you to do the following (going from top left to bottom right):

- Customize the current theme, but only if the theme provides some customization features (not all themes do)
- Change the current theme to a new one
- Write your first blog post
- Add an About page, which is usually the most visited page on most WordPress sites
- View your site
- Manage menus and widgets
- Turn comments on or off, by default they are on
- Learn more about how to get started with WordPress, which is an external link pointing to `https://codex.wordpress.org/First_Steps_With_WordPress`

For now, we're not going to focus on this welcome panel because first, we need to understand what its content means, in order to use it effectively. In this chapter and the following chapters, we will get to know all of the crucial methods of managing a WordPress site, and once we gain some experience, with time, this welcome panel can make our everyday work much quicker. Therefore, let's jump right into the general site settings section.

In this book, instructions regarding which page within the wp-admin to navigate to are indicated by phrases such as *navigate to Settings | General* or *navigate to Posts | Add New*. This always describes the path you should take to get there via the main menu.

Changing general blog information

You may need to change and add some general blog information (such as blog title or one-sentence description) after a successful installation to get your website set up with the correct information. To get started with this, navigate to **Settings** in the main menu.

There are many options you can set here, most of which are self-explanatory. We'll look at the most important ones, and you can explore the rest on your own. Obviously, you can change your blog's title. Mine is called *Daily Cooking*, for example. You can also change the blog description, which is used in most themes as a subtitle for the blog, like the subtitle of a book. The default description is *Just another WordPress site*. You'll probably want to change that. Let's change ours to `Exploring cooking every day of the week`.

One of the things you probably want to take a look at on this page is the **Timezone** option. Whether you have a blog (with timestamps on every post) or not, it's important that WordPress knows what time zone you're in. Particularly when you want to schedule a page or post for the future, show users accurate time stamps, or even just make sure that email notifications are correctly time-stamped. Additionally, if you're planning to publish content internationally, meaning that your target audience is located in an entirely different location, it's good to set the time zone to represent your target audience and not yourself.

The pull-down menu will show you different UTC settings, along with the biggest cities around the world. Just choose a city in your time zone. After you save the changes, the time that appears further down the page (next to **Time Format**) will change to the time you chose, so that you can check and make sure it's correct.

Another feature worth considering on this page is whether or not you want to allow user registration on your site. For most sites, this is not particularly useful, but if you're planning to make the site community-driven or utilize some form of crowdsourcing, then this might be worth considering. In that case, it's not advisable to give new users a user role higher than **Subscriber** (the default value).

When you're done making changes to this page, be sure to click on the **Save Changes** button at the bottom of the page.

Finally, there's only one more component you should adjust in your new site's settings before publishing any content: the permalinks. As WordPress defines them, *permalinks* are the permanent URLs to your individual pages, blog posts, categories, and tags. By default, WordPress links to your new posts using a highly unoptimized URL structure. For instance, if you create a post titled *How to Cook the Best Meal Ever*, WordPress will link it as `http://yoursite.com/?p=123` (or something similar). The main problem with this structure is that it doesn't indicate what the page is about. Neither your visitors nor Google will be able to make a guess. In the case of Google, such a structure can also significantly impact your future search engine rankings. Therefore, to set a more optimized structure, you can go to **Settings | Permalinks**. Here are the available settings:

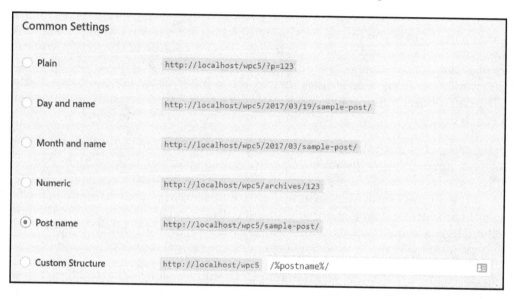

The best setting from a visitor's point of view, as well as from Google's, is the one labeled **Post name**. Going back to the example with the *How to Cook the Best Meal Ever* post, if you set the permalinks to **Post name**, the URL of this post will be `http://yoursite.com/how-to-cook-the-best-meal-ever/`, which is a lot clearer and predictable. You can always review the official information on permalinks anytime at `https://codex.wordpress.org/Using_Permalinks`.

Further down the page, there are also optional settings for **Category base** and **Tag base**. By default, **Category base** is set to `category`. For example, if you have a category called *recipes* then you can view all posts under this category at `http://yoursite.com/category/recipes`.

Some site owners prefer to change this to something more user-friendly, for example, `topics`. Even though this conveys the exact same message, it can be much easier to grasp for visitors who are not that familiar with the standards of web content publishing. In the end, your category base is solely down to your discretion. **Tag base**, on the other hand, rarely needs any adjustments.

Creating your first post

For this chapter and the next few chapters, we'll be focusing on the use of WordPress to run a blog website. In a later chapter, we'll talk more specifically about using WordPress for a non-blog website.

Therefore, with that in mind, let's add the first piece of content to your new blog, a blog post. (This won't be the very first post on the blog itself because WordPress created a post, a comment, and a page for you when it installed. Nevertheless, it will be *your* first post.) To create a post, just click on **New | Post** in the top bar. You'll be taken to the following page:

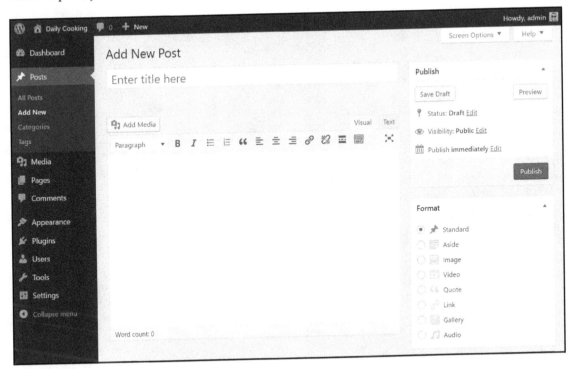

As you can see, there are a lot of options for your post (which we'll explore in more detail in Chapter 3, *Creating Blog Content*). For now, let's just worry about the basics. Every post should have, at a minimum, a *title*, and some *content*. Therefore, go ahead and type in some text in those two fields (the title field and the big content field). When you are happy with it, click on the **Publish** button.

You'll get a green label note informing you that the post has been published. Take a look at the front page of your site by clicking on the name of your site in the top bar. You'll see the following:

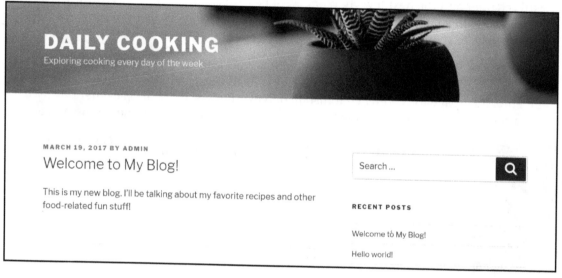

Notice that we are using the default **Twenty Seventeen** theme. If you're using a different one, then the design and the layout of your first post will be different.

Writing your first comment

Now, let's see what it's like to post a comment. One of the great things about blogs is that they give you, the writer, an opportunity to spark a conversation with your readers. WordPress comes with a fantastic commenting system that allows visitors to add comments to your blog. To add your own comment to your first post, just visit the post's permalink URL and scroll down until you see the comment form.

As you're already logged in, all you have to do is write something in the text area and click on **Post Comment**. The comment form you'll see is basic and doesn't leave much room for error:

However, those who are not logged in to the wp-admin will see a slightly different one as shown in the following screenshot:

Later, we'll explore how we can control which comments show up right away and which comments have to wait for you to verify them as valid, as well as which fields are required for visitors.

Retrieving a lost password

If you have lost your password and can't get into your wp-admin panel, you can easily retrieve it by clicking on the **Lost your password?** link on the login page. A newly generated password will be emailed to you at the email address you provided during the installation process. This is why you need to be sure that you enter a valid email address. Otherwise, you will not be able to retrieve your password.

Getting a Gravatar

One final point that's worth discussing in this chapter is the matter of WordPress avatars. Although WordPress provides a number of possibilities in this area, the most popular one revolves around an external service, **Globally Recognized Avatar (Gravatar)**. Gravatar started as a tool meant to provide people with the capability of using the same profile picture (avatar) across the entire web.

What this means in plain English is that whenever you sign up for a web service, and if the service is Gravatar-compatible, so to speak, then it will fetch your profile picture from Gravatar automatically, instead of forcing you to upload it manually from your computer. Apart from the profile picture, Gravatar also gives you a personal online profile that anyone can see whenever they click on your (Gravatar) profile picture or something called Hovercard. Now, what does all this have to do with WordPress, right? Well, WordPress is one of those services and tools that widely support Gravatar in all possible areas of the platform. For example, if you create a new blog and use an admin email address that's hooked up to Gravatar, your profile picture in WordPress will immediately be replaced with the one provided by Gravatar. Moreover, if you ever comment on any WordPress blog with a Gravatar email address, your profile picture will be set as the avatar for the comment itself.

To set your own Gravatar, just go to http://gravatar.com/ and click on the **Sign In** button in the right corner of the screen. You'll be presented with a login form and a small sign-up link labeled **Create an Account**. If you already have a WordPress.com account, then you can safely login with it. If not, click on the **Create an Account** link, which will redirect you to the sign-up page. The fields are quite standard, with you being prompted to enter your email address and your preferred username and password. Once you've completed the sign-up process, you can finally set your Gravatar. On the main **Manage Gravatars** page (accessible via the top menu), there's a link labeled **Add a new image**, this is where you can upload a Gravatar.

The good thing about Gravatar is that you can choose where you want to get the picture from. You can either upload it from your computer, get it from some other place on the web (for example, from a direct link to your Facebook profile image), or use an image that you've uploaded as your Gravatar previously. In the next step, Gravatar allows you to crop and adjust your image. When you're finally happy with the result, you can click the big button and proceed to the rating settings of your image. Every Gravatar can be classified as **G rated**, **PG rated**, **R rated**, or **X rated**. The fact is that if you select anything other than **G rated**, your Gravatar won't be displayed on all sites. Thus, it's a good practice to upload only appropriate images.

When you're done with this step, from now on, your Gravatar is set up and ready to use. Gravatar also enables you to hook up more than one email address to a single account, as well as use more than one image. This is actually a great feature because you can manage each of your email addresses and every form of your online presence with just one Gravatar account.

Now you can go back to your WordPress blog and check whether your new Gravatar has appeared in the profile section within the wp-admin (provided that you've used the same email address for the account).

Summary

You have learned a lot in this chapter. Now, you can install WordPress on a remote server, change the basic default settings of your website, write posts, and comment on those posts. You also have a basic understanding of how WordPress.com works, and how to handle your online image or brand via Gravatar.

In the next chapter, you will learn about all the other aspects of a blog post that you can control, additional ways to add posts, as well as the intricacies of managing and controlling comments and discussions on your blog.

3
Creating Blog Content

Now that your WordPress installation is up and running, you are ready to start creating content. In this chapter, you will learn:

- How the WordPress admin dashboard works (also commonly referred to as wp-admin) and how to find your way around it
- How to control all of the information associated with a blog post, not just the title and content, but also images and media
- How to work with comments – what they are for and how to manage them
- How to keep your content organized and searchable using tags and categories

WordPress admin conventions

In the wp-admin, you have the ability to manage a number of different types of content and content sorting types, including posts, categories, pages, links, media uploads, and more. WordPress uses a similar format for various screens. Let's explore them here.

Lists of items

For every piece of content in WordPress that you might want to manage, there will be a screen listing them. For example, let's have a look at what a list of posts might look like:

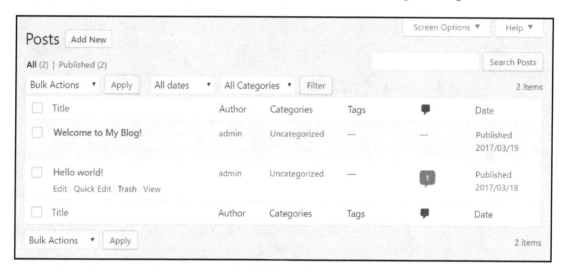

As you can see, the name of the post type is at the top, and the list of items has columns. Let's take a look at the important elements:

- Each item in the list shows its title. You can always click on an item title to edit it.
- If you hover your mouse over a specific row, as I hovered over **Hello world!** in the preceding screenshot, you will see four additional links. The first three are always the same (**Edit, Quick Edit, and Trash**), while the fourth varies between **View** and **Preview**, depending on whether we're dealing with an already published post or one that's pending. The **Edit, Trash** and **View/Preview** links are pretty self-explanatory, but the **Quick Edit** link deserves an additional word. When you click on it, you will see a panel allowing you to perform some simplified editing (just the basic details and parameters, with no actual content editing):

- You can make changes and then click on **Update,** or click on **Cancel** if you've changed your mind.
- The area above the list of posts lets you choose whether to view **All** (posts), **Published** (posts), and also **Drafts**, **Pending**, and **Trash**. At the moment, I have only **All** posts and **Published** posts on my list. But with time, the list is bound to get populated some more, as we're going to continue writing new posts (and the same goes for your own site).
- Just below those links is the **Bulk Actions** menu and its corresponding **Apply** button. Choose one or more posts by clicking on their checkboxes (or check the top checkbox to select every item). Then, choose **Edit** or **Move to Trash** from the **Bulk Actions** menu, and after clicking on **Apply,** you'll be able to bulk delete or bulk edit those posts. Additionally, further down the road, so to speak, when you install some third-party plugins, you'll notice that this **Bulk Actions** menu might contain more options on top of the standard two, editing and deleting.
- The **Filters** menu lets you choose options from the *dates* and *categories* pull-down lists, and then clicks on the **Filter** button to only show items that meet those criteria.
- The search field along with the **Search Posts** button provides yet another way of filtering through your posts, to find the specific one you're looking for. This might not seem like a particularly useful feature at first, but once you have more than, say, 200 posts published on the site, finding individual entries becomes quite a challenge.
- At the very top is the **Screen Options** dropdown. This tab, which appears on every screen on the WordPress dashboard, will allow you to hide or show particular columns, and choose the number of items to show per page.

Posting on your blog

The central activity you'll be doing with your blog is adding posts. A post is like an article in a magazine; it needs a title, content, and an author (in this case, you, though WordPress allows multiple authors to contribute to a blog). A blog post also has a lot of other information attached to it, such as a date, excerpt, tags, and categories. In this section, you will learn how to create a new post, and what kind of information to attach to it.

Adding a simple post

Let's review the process of adding a simple post to your blog, which we carried out in the previous chapter. Whenever you want to add content or carry out a maintenance process on your WordPress website, you have to start by logging in to the **WordPress administration panel (wp-admin)** of your site. To get to the admin panel, just point your web browser to `http://yoursite.com/wp-admin`.

 Remember that if you have installed WordPress in a subfolder (for example, `blog`), then your URL has to include that subfolder (for example, `http://yoursite.com/blog/wp-admin`).

When you first log in to the wp-admin, you'll land at the **Dashboard.** The Dashboard has a lot of information on it, so don't worry about that right now.

The quickest way to get to the **Add New Post** page at any time is to click on **New** (link in the top bar of wp-admin) and then on **Post**. This is the **Add New Post** panel:

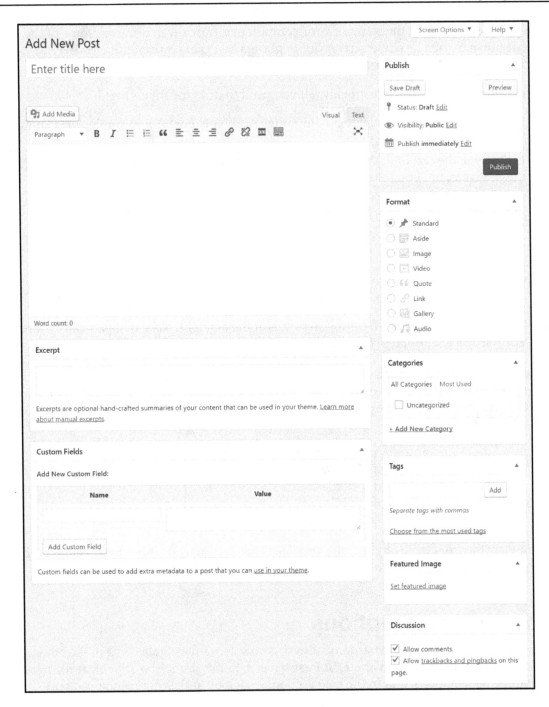

Note that depending on the setup of your computer and your web browser, some of the blocks shown in the preceding screenshot might not be visible by default. However, everything that's crucial for content publication will definitely be on the screen.

To add a new post to your site quickly, all you need to do is the following:

1. Type in a title into the text field under **Add New Post** (for example, `My Top 3 Favorite Dishes`).

2. Type the text of your post in the main content box. Note that the default view is **Visual**, but you have a choice of the **Text** view as well:

3. Click on the **Publish** button, which is at the far right. Note that you can choose to save a *draft* or *preview* your post as well.

Once you click on the **Publish** button, you have to wait while WordPress performs its magic. When the process completes, you'll see yourself still on the same screen, but now the following message will have appeared telling you that your post was published and giving you a **View post** link:

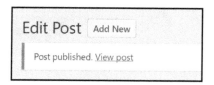

If you view the front page of your site, you'll see that your new post has been added at the top (newest posts are always at the top).

Common post options

Now that we've reviewed the basics of adding a post, let's investigate some of the other options on the **Add New Post** and **Edit Post** screens. In this section, we'll look at the most commonly used options, and in the next section, we'll look at the more advanced ones.

Categories and tags

Categories and tags are two types of information that you can add to a blog post. We use them to organize the information in your blog by topic and content (rather than just by date) and to help visitors find what they are looking for on your blog.

Categories are primarily used for structural organizing. They can be hierarchical, meaning a category can be a parent of another category. A relatively busy blog will probably have at least 10 categories, but probably no more than 15 or 20. Each post in such a blog is likely to have between one and four categories assigned to it. For example, a blog about food and cooking might have these categories: *Recipes, Food Talk, In The Media, Ingredients,* and *Restaurants*. Of course, the numbers mentioned are just suggestions; you can create and assign as many categories as you like. The way you structure your categories is entirely up to you as well. There are no true rules regarding this in the WordPress world, just guidelines like these.

Tags are primarily used as shorthand for describing the topics covered in a particular blog post. A relatively busy blog will have anywhere from 15 to even 100 tags in use. Each post in that blog is likely to have three to ten tags assigned to it. For example, a post on a food blog about a recipe for butternut squash soup may have these tags: *soup, vegetarian, autumn, hot,* and *easy*. Again, you can create and assign as many tags as you like.

Let's add a new post to the blog. After you give it a title and some content, let's add tags and categories. When adding tags, just type your list of tags into the **Tags** box on the right-hand side of the interface, separated by commas:

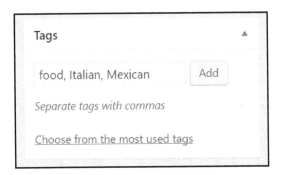

Then, click on the **Add** button. The tags you just typed in will appear below the text field with little x buttons next to them. You can click on any x button to delete a tag. Once you've used some tags on your blog, you'll be able to click on the **Choose from the most used tags** link in this box so that you can easily reuse tags.

Categories work a bit differently than tags. Once you get your blog going, you'll usually just check the boxes next to existing categories in the **Categories** box. In this case, as we don't have any existing categories, we'll have to add one or two.

In the **Categories** box on the right, click on the **+ Add New Category** link. Type your category into the text field, and click on the **+ Add New Category** button. Your new category will show up on the list, already checked. Look at the following screenshot:

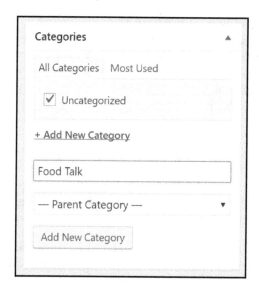

If, in the future you want to add a category that needs a parent category, select **Parent category** from the pull-down menu, before clicking on the **+ Add New Category** button. If you want to manage more details about your categories, move them around, rename them, assign parent categories, and assign descriptive text, you can do so on the **Categories** page, which we'll see in detail later in this chapter.

Click on the **Publish** button, and you're done (you can instead choose to schedule a post; we'll explore that in detail in a few pages). When you look at the front page of your site, you'll see your new post on the top, your new category in the sidebar, and the tags and category (that you chose for your post) listed under the post itself.

Images in your posts

Almost every good blog post needs an image! This will give the reader an instant idea of what the post is about, and the image will draw people's attention in as well. WordPress makes it easy to add an image to your post, control default image sizes, make minor edits to that image, and designate a *featured* image for your post.

Adding an image to a post

Luckily, WordPress makes adding images to your content very easy. Let's add an image to the post we've just created a minute ago. You can click on **Edit** underneath your post on the front page of your site to get there quickly. Alternatively, go back to the wp-admin, open **Posts** from the main sidebar menu, and then click on the post's title.

To add an image to a post, first, you'll need to have that image on your computer or know the exact URL pointing to the image if it's already online. Before you get ready to upload an image, make sure that your image is optimized for the web; for instance, you can use a service like **TinyPNG** (`https://tinypng.com/`). Huge files will be uploaded slowly and slow down the process of viewing your site. Just to give you a good example here, I'm using a photo of my own so I don't have to worry about any copyright issues (always make sure to use only the images that you have the right to use, copyright infringement online is a serious problem, to say the least). Once you have a picture on your computer and know where it is, carry out the following steps to add the photo to your blog post:

1. Click on the **Add Media** button, which is right above the content box and below the title box:

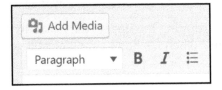

2. The box that appears allows you to do a number of different things regarding the media you want to include in your post. The most user-friendly feature here, however, is the drag-and-drop support. Just grab the image from your desktop, and drop it in the center area of the page, labeled **Drop files anywhere to upload**:

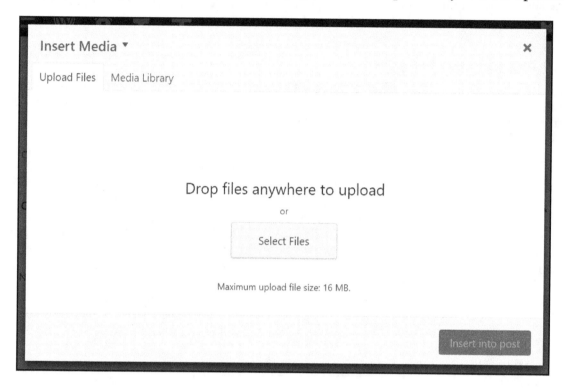

3. Immediately after dropping the image, the uploader bar will show the progress of the operation, and when it's done, you'll be able to do some final fine-tuning:

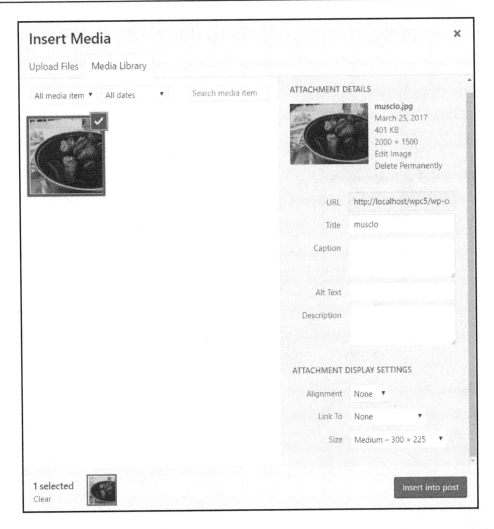

4. The fields that are important right now are **Title**, **Alt Text**, **Alignment**, **Link To,** and **Size. Title** is a description for the image, **Alt Text** is a phrase that's going to appear instead of the image in case the file goes missing or any other problems present themselves; **Alignment** will tell the image whether to have text wrap around it and whether it should be right, left, or center; **Link To** instructs WordPress whether or not to link the image to anything (a common solution is to select **None**); and **Size** is the size of the image (you can select from a couple of presets).

5. Once you have all of these fields filled out, click on **Insert into post**. This box will disappear, and your image will show up in the post--right where your cursor was prior to clicking on the **Add Media** button, on the edit page itself (in the Visual editor, that is; if you're using the Text editor, then the HTML code of the image will be displayed instead).

6. Now, click on the **Update** button, and go look at the front page of your site again. There's your image!

Controlling default image sizes

You may be wondering about those image sizes that I mentioned a couple of paragraphs earlier. What if you want bigger or smaller thumbnails? Whenever you upload an image, WordPress creates three versions of that image for you. You can set the pixel dimensions of those three versions by opening **Settings** in the main sidebar menu, and then clicking on **Media**. This takes you to the **Media Settings** page:

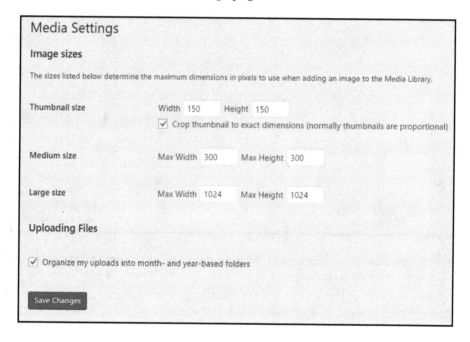

Here, you can specify the size of the uploaded images for the following:

- **Thumbnail size**
- **Medium size**
- **Large size**

If you change the dimensions on this page and click on the **Save Changes** button, only the images you upload in the future will be affected. Images you've already uploaded to the site will stay at their original thumbnail, medium and large versions. It's a good idea to decide what you want your three media sizes to be early on in your site's lifespan, so you can set them and have them applied to all images, right from the start.

Another thing about uploading images is the craze for HiDPI displays, also called Retina displays, or **Ultra High Definition** (**UHD**). Currently, WordPress is a kind of a transitional phase when it comes to images and being in tune with modern display technology; retina-ready functionality was introduced not that long ago in WordPress 3.5. In short, if you want to make your images retina compatible (meaning that they look good on iPads, modern Android phones, and other devices with HiDPI screens), you should upload the images at twice the intended dimensions. For example, if you want your image to be presented as 800 pixels wide and 600 pixels high then upload it as 1600 pixels wide and 1200 pixels high. WordPress will manage to display it properly anyway, and whoever visits your site from a modern device will see a high-definition version of the image. In future versions, WordPress will provide a more managed way of handling retina-compatible images.

Editing an uploaded image

Every image that has been previously uploaded to WordPress can be edited. In order to do this, go to the **Media Library** by clicking on the **Media** button in the main sidebar. What you'll see is a new kind of listing, introduced in one of the latest versions of WordPress. Instead of a traditional list, what you get to work with now is a grid-based archive that gives each piece of media much better visibility. Right now, we only have one image in the library, but as you continue working with your site, the list will become much more impressive:

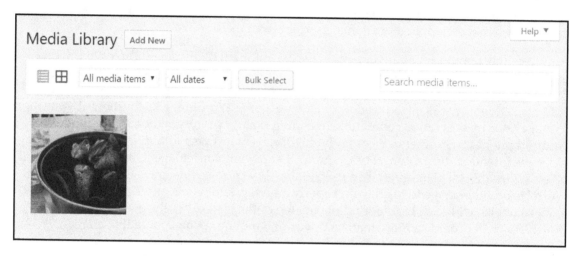

When you click on the image and then on the **Edit Image** button at the bottom of the pop-up window that's going to appear, you'll enter the **Attachment Details** section. Here, you can perform a number of operations to make your image just perfect. As it turns out, WordPress does a good-enough job of simple image tuning so that you don't really need an expensive software such as Adobe Photoshop for this. Among the possibilities, you'll find the option of cropping, rotating, scaling, and flipping vertically and horizontally:

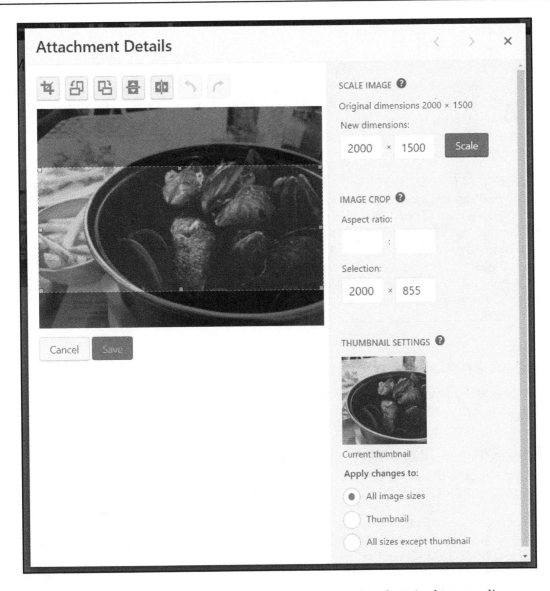

For example, you can use your mouse to draw a box, as I have done in the preceding screenshot. On the right, in the box marked **Image Crop**, you'll see the pixel dimensions of your selection. Click on the *crop* icon (top left), then the **Thumbnail** radio button (on the right), and then **Save** (just below your photo). You now have a new thumbnail! Of course, you can adjust any other version of your image just by making a different selection prior to hitting the Save button. Play around a little until you become familiar with the details.

Designating a featured image

As of WordPress 2.9, you can designate a single image that represents your post. This is referred to as the featured image. Some themes will make use of this, and some will not. The default theme, the one we've been using, is named **Twenty Seventeen**, and it uses the featured image to create a great looking, full-width bar right above the main content of the post. It also includes featured images on the front page, alongside every post. Depending on the theme you're using, its behavior with featured images can vary, but in general, every modern theme supports them in one way or the other.

In order to set a featured image, go to the **Edit Post** screen. In the right sidebar, you'll see a box labeled **Featured Image**. Just click on the **Set featured image** link. After doing so, you'll see a pop-up window, very similar to the one we used when uploading images. Here, you can either upload a completely new image or select an existing image by clicking on it. All you have to do now is click on the **Set featured image** button in the bottom-right corner. After completing the operation, you can finally see what your new image looks like on the front page. Also, keep in mind that WordPress uses featured images in multiple places, and not only the front page. As mentioned before, much of this behavior depends on your current theme.

Videos and other media in your posts

These days, the newest versions of WordPress are capable of not only including images in our blog posts but other types of media too, such as audio files and videos.

Adding videos to blog posts

Luckily for us, the process of adding a video to a standard blog post or page has been made as easy as possible. Let's discuss this step by step.

We're going to start by creating a whole new post. The title we can use is, *Great Baby Back Ribs Recipe*. Creating the post itself is pretty basic. All you need to do is navigate to **Posts | Add New**. You'll see a screen that we've already covered earlier in this chapter. Let's put some example content in place, and try including a video right away. All we have to do in order to achieve this is copy and paste the URL of the video that we'd like to have included in our content. Just a standard copy-and-paste, and nothing else.

 When copying the URL of the video, it's important to make sure that the link is copied as-is in raw-text form (not hyperlinked anywhere: that is, not clickable).

The example I'm going to use here is the video at `http://www.youtube.com/watch?v=` `hDyHbTxTL-A`.

As you would have guessed, it's a nice video recipe for some baby back ribs! So in order to include this video in a blog post, all I need to do is take its URL and just paste it in. This is the raw-text content of the new post that I'm working on now:

```
Here's a great video recipe for some killer baby back ribs:

http://www.youtube.com/watch?v=hDyHbTxTL-A

(by Laura Vitale)
```

Now, when I save such a post, the URL of the video will be turned into a live video automatically. This will happen both on the front page of the website and even on the **Edit Post** screen itself. Refer to the following screenshot:

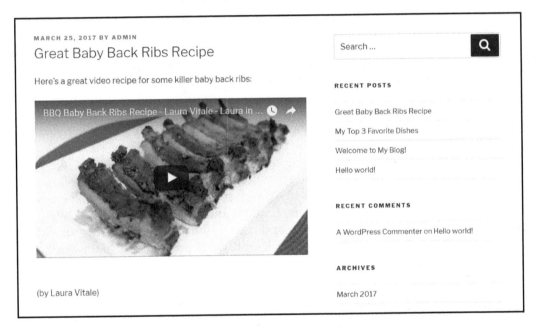

To give the post some more unique presence, I also added a new category, **Recipes**, and I assigned the post to a new content type, **Video**. This is done through the sidebar on the **Edit Post** screen. We will talk more about different content types later in this chapter. Take a look at the following screenshot:

The process described here explains how to embed YouTube videos and make them a part of your blog posts, but the same goes for other popular platforms like Vimeo, TED, Hulu, WordPress.tv, and others. To get the full list of the supported platforms, please visit `https://codex.wordpress.org/Embeds`.

One more method of adding videos to blog posts, which we left out initially, is uploading the raw video files manually (instead of using a third-party platform like YouTube). Although this is possible in WordPress, you can drag and drop a video file just like you'd do with an image, it's not a recommended solution. Video files are always quite large in size, and having them hosted on your standard web server can become very expensive (bandwidth costs), should the video become popular and end up being viewed by thousands of people. It's a lot more efficient and user-friendly to just upload your video to YouTube or a similar platform, and then have it embedded on your site, like we've explained a minute ago.

Adding audio to blog posts

Not surprisingly at this point, it turns out that WordPress makes adding audio to your blog posts, just as easy as adding a video. To demonstrate this, I'm going to create an entirely new post and call it, *Some Paleo Wisdom With Robb Wolf*. In it, I'm going to share a podcast episode of Robb's. To do that, just like with videos, I have to get a direct URL of the audio file that I want to share on the blog.

Going to Robb's site, I quickly find the episode I'm after available at `http://traffic.`
`libsyn.com/robbwolf/PaleoSolution-240.mp3`. So, I take this URL, and just like with
video, I paste it right into my new blog post's content box as follows:

```
Check out this great podcast episode by Robb Wolf:
http://traffic.libsyn.com/robbwolf/PaleoSolution-240.mp3
```

WordPress will pick that URL immediately and turn it into a live audio streaming. When I
publish my new post, this becomes visible right away. The next screenshot presents what
my new post looks like on the front page:

Now, in this example, I used a direct URL address of an audio file (the MP3 podcast), but I
can also use a direct URL of an audio recording at SoundCloud, Spotify, or Rdio, plus a
bunch of other services. Again, to get the full list of supported platforms, feel free to visit
`https://codex.wordpress.org/Embeds`.

Adding raw audio files is possible too. However, this presents the same problems as we
mentioned when talking about video files. Even though audio files are always smaller in
size than videos, they can still cost you a lot of money if you're attempting to host them on
your standard web server. It's, therefore, usually a better solution to upload your audio
somewhere else (such as, SoundCloud, for example), and then just embed the audio inside
of a blog post like we're describing here.

Limited editing possibilities

Unlike with images, WordPress doesn't really give us any editing possibilities when it
comes to media like audio or video. It's understandable that images can be manipulated in a
lot of ways, for example, they can be rotated, cropped, scaled, and so on. However, there's
no such possibility with videos. Once a video file or audio file is produced, we can't alter it
in any way. We can only take it and display it on our sites as is.

Using the Visual editor versus the Text editor

WordPress comes with a **Visual** editor, otherwise known as a WYSIWYG editor (pronounced *wissy-wig*, and stands for **What You See Is What You Get**). This is the default editor for typing and editing your posts. If you're comfortable with HTML, you may prefer to write and edit your posts using the **Text** editor--particularly useful if you want to add special content or styling. To switch from the rich text editor to the **Text** editor, click on the **Text** tab next to the **Visual** tab at the top of the content box:

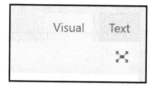

You'll see your post in all its raw HTML glory, and you'll get a new set of buttons that let you quickly bold and italicize text, as well as add link code, image code, and so on. You can make changes, and swap back and forth between the tabs to see the result.

For example, going back to the post we were building just a minute ago, the one with the embedded podcast episode--when we switch between **Visual** and **Text**, we'll see that in the **Visual** editor mode, the link to the audio file has already been turned into a live audio player, while in the **Text** editor mode, we can still see the URL in its raw form. The next screenshot presents this side by side:

Even though the **Text** editor allows you to use any HTML element in existence, it's not a fully fledged HTML support. For instance, using <p> tags is not necessary for the **Text** editor, as they will be stripped by default. In order to create a new paragraph in the **Text** editor, all you need to do is press the *Enter* key twice. That being said, at the same time, the Text editor is currently the only way to use HTML tables in WordPress (within posts and pages).

You can easily place your table content inside `<table>`, `<tr>`, and `<td>` tags and WordPress won't alter them in any way, effectively allowing you to create the exact table you want. Another thing the Text editor is most commonly used for is introducing custom HTML parameters in `<img/>` and `<a>` tags, and also custom CSS classes in other popular tags. Some content creators actually prefer working with the Text editor, rather than the Visual editor because it gives them much more control and more certainty regarding the way their content is going to be presented on the frontend.

Lead and body

One of the many interesting publishing features WordPress has to offer is the concept of the lead and the body of the post. This may sound like a strange thing, but it's actually quite simple. When you're publishing a new post, you don't necessarily want to display its whole contents right away on the front page. A much more user-friendly approach is to display only the lead, and then display the complete post under its individual URL. Achieving this in WordPress is very simple. All you have to do is use the Insert Read More Tag button, available in the **Visual** editor (or the more button in the **Text** editor). Simply place your cursor exactly where you want to break your post (the text before the cursor will become the lead), and then click the Insert More Tag button:

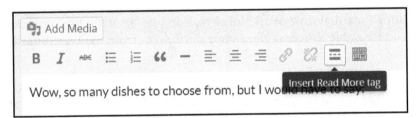

An alternative way of using this tag is to switch to the **Text** editor and input the tag manually, which is `<!--more-->`. Both approaches produce the same result. Clicking on the main **Update** button will save the changes.

On the front page, most WordPress themes display such posts by presenting the lead along with a **Continue reading** link, and then the whole post (both the lead and the rest of the post) is displayed under the post's individual URL.

Drafts, pending articles, and timestamps

There are three additional items I'd like to cover in this section: drafts, pending articles, and timestamps.

Drafts

WordPress gives you the option to save a draft of your post, so that you don't have to publish it right away, but can still save your work. If you've started writing a post and want to save a draft, just click on the **Save Draft** button at the right (in the **Publish** box), instead of the **Publish** button. Even if you don't click on the **Save Draft** button, WordPress will attempt to save a draft of your post for you, about once a minute. You'll see this in the area just below the content box. The text will say **Saving Draft...** and then show the time of the last draft saved:

At this point, after a manual save or an autosave, you can leave the **Edit Post** page and do other things. You'll be able to access all of your draft posts from the **Dashboard**, or from the **Edit Posts** page.

In essence, drafts are meant to hold your *work in progress*, which means all articles that haven't been finished yet, or haven't even been started yet, and obviously everything in between.

Pending articles

Pending articles is a functionality that's going to be a lot more helpful to people working with multi-author blogs, rather than single-author blogs. In a bigger publishing structure, there are individuals responsible for different areas of the publishing process. WordPress, being a quality tool, supports such a structure by providing a way to save articles as **Pending Review**. In an editor-author relationship, if an editor sees a post marked as **Pending Review**, they know that they should have a look at it and prepare it for publication.

That's it for the theory, and now how to do it. When creating a new post, click on the **Edit** link right next to the **Status: Draft** label:

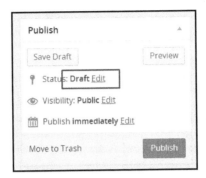

Right after doing so, you'll be presented with a new drop-down menu from which you can select **Pending Review**, and then click the **OK** button. Now, just click the **Save as Pending** button that will appear in place of the old **Save Draft** button, and you have a shiny new article that's pending review.

Timestamps

WordPress will also let you alter the timestamp of your post. This is useful if you are writing a post today that you wish you'd published yesterday, or if you're writing a post in advance and don't want it to show up until the right day. By default, the timestamp will be set to the present moment. To change it, just find the **Publish** box, and click on the **Edit** link (next to the calendar icon and **Publish immediately**). New fields will show up, and you will be able to alter the publication date:

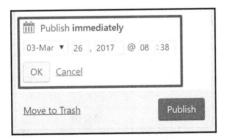

Change the details, click on the **OK** button, and then click on **Publish** or **Schedule** (depending on whether your new publication date is set in the past or in the future).

Advanced post options

By now, you have a handle on the most common and simple options for posts, and you may be wondering about some of the other options on the **Edit Post** page. We'll cover them all in this section.

A quick display tip

When you first visit the **Edit Post** page, some of the advanced options (**Excerpt, Custom Fields, Discussion, Revisions, Author,** and **Format**) are *open* below the post content. If you never use them and want to clean up the look of this page, you can single-click each bar and they'll collapse. You can also rearrange them by dragging them to form a new order. You can also use **Screen Options** (top right of the page) to uncheck certain boxes, and thus not display them at all.

Excerpt

WordPress offers theme designers the option to show a post's **Excerpt** (instead of its full content or lead+body) on pages within the theme:

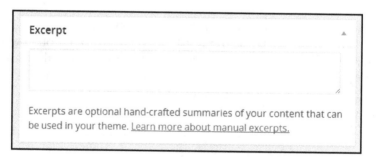

This is how the excerpt works:

- If you enter some text into the **Excerpt** box on the **Edit Post** page, that text will be used as the post's excerpt on the pages that call for it.
- If you do not enter any text into the **Excerpt** box, WordPress will use the first 55 words of the post's content (which is stripped of HTML tags) followed by [...] (which is not a link).
- If you do not enter any text into the **Excerpt** box, and the theme you are using does something special, the number of words and the final text could be different.

You are never required to enter excerpt text. However, it is advisable that you do take advantage of this possibility. Excerpts can introduce big readability improvements to your site, and make your content easier to grasp for the reader, provided that your current theme uses excerpts in one way or the other. In some cases, excerpts also give your site additional SEO benefits - provided that your theme displays them in places where Google and the other search engines can see them.

The `more` tag (`<!--more-->`), which has been described in one of the previous sections in this chapter, should not be confused with the excerpt. It is different from the excerpt because of you, not the theme designer, controls its use. Additionally, the `more` tag is supported by every theme and has a slightly different task than the excerpt. It's meant to present the lead of the post, the part that's going to convince the reader to visit the complete post, while the excerpt is a summary of the post's contents.

Discussion

The **Discussion** box on the post editing screen (sometimes needs enabling through **Screen Options**) has two checkboxes in it: one for allowing comments, and the other for trackbacks and pingbacks. When you first install WordPress, both these checkboxes will be checked by default. You have to uncheck them if you want to turn off the comments or trackbacks and pingbacks for the post:

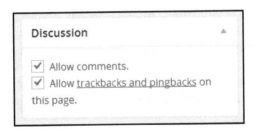

If you uncheck the **Allow comments** box, visitors will not be able to comment on that given blog post.

If you uncheck the **Allow trackbacks and pingbacks on this page** box, when other people mention your blog post and link to it on their own websites, your blog won't notice this fact. If the box stays checked, other people's pingbacks about this post will show up under your post along with standard comments, if any.

If you want either or both of these boxes to be unchecked by default, go to **Settings**, and then **Discussion** in the main menu. You can uncheck either or both of the boxes labeled, **Allow link notifications from other blogs (pingbacks and trackbacks) on new articles** and **Allow people to post comments on new articles.**

A word on trackbacks and pingbacks

Originally, the trackback and pingback functionality was meant to provide you with a way to communicate with other websites--to let them know that you've published a post mentioning them in one way or the other (usually through a link). However, nowadays, trackbacks, and pingbacks are becoming somewhat out-of-date and most bloggers don't even bother to check the trackbacks/pingbacks that they're receiving. For what it's worth, you can probably safely ignore trackbacks and pingbacks altogether. Nevertheless, the decision whether or not to support them on your site is entirely up to you.

If you want to learn more about trackbacks and pingbacks, you can go to the Codex at `https://codex.wordpress.org/Introduction_to_Blogging#Trackbacks` and `https://codex.wordpress.org/Introduction_to_Blogging#Pingbacks`.

Custom Fields

Custom Fields are WordPress' way of giving you the possibility to include some additional information in your blog posts (information that you don't want to display directly on the frontend). In essence, **Custom Fields** are a kind of semi-programming tool--they are not exactly *code* as understood by PHP programmers, yet they do give you the possibility to tweak your content in a certain, non-stock way. Many WordPress themes use various **Custom Fields** to style the individual aspects of posts. For example, some theme creators use **Custom Fields** to disable the sidebar on certain posts or include various typographic elements.

As another example, let's say you are a gadget reviewer and every blog post is a review of some cool new thing. Every time you write a review, you're writing it about a product that's made by some company, and you'd like to have that company's logo associated with the blog post. You can make a custom field called `company_logo` and the value can be the path to the logo image:

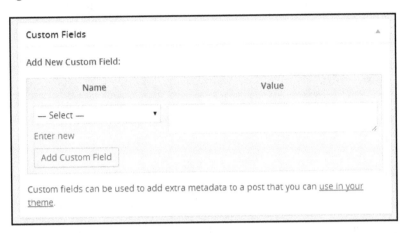

To display or make use of this Custom Field information, you either have to modify your theme files manually or use a plugin.

Learning More

Read more about custom fields in the WordPress Codex at `https://codex.wordpress.org/Using_Custom_Fields`.

Working with post revisions

Apart from many content formatting features, WordPress also allows some basic version control for your posts. What this means is that WordPress keeps every subversion of your every post. Or in plain English, every time you press the **Update** button, instead of overwriting the previous version of your post, WordPress creates a completely new one. Although this feature doesn't seem like the most useful one at first, it's actually very important for sites where the content is managed by more than one person. In such a scenario, it's easy to get the newest versions of the posts mixed up, so it's always good to have the possibility to return to the previous one.

To take full advantage of this functionality, what you need to do first is enable **Revisions** in the upper slide-down **Screen Options** menu on the post editing screen. Once you do so, a small box titled **Revisions** will appear at the bottom of the screen:

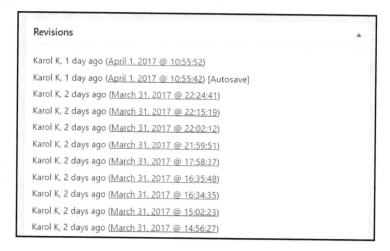

If you click on any of the links displayed inside this box, you will be taken to a page where you can compare individual revisions, and then restore the one you want to work with from now on. The interface provides the main slider that can be used to select individual revisions of the post. This is visible in the following screenshot:

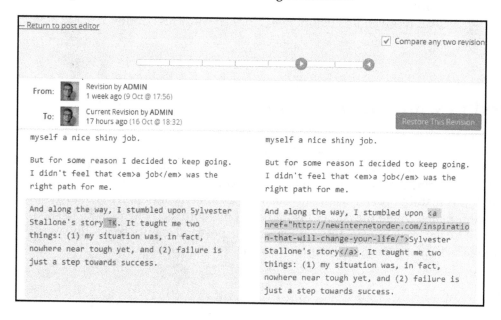

The revision functionality has two main versions. The first one is when the **Compare any two revisions** box isn't checked, and it lets you compare the revision that's currently selected (on the slider) to the revision directly preceding it. The second version is when the **Compare any two revisions** box is checked. In this case, you can select the revisions you want to compare individually which essentially allows you to compare any two revisions, just like the box suggests. The revision on the left is always the *previous* revision, while the one on the right is the next or *current* one (visible in the preceding screenshot). For every paragraph where there is a difference found, this will be highlighted in red and green, and every individual difference will have additional highlighting. Clicking on the **Restore This Revision** button will restore the revision on the right, and you will be brought back to the post editing screen automatically.

If you feel that revisions won't be of any particular use to your site, then you can simply choose to not pay attention to the **Revisions** box. When you work with your content normally, not worrying about the revisions, WordPress will always display the most recent versions of your posts by default.

Changing the author of the post

This is a very basic feature in WordPress, so let's only take a minute to discuss it. Basically, every post and page in WordPress has an author, which is quite obvious in itself. However, if you want to, you can change the assigned author of any given entry. In order to do it, just go to the post editing screen or the page editing screen, and scroll down until you see the **Author** box. If it's not visible, enable it from the pull-down **Screen Options** menu. Refer to the following screenshot:

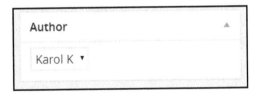

The box contains just one drop-down menu that lists every user account on your site. Just select a new author, and click on the **Update** button. That's all. If you only have one user, the admin account, on your site, then the box will only contain one name.

Protecting content

WordPress gives you the option to hide posts. You can hide a post from everyone but yourself by marking it **Private** (although the user roles of *admin* and *editor* will still see it), or you can hide it from everyone, but the people with whom you share a password by marking it as **Password protected**. To implement this, look at the **Publish** box at the upper right of the **Edit Post** panel. If you click on the **Edit** link next to **Visibility: Public**, a few options will appear:

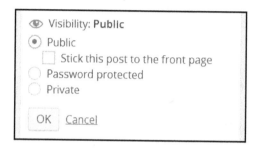

If you click on the **Password protected** radio button, you'll get a box where you can type a password (limited to 20 characters). Visitors to your blog will see the post title, along with a note that they have to type in a password to read the post.

If you click on the **Private** radio button, the post will not show up on the blog at all to any viewers, unless you are the viewer, and you are logged in. The post will also appear if the person browsing the site is a logged-in editor (having the user role of **Editor**).

If you leave the post **Public** and check the **Stick this post to the front page** checkbox, this post will be the first post on the front page, regardless of its publication date.

Be sure to click on the **OK** button, if you make any changes.

Pretty post slug

We've already talked about tuning the permalinks settings of your site in Chapter 2, *Getting Started with WordPress*. Now is a good moment to expand on this knowledge and discuss a little something called the **post slug**. One of the most accurate definitions of what a post slug comes from the WordPress Codex itself. The one provided at https://codex. wordpress.org/Glossary#Post_Slug teaches us that the post slug is made from a few lowercase words separated by dashes, describing a post and usually derived from the post title to create a user-friendly permalink.

In other words, the post slug is what comes after your domain name in the post's URL. For example, my post about my top three favorite dishes uses this URL: `http://localhost/wpc5/my-top-3-favorite-dishes/`, where the last part--`my-top-3-favorite-dishes`, is the slug. Just like the official definition says, WordPress chooses the slug by taking my post title, making it all lowercase, removing all punctuation, and replacing spaces with dashes. If I'd prefer it to be something else, such as `3-favorite-dishes`, I can change it in the area just below the post's title:

Just click on **Edit** to change the slug. Readable URLs are something that Google Search loves, so using them helps to optimize your site for search engines. It also helps users figure out what a post is about before clicking on the URL.

Custom post format settings

Since you will most likely start your WordPress journey with the default theme--Twenty Seventeen, I should probably say a few words about one more box that's visible on the post editing screen--the one titled **Format**. We've already touched upon this briefly when talking about publishing videos and audio files along with your posts:

Some themes provide basic, ready-made formatting styles for certain types of posts. However, Twenty Seventeen isn't one of the most functional themes in this regard. In its current version, there's no visual difference at all between the various **Format** options. However, there are hundreds of other themes out there that support the **Format** functionality more broadly. Here are some examples derived from the previous default theme, Twenty Thirteen. First, we have a post saved as Standard:

Then the same post saved as Quote:

And, finally, saved as Status:

Additional writing options

In addition to simply logging into the wp-admin, you have a couple of other possible ways for adding posts to your blog.

Press This

WordPress offers a neat bookmarklet called **Press This**. You can put it into your browser's bookmarks or favorites, and it will let you quickly write a blog post about the website you're visiting. You may have encountered this same feature as offered by Facebook, and other social networking sites.

You just have to add **Press This** to your browser once, and then you can use it anytime. To add the **Press This** link to your browser, in the wp-admin, go to the **Tools** page. At the top of the page is the **Press This** box. Just use your mouse, and drag the button up to your browser's bookmarks bar as shown in the following:

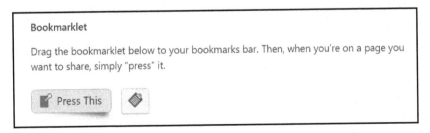

Now you can use it! For example, if you're browsing through a website and you've just read an article you'd like to mention in a blog post, just click on the **Press This** bookmark. A window will pop up with the post editing screen in it. You can write whatever text you want, add tags and categories, and then either save the post as a draft or publish it right away.

Calypso by WordPress.com

Calypso is a piece of software developed by the WordPress.com guys. It's a desktop-based blogging tool. You can download it for free from `https://apps.wordpress.com/desktop/`. There are versions for both Windows and Mac available. Calypso works similarly to any other software that you happen to have on your computer right now. After you install it, you can log in to your WordPress.com account, and then manage all your websites that are hooked up to that WordPress.com account from within the Calypso software.

The tool itself is very easy to use and very efficient. However, it does require a live internet connection to work. Think of it as an alternative way of accessing your WordPress.com account, via your desktop instead of a web browser. The user interface itself looks exactly like your dashboard at the WordPress.com website.

To learn more about Calypso and how to use it, you can visit this in-depth guide: `https://premium.wpmudev.org/blog/calypso-tour/`.

Mobile apps for iOS and Android

This final method of posting content on WordPress is growing stronger every year, or even every month. The mobile usage of the web is constantly rising, and this is reflected in the way people interact with their WordPress sites or blogs. It's not surprising that there's a great wealth of blogging tools and apps for the two most popular mobile platforms, iOS, and Android. Both systems have the native WordPress app available. You can get these apps at `https://apps.wordpress.com/mobile/`. The user interfaces of the apps have some minor differences depending on what device you're using to access the app with, but the core functionality remains the same.

The app is very user-friendly and guides you through all the crucial steps of setting up a connection with your blog. You can add a new site from the **Settings** menu. Once you do so, you get to use a standard set of features that let you in on a variety of actions that you can perform on your site's content. You can create and edit posts, do the same with pages, moderate comments, and hop over to the site's wp-admin via a direct link. Everything is available from a clear menu in the center of the screen. Here's what the main screen of the app looks like in the iPad edition:

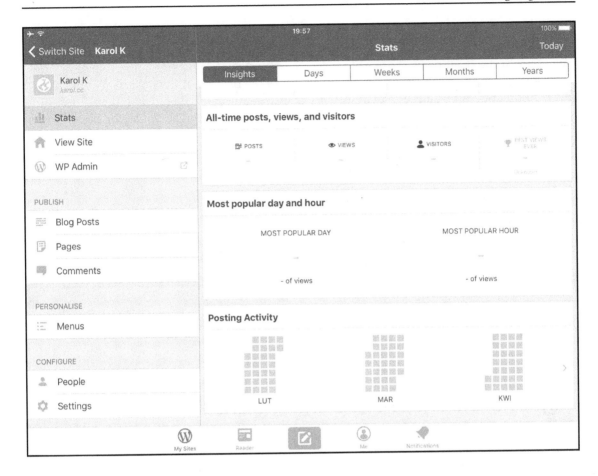

Discussion on your blog – comments

Comments are an important element for most blogs. While you are the only person who can write blog posts, the visitors to your blog can add comments to your posts. This can fuel a sense of community within a blog, allow people to give you feedback on your writing, and give your visitors a way to help or talk to other visitors. The only downside of commenting is that unscrupulous people will try to misuse your blog's ability to accept comments, and will try to post spam or advertisements on your blog instead of relevant comments. It's actually reported by Akismet, one of the leaders in spam fighting on WordPress blogs, that there are 7.5 million spam comments being processed every hour. What this means is simple--whether we like it or not, spam is an integral part of our online journey. Luckily, the WordPress community is always developing more ways of fixing the problem.

Adding a comment

If you look at the front page of your blog, you'll see that every post has a link that says **Leave a Reply**. Clicking on that link will take you to the bottom of the post page, which is where comments can be added, as we saw in Chapter 2, *Getting Started with WordPress*.

If you're logged into the wp-admin, you'll see your name and a space to write your comment. If you're not logged in, you'll see a comment form that any other visitor will see. This form includes fields to fill in name, email, and website, along with the commenting text area.

Once you type in the required information and click on the **Post Comment** button, the comment will be entered into the WordPress database, along with all of your other blog information. How soon it shows up on the site depends on your discussion settings. Take a look at the following screenshot:

Discussion settings

In the preceding screenshot, notice that **Name*** and **Email*** fields are both marked as required (*). As the owner of the blog/site, you can change the requirements for comments. First, log into the wp-admin and navigate to **Settings** | **Discussion**. We explored the first box (**Default article settings**), earlier in this chapter.

Submission, notification, and moderation settings

Let's focus on the checkboxes on this page that relate only to submission, notification, and moderation. The boxes that are checked on this page will determine how much moderation and checking a comment has to go through before it gets posted on the blog.

The default settings are relatively strict. The only way to make a more strictly controlled discussion on your blog is to check **Comment must be manually approved**. This option means that no matter what, all comments go into the moderation queue, and do not show up on the site until you manually approve them.

Let's look at the settings having to do with the comment submission that are visible under **Other comment settings**. The first two options control what the user has to do before even being able to type in a comment:

- **Comment author must fill out the name and email**: As you noticed in the screenshot in the adding a **Comment** section, **Name*** and **Email*** fields are required. If you leave this checked, then anyone posting a comment will encounter an error if they try to leave either of the fields blank. This doesn't add a huge amount of security because robots know how to fill out a name and an email and because anyone can put fake information in there. However, it does help your blog readers to keep a track of who is who if a long discussion develops, and it can slightly discourage utterly impulsive commenting. Also, visitors who have a Gravatar account (mentioned in the previous chapter), are quite willing to provide their email addresses anyway. That's because using an email address that's connected to Gravatar will result in their profile picture (avatar) being displayed along with the comment, making it much more personal and visible among all the other comments.

- **Users must be registered and logged in to comment**: Most bloggers do not check this box because it means that only visitors who register for the blog can comment. Most bloggers don't want random people registering, and most visitors don't want to be compelled to register to your blog. If you check this box, there's a good chance you'll get no comments (which may be what you want). Alternatively, if you're setting up a blog for a closed community of people, this setting might be useful.

- **Automatically close comments on articles older than X days**: Here, you can set any number of days, after which the comments on your content will be closed. Although this feature might not seem like a useful one at first, it can actually be valuable to various kinds of news sites or other online publications, where allowing comments on old events makes very little sense.

- **Enable threaded (nested) comments X levels deep**: This option is enabled by default, and it's yet another way of making your site more readable and user-friendly. Sometimes commenters want to be able to respond to someone else's comments, simply as part of an ongoing discussion. This is the feature that allows them to do so. Also, it gives you, the author, a great way of interacting with your audience, through direct responses to every comment of theirs.

- **Break comments into pages [...]**: This feature won't be of any value to you unless you're getting more than 200 comments per post. So you can confidently leave it unchecked for now.

Now, let's look at the settings that have to do with moderation visible under **Before a comment appears**. These two options have to do with the circumstances that allow comments to appear on the site.

- **Comment must be manually approved**: As I mentioned earlier, if this box is checked, every comment has to be manually approved by you before it appears on the site.

- **Comment author must have a previously approved comment**: If you uncheck the box above this, but check this one, then you've relaxed your settings a little bit. This means that if the person commenting has commented before and had his or her comment approved, then the person's future comments don't have to be verified by you; they'll just appear on the website immediately. The person just has to enter the same name and email as the one in the previously approved comment.

Now, let's look at the settings that have to do with notifications. These two options are under the **Email me whenever** header. These options are related to the circumstances of receiving an email notification about the comment activity:

- **Anyone posts a comment**: This is generally a good setting to keep. You'll get an email whenever anyone posts a comment-whether or not it needs to be moderated. This will make it easier for you to follow the discussion on your blog, and to be aware of a comment that is not moderated, and requires deletion quickly.
- **A comment is held for moderation**: If you're not particularly interested in following every comment on your blog, you can uncheck the **Anyone posts a comment** checkbox, and only leave this one checked. You will only get an email about legitimate-looking comments that appear to need moderation and need your approval.

When to moderate or blacklist a comment

If you scroll down the page a bit, you'll see the **Comment Moderation** area:

This is an extension of the moderation settings from the top of the page. Note that if you've checked the **Comment must be manually approved** checkbox, you can safely ignore this **Comment Moderation** box. Otherwise, you can use this box to help WordPress figure out which comments are probably okay, and which might be spam or inappropriate for your blog. You can tell WordPress to suspect a comment if it has more than a certain number of links, as spam comments often are just a list of URLs.

The larger box is for you to enter suspect words and IP addresses:

- Here, you can type words that are commonly found in spam (you can figure this out by looking through your junk mail in your email), or just uncouth words in general.
- The IP addresses you will enter into this box would be those of any comments you've gotten in the past from someone who comments inappropriately or adds actual spam. Whenever WordPress receives a comment on your blog, it captures the IP address for you so that you'll have them handy.

Scroll down a bit more, and you'll see the **Comment Blacklist** box:

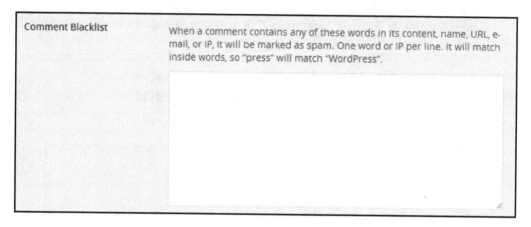

Unlike the **Comment Moderation** box we just saw, which tells WordPress how to identify suspect comments, the **Comment Blacklist** box tells WordPress how to identify comments that are almost definitely bad. These comments won't be added to the moderation queue, and you won't get an email about them; they'll be marked right away as spam.

Avatar display settings

The final box on this page is the **Avatars** box. Just as I mentioned in `Chapter 2, Getting Started with WordPress`, an avatar is an image that is a person's personal icon. Avatars in WordPress are provided through Gravatar--a service available at `http://gravatar.com/` that lets you create your personal online profile, which is going to then be consistently used on other websites across the web. By default, avatars will show up on your blog if you leave the **Show Avatars** radio button checked, which is visible near the bottom of the discussion settings page.

The second box, **Maximum Rating**, will tell WordPress when it should not show avatars that have been rated as too explicit. Remember the rating we were setting when uploading a new picture to Gravatar? This setting here is the place where you can choose which pictures you want to allow on your own site (selecting the **G** rating is advisable).

The third box, **Default Avatar**, tells WordPress what avatar to use for visitors who do not come with their own gravatar.

Moderating comments

Now that we've thoroughly explored the settings for which comments need to be moderated, let's discuss what you actually need to do to moderate comments. *Moderating* means that you look over a comment that is in limbo and decide whether it's insightful enough that it can be published on your site. If it's good, it gets to appear on the frontend of your website; and if it is bad, it's either marked as spam, or is deleted and is never seen by anyone but you, and the person who wrote it.

To view comments waiting for moderation, log in to your wp-admin and navigate to **Comments** in the main menu. If you have any comments waiting for moderation, there will be a little number in the main menu telling you how many comments await moderation:

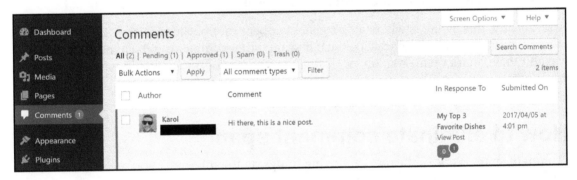

This main **Comments** page is fully featured, just like the **Posts** page. For each comment, you see the following information from left to right:

- Commenter avatar, name, website address (if there was any given), email address (if there was any given), and IP (if there was any given)
- Comment text, along with links to approve it so that it shows up on the site (the links appear when you hover your mouse over the comment), you can also mark it as **Spam**, **Trash** it, **Edit** it, **Quick Edit** it, or **Reply** to it

- Comment submission time and date
- The title of the post on which the comment was made (which is also a link to edit that post), a number in parentheses indicating how many approved comments are already there on that post (which is also a link that will filter the comments list so that it shows only comments on this page), and a link to the post itself (labeled **View Post**)

Comments that are awaiting moderation have a red-ish background, like the first comment in the preceding screenshot (you can also see my Gravatar).

You can click on the **Quick Edit** link for any comment to open form fields right within this list. This will allow you to edit the text of the comment and the commenter's name, email, and URL.

You can use the links at the top--**All**, **Pending**, **Approved**, **Spam**, and **Trash**, to filter the list based on those statuses. You can also filter either pings or comments with the **All comment types** pull-down filter menu. You can check one or more comments to apply any of the bulk actions available in the **Bulk Actions** menus at the top and bottom of the list.

Another quick way to get to this page, or to apply an action to a comment, is to use the links in the email that WordPress sends you when a comment is held for moderation (provided you've selected this option in the **Settings | Discussion** section).

Additionally, this listing is where all pingbacks appear for your moderation. From a blog owner's point of view, pingbacks look just like any other comments, which means that you can edit them, mark them as spam, or trash them like you normally would with standard comments.

How to eliminate comment spam

Comment spam is one of the most annoying things on the Internet if you're an online publisher. Basically, a spam comment is a comment that has been submitted for the sole purpose of getting a link back to a specific website. The main reason why people submit spam comments is **Search Engine Optimization (SEO)**--the number of links pointing to a site is a known SEO factor, and website owners around the world do whatever they can to get as many links as possible. Unfortunately for us, sometimes it means using various spam methods as well.

The way WordPress comments are set up by default makes it possible for anyone to get a link from your site just by submitting a comment and providing a website address in one of the comment fields. If they do so and the comment gets approved, whatever was typed into the **Name** field of the comment becomes the text of the link, and the **Website** becomes the link's destination.

The worst thing about comment spam is that once your site gets even remotely popular, you can start getting hundreds of spam comments a day; hence dealing with them by hand becomes almost impossible.

Unfortunately, fighting comment spam is not something built into WordPress by default. This means that you have to get some plugin(s) to enable this functionality. For now, let's focus on the most popular spam protection plugin at the moment--**Akismet**. The good thing about it is that it comes along with the standard WordPress installation, so you should be able to find it in the **Plugins** section in your wp-admin. We will cover plugins in detail later in this book, for now, let's just review how to get Akismet working on your blog. If your blog is built on WordPress.com, then Akismet is already activated by default. For a standard, standalone blog, you'll have to activate it first.

Learning more
You can learn more about the Akismet spam-fighting service at https:// akismet.com/. Also, if you're interested in some alternative solutions then please visit https://wordpress.org/plugins/antispam-bee/.

Working with Akismet

If you want to enable spam protection with Akismet, the first thing you need to do is enable the Akismet plugin. To do that, go to **Plugins** in the wp-admin. From there, click on the **Activate** link that's directly below the Akismet plugin listing:

	Plugin	Description
☐	Akismet Anti-Spam	Used by millions, Akismet is quite possibly the best way in the world to **protect your blog from spam**. It keeps your site protected even while you sleep. To get started: activate the Akismet plugin and then go to your Akismet Settings page to set up your API key.
	Activate | Edit | Delete	Version 3.3 | By Automattic | View details

Right away, you'll see an on-screen prompt to set up your spam protection--a big blue button labeled **Set up your Akismet account** will pop up at the top of the screen. Click it.

The Akismet plugin requires that you have a special API key. Getting this API key isn't something particularly difficult, but we still need to go through a couple of steps. First, click on the **Get your API key** button:

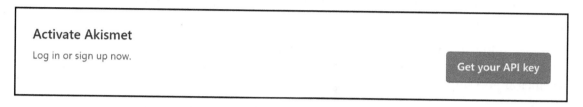

You will be redirected to akismet.com (`https://akismet.com/`) where you will be able to complete the process. The on-screen instructions are very clear and take you by the hand through everything. To get started, you first need a WordPress.com profile account. If you don't have one yet, you will be prompted to create one first. Nothing fancy, just standard information is needed during signup. We covered this in an earlier chapter.

When you do have the account and begin setting up Akismet, the thing you should pay special attention to is the specific subscription plan that you're going to select. At the time of writing, there are three available: Basic (free), Plus ($5), Premium ($9). To get standard spam protection, you can confidently go with Basic as shown in the following screenshot:

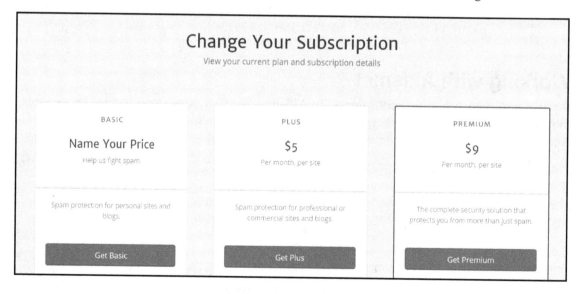

Now, this is tricky. The plan you've selected is based on voluntary donations. If you're not willing to spend any money, just take the slider that's in the center and slide it to the left, all the way to $0.00/yr:

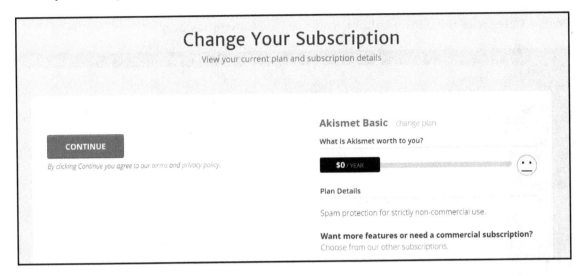

After clicking on the final activation link, you will be redirected back to your WordPress website, and the API key is going to be already put in the right field in Akismet settings.

If you're feeling confident, you can check the box labeled **Silently discard the worst and most pervasive spam so I never see it**. Akismet is relatively good at identifying which comment is actually spam, and checking this box will make those comments disappear. However, if you're concerned about Akismet misidentifying comments, leave this unchecked.

All you have to do is click on the **Save Changes** button, and your blog is now protected from comment spam!

Adding and managing categories

Earlier in this chapter, you learned how to add a category quickly when adding a post. Now, let's talk about how to manage your categories in a bigger way. First, navigate to **Posts | Categories** in your wp-admin. You'll see the **Categories** page:

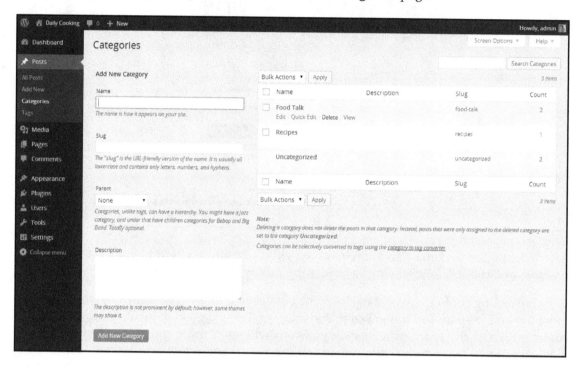

This is a useful page that combines the ability to add, edit, and review all of your categories. As you can see, any category that you've added via the **Edit Post** page is listed here. You can Edit, Quick Edit, or Delete any category by clicking on the appropriate link in the list.

If you add a category on this page, you can also choose its **Slug**. The slug is the short bit of text that shows up in the URL of your site if you have pretty permalinks enabled. If you don't choose a slug, WordPress will create one for you by taking the category name, reducing it to all lowercase, replacing spaces with dashes, and removing any other punctuation mark (similar to what's being done with slugs for posts).

Another thing you can do on this page is to choose a parent category for any category. Some themes support displaying categories hierarchically, but not all do. In a good, modern theme, if you create a custom menu for categories, all child categories will be displayed as sub menus.

The ability to create a hierarchy of categories is actually the main technical thing that separates categories from tags. Other than that, both elements are quite similar in construction, although they still have different purposes.

Summary

In this chapter, you learned everything you need to know in order to add content to your blog, and then manage that content. You learned about posts, categories, and comments. You discovered tags, spam (unfortunately), and excerpts. You also learned about adding and editing images, working with video and audio content, using the Visual editor (and the Text editor), changing timestamps, customizing excerpts, and the different ways of posting.

Your control over your blog content is complete, and you are well equipped to set your blog on fire!

In the next chapter, you'll learn about all the other types of content that you can manage on your website with WordPress.

4
Pages, Media, and Importing/Exporting Content

You now have the blog part of your website fully under control. By now, you've probably noticed that WordPress offers you a lot more than simply posts, comments, tags, and categories.

In this chapter, we will explore and control all the other types of content that WordPress already has. You'll be able to create static pages that aren't a part of your ongoing blog, add various types of media to your posts, and create appealing image galleries to display photos and other images (working with the new media library).

Pages

At first glance, pages look very similar to posts. Both pages and posts have a title and a content area in which we can write extended text. However, pages are handled quite differently from posts. First of all, pages don't have categories or tags (pages don't need to be categorized, since on most websites, there are a lot fewer pages than posts). Moreover, posts belong to your blog and are meant to be a part of an ongoing, expanding section of your website. Posts are added regularly, whereas pages are more static and aren't generally expected to change that much.

In short, I would advise you to think of pages as pieces of static content, and posts as a series of articles published in a timely manner. In other words, pages are meant to hold content that is equally up to date, no matter when someone reads them. For instance, the things that people publish via WordPress pages are most commonly details about their company or business, team - *"who are we,"* and other related and evergreen details. Posts are often very time sensitive and present advice/news that's important today/now. For most blogs, posts are the pillars of their content and make up more than 90 percent of the whole content.

When you installed WordPress, a page was automatically created for you (along with the first post and the first comment). You can see this by going to `http://YOURSITE.com/sample-page/`:

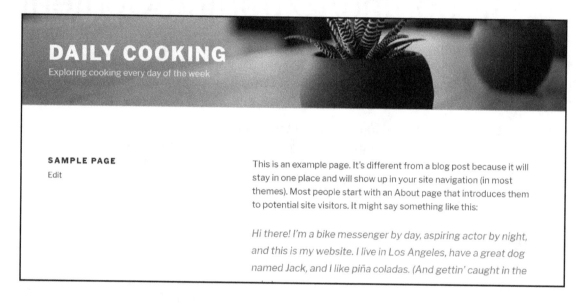

Adding a page

To add a new page, go to your wp-admin and navigate to **Pages** | **Add New,** or use the drop-down menu in the top dark menu by clicking on **New** and then **Page**. This will take you to the **Add New Page** screen:

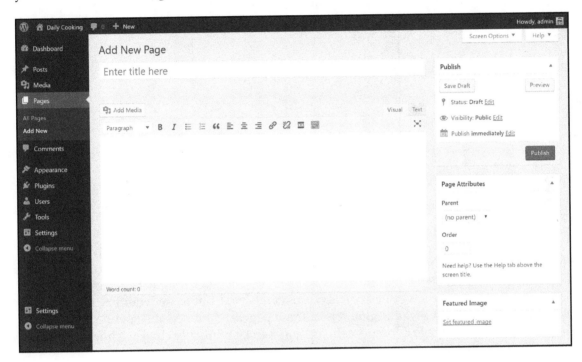

The minimum you need to do in order to create a new page is type in a title and some content. Then, click on the blue **Publish** button, just as you would for a post, and your new page will become available under its unique URL.

You'll recognize most of the fields on this page from the **Add New Post** page. They work the same for pages as they do for posts. Let's talk about the one section that's new--the box called **Page Attributes**, consisting of elements such as **Parent** and **Order**:

Parent

WordPress allows you to structure your pages hierarchically. This way, you can organize your website's pages into main pages and subpages, which is useful if you're going to have a lot of pages on your site. For example, if I was to write a blog along with three other authors, we would each have one page about us on the site, but those would be subpages of the main **About** page. If I was adding one of these pages, I'd first create a new **About** page, then create another page just for me, called *About Karol*, and finally choose **About** as the parent page for this new page.

Order

By default, the pages on your page list in the sidebar (or in the main navigation of your blog) will be in alphabetical order by page title. If you want them in some other order, you can specify it by entering numbers in the **Order** box for all your pages. Pages with lower numbers (for example, 0) will be listed before pages with higher numbers (for example, 5). You can easily test this by editing some of your pages and assigning various numbers to them. That being said, to be honest, this isn't a very clear method of rearranging pages inside menus. You can do it much more easily with a functionality called **Custom Menus** (described later in this chapter). In the end, I would advise you to save all of your pages with the order value of 0.

Managing pages

To see a list of all the pages on your website in the wp-admin, navigate to **Pages** | **Edit** in the main menu. You'll see the **Pages** screen, as shown in the following screenshot:

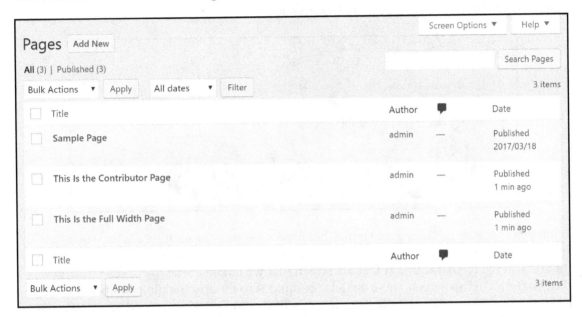

By now, this list format should begin to look familiar to you. You've got your list of pages, and in each row, there are a number of useful links allowing you to **Edit**, **Quick Edit**, **Trash**, or **View** the page. You can click on an author's name to filter the list by that author. You can use the two links at the top, **All** and **Published**, to filter the pages by status (if you have pages saved as **Drafts** or **Pending Review**, then they will also appear here). There's also filtering by date, through the drop-down menu just above the list of pages. Additionally, you can check certain boxes and mass-edit pages using the **Bulk Actions** menu at the top and bottom of the list. You can also search your pages with the search box at the top.

Media Library

The **Media Library** is where WordPress stores all of your uploaded files such as images, PDFs, music, videos, and so on. To see your **Media Library**, navigate to Media in the main menu (probably not a lot of media there at the moment):

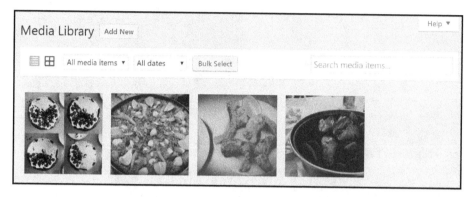

What you're seeing is a nice grid layout that makes looking through media very user-friendly. My **Media Library** has four photos in it at the moment. Once I click on any of them, I will see the **Attachment Details** screen that we talked about in `Chapter 3`, *Creating Blog Content*. On this screen, there are a lot of options to modify the file that's been selected. We can edit details, such as **Title**, **Caption**, **Alt Text**, and **Description**, and also delete the file permanently or view it on the frontend of the site:

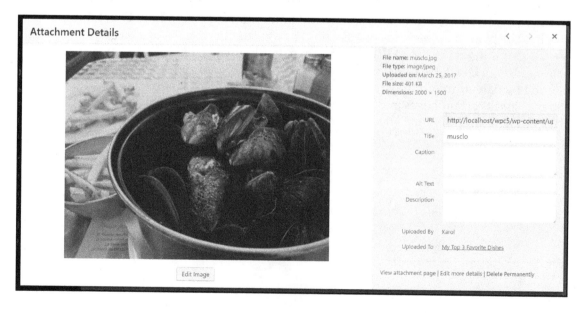

You can also add a new file to your **Media Library**. Navigate to **Media Library** | **Add New** to access a page similar to the upload media page that you got while uploading a file for a post. When you click on the **Select Files** button and select the file to be uploaded, or drag and drop it directly from your desktop, it will upload the file and then display it along with the rest of the media files in the library. Your new item will be unattached to any post or page at this point.

To include it somewhere (in a post or page), just go to the **Add/Edit Post** or **Add/Edit Page** screen and click on the **Add Media** button as you were doing previously. However, instead of uploading a new file, just select it from the **Media Library** (the default screen after clicking on the **Add Media** button):

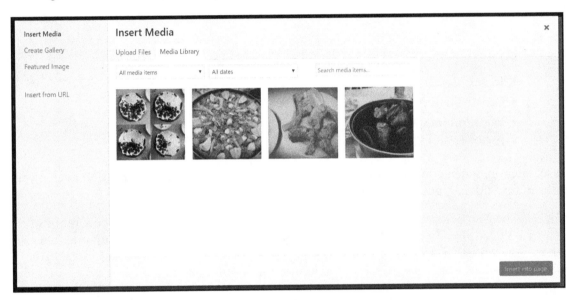

When you click on any image displayed on this **Insert Media** screen, you'll see the same set of options you got after uploading an image. Now, you can click on the **Insert into post** or **Insert into page** button. The media item will now appear as **Uploaded To** that post or page:

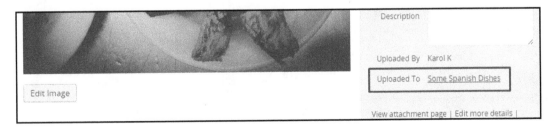

By the way, as you can see, I've created a whole new post for that image and titled it **Some Spanish Dishes**.

Media Manager

The aforementioned **Insert Media** screen that's visible in the preceding screenshots is also known as the **Media Manager**. You can always access the Media Manager from within the **Add/Edit Post** or **Add/Edit Page** screen by clicking on the **Add Media** button. We've already discussed two ways of using it--uploading new media and attaching media that has been previously uploaded; but that's not all. The Media Manager has a lot more interesting stuff under the hood.

First of all, if we take a look at the left sidebar, there are four links there (review the preceding screenshots). Starting from the top, these are as follows:

- **Insert Media**
- **Create Gallery**
- **Featured Image**
- **Insert from URL**

Also, later on, when you have some third-party plugins installed, you might find even more links in that sidebar, but for now, four it is.

Clicking on any of them will reload the center part of the screen to present a new range of features. We've already covered most of the **Insert Media** tab that is the default one. This is where you can either upload new files or select existing ones from the Media Library. This tab also provides a handy search box and a filtering dropdown:

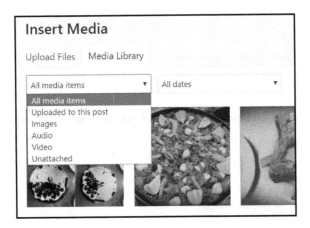

The filtering dropdown won't be of much use right now, but once you have hundreds of different media in the media library, being able to sort through them will become invaluable. The filtering dropdown simply lets you display media only of a specific type (the types are **Uploaded to this post**, **Images**, **Audio**, **Video**, **Unattached**, and **All media items**). Also, the dropdown right next to it delivers the possibility to filter by date. The search field is simply a *search field* and works immediately as you type (there's no submit button).

The second tab is **Create Gallery**. This is a completely new gallery creation mechanism. The number of things we can do in this module is truly impressive. It's all explained in the section ahead.

The third tab in the Media Manager is **Featured Image**. This offers you yet another way to assign a featured image to your posts (the first method was from within the box on the post editing screen itself). This is a very simple task. All you need to do is click on the image you want to save as the featured one and then click on the **Set featured image** button in the bottom-right corner.

Finally, we have the last tab, called **Insert from URL**. Apart from the possibility to upload your own images, WordPress also allows you to pick an image from the web and have it displayed on your site. As always, in such situations, you have to be careful not to take a copyrighted image, but from the technical point of view, WordPress is capable of importing any image that you input into the main field, as shown in the following screenshot:

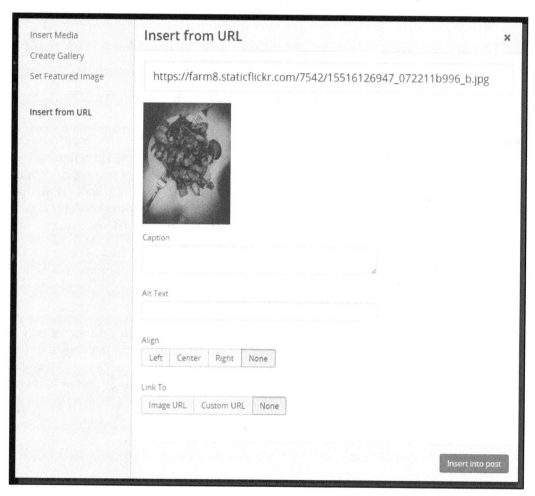

As you can see, I've used a link to an image on Flickr (an image from my personal account, actually). There are some additional settings here that you should use. Apart from the **Caption** and the **Alt Text** options (this is the text that gets displayed in case the image fails to load for whatever reason), there are also settings for the alignment and the URL destination of the link (if you want to link your image to something).

The important thing worth pointing out here is that WordPress doesn't import this external image into your Media Library. Instead, it *hot-links* the image from the source. In other words, the image is still on another server. What this means for you is that you don't have any actual control over this image. It can be removed overnight or replaced with another image without your knowledge. That's why, in 90 percent of cases, it's actually better to download any image you want to use and then upload it to your media library, instead of hot-linking it.

Adding an image gallery

Just like I've mentioned in the previous section, the gallery module that you can find inside the Media Manager provides a completely redesigned, modern way of working with image galleries. Just to remind you, this new gallery module can be accessed by clicking on the **Add Media** button when editing a post or a page and then clicking on the **Create Gallery** link in the left sidebar.

One of the most user-friendly aspects of creating image galleries in WordPress is that you can drag and drop multiple images at once. And WordPress will immediately start turning them into a gallery. However, before you can do this, you have to choose where you want to display your new gallery, and that's what we're going to do next.

Choosing a post or page

This is a very simple step, and we've been doing this previously, so here we go. You can add a gallery (or multiple galleries) to any new or existing page or post. I, for example, went with one of my existing posts, which you can see in the following screenshot:

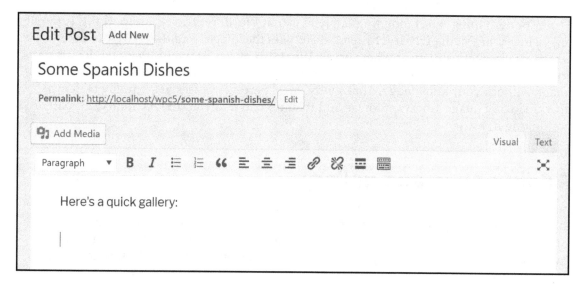

Notice where I have left my cursor (it's right at the bottom if you can't see it). I made sure to leave it in a spot on the page where I want my gallery to appear, that is, underneath my introductory paragraph.

Selecting or uploading images

You can start either by uploading some new images or selecting the ones already in your media library. If it's the former you're after, then simply click on **Add Media** and then the **Create Gallery** link on the left, grab some images from your desktop and drag and drop them onto the upload area.

If you want to work with some of your existing images that are already in the media library, then just click on the **Media Library** tab as shown in the following screenshot. As an example, I've selected three images that I want to use (they have a checkbox in the upper-right corners):

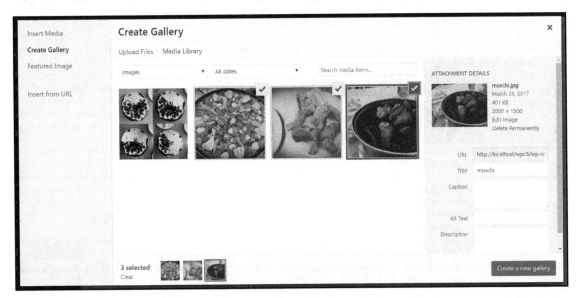

At this stage, you can adjust the titles and descriptions of the images if you want to, and then click on the **Create a new gallery** button. In the next step, you have the opportunity to rearrange your images by dragging them around the display area. You can also adjust the captions (the captions will be saved so that they can be reused later on if you're creating a gallery using the same images). On the right side, under **Link To**, there's a drop-down menu where you can change the link destination for each image. The way a gallery works in WordPress is that when visitors click on any image, they will be redirected either to the media file itself, to the attachment page (an individual page created for each image by default), or nowhere at all. Going with the default value of media file is the recommended choice.

The other three options on this page--the number of columns, the **Random Order** checkbox, and **Size**--are pretty self-explanatory. When you're done, just click on the **Insert gallery** button:

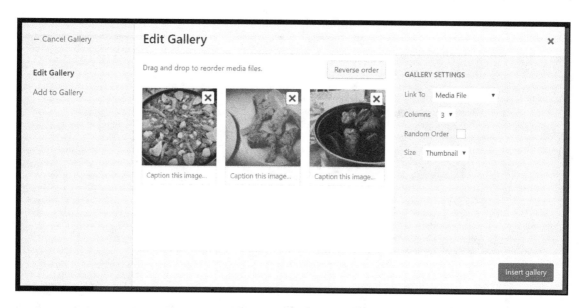

On the post editing screen, the gallery block itself has a nice preview. There's a small space, and in it, we can see the images that will appear as a part of the gallery:

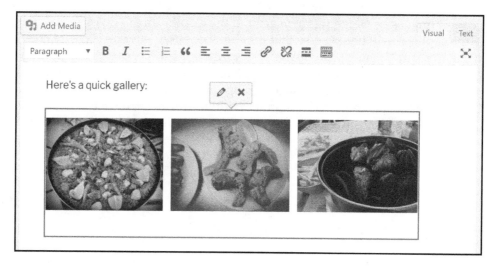

However, when you view the gallery on the frontend of your site, it's going to look great. The degree of its greatness depends closely on the theme you're using, though. When you click on any of the images, you'll be taken to a larger version of the image.

Also, while on the post editing screen, you can edit any image and any gallery by clicking on the preview and then on one of the buttons that are going to appear. You can see this in the preceding screenshot.

One more note, if you're in the **Text** view, you'll see the gallery shortcode instead of the visual gallery block:

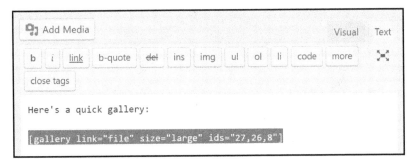

In this case, the gallery is inserted through a simple shortcode, which is [gallery link="file" size="large" ids="27,26,8"]. These IDs are the individual IDs of the media files that are a part of the gallery. What this means is that you can also edit your gallery by hand, simply by replacing the IDs or adding some new ones.

 We're going to talk about shortcodes in more detail in Chapter 10, *Developing Plugins, Widgets, and an Introduction to the REST API*. For now, all you need to know is that they allow you to include quite complex functionality just by using short trigger codes; hence the name *shortcodes*.

Note that because I'm uploading the photos while editing this particular post, all of these photos will be attached to this post, which is a nice way of indicating which images go where.

 The [gallery] shortcode is quite powerful! Take a look at the codex to get all of its parameters, at https://codex.wordpress.org/Gallery_Shortcode.

Importing/exporting your content

The final thing I want to describe in this chapter is the feature of importing and exporting your content. By default, WordPress allows you to *take* content from other places and publish it on your site. There are a number of platforms supported, including **Blogger**, **LiveJournal**, **Tumblr** blogs, and more. You can see the complete list by navigating to **Tools | Import** (it's also the starting point when importing content):

Import

If you have posts or comments in another system, WordPress can import those into this site. To get started, choose a system to import from below:

Blogger
Install Now | Details

Import posts, comments, and users from a Blogger blog.

Blogroll
Install Now | Details

Import links in OPML format.

Categories and Tags Converter
Install Now | Details

Convert existing categories to tags or tags to categories, selectively.

LiveJournal
Install Now | Details

Import posts from LiveJournal using their API.

Movable Type and TypePad
Install Now | Details

Import posts and comments from a Movable Type or TypePad blog.

RSS
Install Now | Details

Import posts from an RSS feed.

Tumblr
Install Now | Details

Import posts & media from Tumblr using their API.

WordPress
Install Now | Details

Import posts, pages, comments, custom fields, categories, and tags from a WordPress export file.

If the importer you need is not listed, search the plugin directory to see if an importer is available.

Importing content

If you want to import content from any source, you first need to click on either of the **Install Now** links that are under the available platforms (visible in the preceding screenshot). WordPress uses additional plugins to handle the importing, and it first needs to install them in order to carry out the procedure.

Importing content from each of the available platforms is a bit different, but the general process looks similar, so we're going to use another WordPress site as an example here (that is, we're going to import content from another WordPress website). For that to work, all we need to do is click on the **Install Now** link that's within the **WordPress** section (it's the last one in the preceding screenshot), and then when the installation completes, click on the new **Run Importer** link that has just appeared. Refer to the following screenshot:

WordPress   Import posts, pages, comments, custom fields, categories, and tags from a WordPress
Run Importer | Details   export file.

This will take you straight to the importer panel:

It is a very simple interface where all you have to do is take a WordPress export file and upload it to your site. The platform will take care of extracting the archive and importing the content into it. As a result, your site is going to be filled with new posts, pages, even comments, custom fields, and navigation menus.

The main purpose of this feature is to help everyone who's migrating their sites from platforms such as **Blogger** or **LiveJournal**. Imagine if someone had a Blogger blog with over a hundred posts in it. Going through each one individually and inputting it to WordPress by hand would be too time-consuming. With this feature, it can be done in under a minute.

Exporting content

Exporting content is even simpler than importing. To start, navigate to **Tools | Export**:

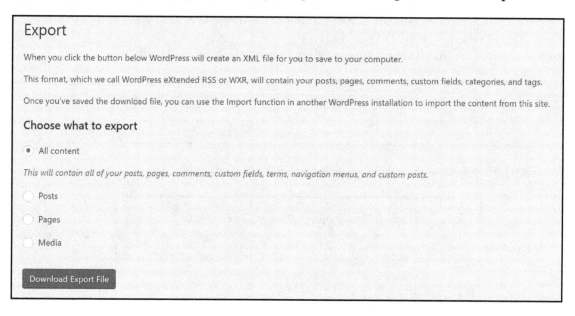

There's not much you can do here except select what you want to export and then click on the big button to download your WordPress export file.

Selecting **All content** will export your posts, pages, comments, custom fields, terms, navigation menus, and custom posts. Selecting just **Posts** or **Pages** is pretty self-explanatory.

When you click on the **Download Export File** button, you will end up with a file that's just like the one we used when importing. This means that you can take that file and create a mirror copy of your site somewhere else under another domain name.

Summary

In this chapter, we explored the content that WordPress can handle that's not directly about blogging. You learned about static pages, the Media Library (and the Media Manager), image galleries, and importing/exporting your content.

You are now fully equipped to use the WordPress Admin panel to control all of your website's content. Next, you'll learn how to expand your site's functionality by installing new plugins, which we'll be discussing in the following chapter.

5
Plugins - What They Are and Why You Need Them

The topic of plugins has grown a lot in recent years. Nowadays, it's hard to imagine any WordPress site that could operate without at least a handful of (essential) plugins installed.

In this chapter, you will get to know what plugins are, why to use them, how to use them, where to get them, and how to be up-to-date with any new useful plugins that get released to the community. We will also talk about some of the most basic and popular plugins in the WordPress world, and why having them might be a good idea. Okay, let's get on with it!

Breaking down plugins - what are they?

Simply speaking, plugins are small scripts (files with executable PHP code) that allow you to include new functionality in your WordPress site--functionality that is *not* available or enabled by default. One of the best advantages of WordPress is that it's quite an optimized platform. It makes your site load fast and doesn't contain much redundant code. However, WordPress itself only offers the absolute essential range of features--the features useful to everyone. At the same time, the platform provides a straightforward way of expanding the abilities of your site by introducing, you guessed it, plugins. The idea is simple--if you want your site to be able to handle a specific new task, there's surely a plugin for that. Much like in the Apple world and the popular expression, "there's an app for that."

Why use plugins

The best thing about plugins is that you don't need any specific programming knowledge in order to use them. Essentially, they are just like standard applications for iOS or Android-- you can install them and enjoy the things they have to offer without knowing what's going on inside. This being said, not all plugins are safe to use in terms of data security or code quality. We will discuss this topic later in the chapter.

Furthermore, the right combination of plugins can make your site more optimized, more user-friendly, more attractive, more social-media-friendly, properly backed up, protected against spam, and, ultimately, unique. Plugins really are one of the best things about WordPress.

You see, before content management systems like WordPress were popularized, there was no easy way for site owners to introduce new functionalities to their sites. Doing so always required hiring a professional programmer and investing in the whole development process. Nowadays, this is no longer the case, and virtually anyone can have an impressive site without losing their shirt.

Where to get plugins

The community behind WordPress plugins is a huge one. There's not a central plugin-building company or anything. Developers all over the world create plugins and then distribute them across the internet. And, very often, they receive no direct compensation whatsoever. The best and the safest place to visit for WordPress plugins is the official directory at `https://wordpress.org/plugins/`:

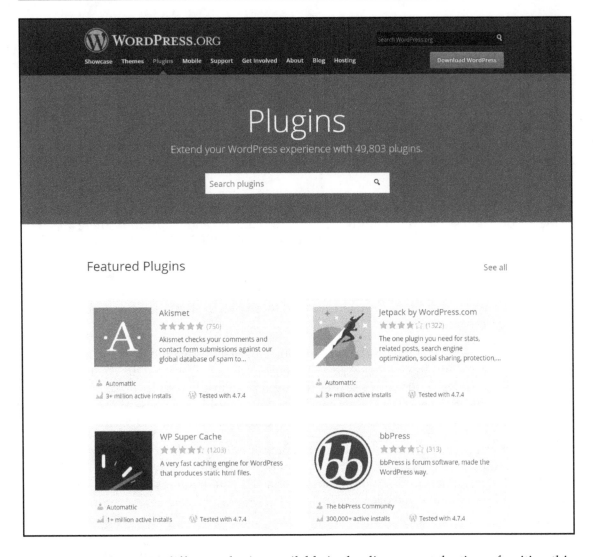

There are nearly 50,000 different plugins available in the directory at the time of writing this book, and that number is constantly expanding with around 100+ new plugins being added every week. This is really impressive considering the fact that many of those plugins are very advanced pieces of web software and not just simple, one-script add-ons.

There's a search field available in the center of the page in the directory (visible in the preceding screenshot), which allows you to search plugins by topic and by tag. You can also view a list of the most popular plugins as well as featured plugins. In short, the official `plugin` directory is where you should always go first when looking for a plugin. It's also a good habit to always check how popular the plugins you're interested in are. Downloading plugins that already have a proven track record of happy users will improve your chances of getting a quality product that you'll enjoy using. This is really important, since your site security should never be underestimated. By getting your plugins from the official WordPress directory, you can at least be certain that the plugins are not malicious in any way.

You can also carry out Google searches. I recommend searching for the problem you're trying to solve and see what plugins other users recommend and why. Often, there are multiple plugins that perform similar functions, and you will find the feedback from other WordPress users valuable in choosing between them. However, as you do this, be sure to keep an eye out for malicious or poorly coded plugins that could break your website or allow someone to hack into it. Be careful when installing new plugins with no reviews, comments, or feedback from users, in addition to those plugins that have bad feedback about them on the internet.

To get even more in-depth into your plugin investigation, you can also check out the changelogs and support forums for each plugin you're considering for your site (every plugin page inside the official `plugin` directory has a tab named **Support**). This should give you an idea of how well or how poorly a given plugin is coded, supported, and so on.

Apart from free plugins, there's also a big set of premium plugins (paid ones). However, you won't find them in the official directory. Most of those plugins have their own websites handling sales, customer support, and usage tutorials. If you're interested, one of the more popular premium plugin directories can be found at `https://codecanyon.net/category/wordpress`.

Finding new plugins

Generally speaking, if a given plugin proves that it's a quality solution and gains some popularity, it will be showcased on the homepage of the official directory in the **Featured Plugins** section. But if you want to be up to date with things as they happen, you can pay attention to what's going on at `https://wordpress.org/plugins/browse/new/`.

Additionally, a great way to discover new plugins is to become a regular on one of the popular blogs about WordPress. Although these blogs are not official creations (they are run by independent owners), they do provide an impressive range of tips and advice, not only on plugins but also on other aspects related to WordPress. The list includes the following:

- https://wptavern.com/
- https://codeinwp.com/blog/
- https://themeisle.com/blog/
- http://www.wpbeginner.com/

Installing a plugin - the how-to

The steps for installing a plugin are simple:

1. Find your plugin.
2. Download it to your WordPress site, either manually or through the automatic installer.
3. Install and activate it.
4. Configure and/or implement it (if necessary).

There are two ways to get the plugin into your WordPress installation:

- Install manually
- Install from within the wp-admin

The first option--installing plugins manually--generally requires a bit more effort than the second one, but sometimes it's the only way to work with certain plugins (mostly premium ones). The second option--installing from within the wp-admin--is generally quicker and easier, but it's not possible in all cases. You need to be on a server that's configured correctly, in a way that lets WordPress add files (we talked about installing WordPress and server configuration in Chapter 2, *Getting Started with WordPress*). Plus, the plugin you want to install has to be available in the WordPress plugin repository, that is, the official plugin directory.

In the following section, we'll go over the manual method first, and then handle auto-installation.

Manual plugin installation

As an example here, I will install a popular plugin called **Jetpack** by WordPress.com. It's quite a large plugin, offering a range of features and effectively making your WordPress site more functional and easier to use at the same time. We'll discuss it in more detail later in this chapter. This being said, the following procedure allows you to install any WordPress plugin you can get your hands on, not only Jetpack.

To install a plugin manually, you must start by downloading the plugin archive either from the official directory at `https://wordpress.org/plugins/` or from some other website or source (usually when dealing with premium plugins).

In this case, the Jetpack plugin is available in the official directory at `https://wordpress.org/plugins/jetpack/`:

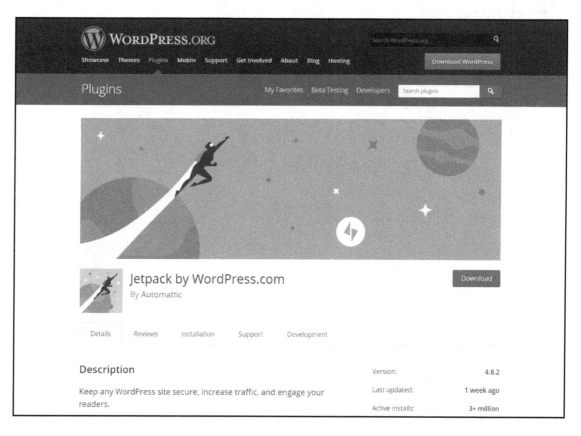

Just click on the blue **Download** button and save the resulting ZIP file on your computer in a place where you can find it easily. Once you have the plugin downloaded, and if your server is set up correctly, you should be able to upload the ZIP file directly via the **Plugins | Add New** page. Go to that page, click on the **Upload Plugin** button at the top and choose the ZIP file of the plugin, as shown in the following screenshot:

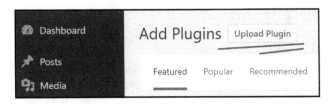

If this automatic uploader doesn't work for you, you can do it the old-fashioned way. First unzip, that is, extract the ZIP file you downloaded so that it's a folder, probably named `jetpack` (at least in this case). Then, using your FTP client, upload this folder inside the `wp-content/plugins/` folder of your WordPress installation. You'll also see the two plugins in that folder that WordPress came with--`akismet` and `hello.php`.

If you need any assistance with FTP software, review `Chapter 2`, *Getting Started with WordPress*, where we talked about the topic of installing WordPress.

After the upload finishes, you will be able to activate the plugin. This is required to effectively "turn the plugin on." This can be done simply by clicking on the **Activate Plugin** button, as shown in the following screenshot. At this point, you're done and the Jetpack plugin is working:

Now, you are ready for the final step--configuring and ultimately making use of the plugin. But, before we shift our attention to this, let's discuss an easier method of dealing with plugin installation, which is also the recommended way.

Auto-installation

If the plugin you want to install is available in the official `plugin` directory at `https://wordpress.org/plugins/` and your server configuration meets the requirements for auto-installation (your web host has to grant you the read/write/modify directory and file permissions; usually the case with the majority of serious hosting companies), then you can search for and install a new plugin from within the wp-admin. Just navigate to **Plugins | Add New**. It just so happens that the plugin I'm using here as the example--Jetpack--is one of the most popular plugins in the directory at the moment. Therefore, you will actually see it on the main screen in the **Plugins | Add New** section. If the plugin you want to install is not in this featured plugins area, you can type its name in the search box to the right (the following screenshot):

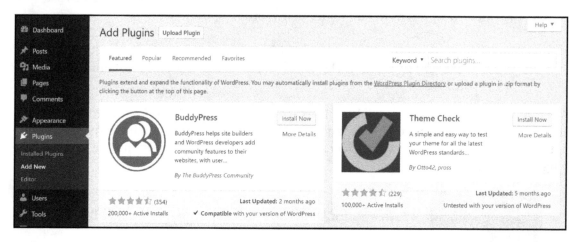

Once you see a plugin that seems interesting, you can click on the **More Details** link to see some more information about the features it has to offer:

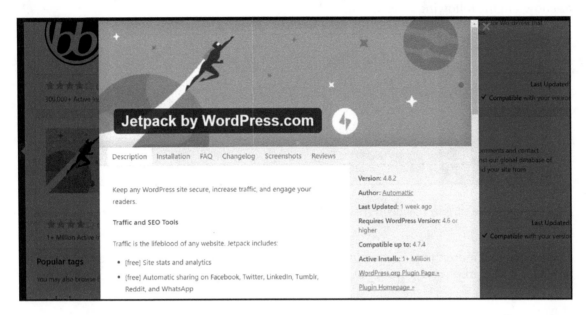

I recommend you always look at this information carefully. Be sure to watch for version compatibility. There's a parameter labeled **Compatible up to** listed with the plugin's details. In some cases, you can risk installing a plugin that's a little outdated, but you should proceed with caution.

After installation, you need to test the plugin carefully and verify that it's behaving correctly. Most of the time, if the **Compatible up to** parameter indicates an older version of WordPress, it doesn't necessarily mean that the plugin will fail to work with a newer version. It just means that it hasn't been thoroughly tested, hence the importance of performing your own tests. However, I strongly advise against installing any plugins that haven't been updated in more than two years. Luckily, whenever you encounter such a plugin, WordPress itself will warn you either through this message on the official plugin page, as shown in the following screenshot. Or, inside the plugin details section in the wp-admin, there's a parameter labeled **Last Updated.**:

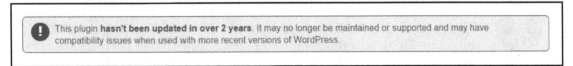

If everything is fine, you can proceed by clicking on the **Install Now** button. The next screen you see will invite you to activate the plugin (just like when installing a plugin manually), as shown in the following screenshot:

At this point, the plugin has been installed and activated. In other words, it should be fully operational.

There's just one more thing. Some plugins are perfectly functional right after activation, while others require some additional tuning up. The following are the four most likely scenarios:

- You may not have to do anything. Some plugins simply change the way WordPress does certain things, and activating them is all you have to do.
- You may have to configure the plugin before it begins to work. Some plugins need you to make choices and set new settings.
- You may also get a set of shortcodes or other elements that you can use to include additional content that the plugin provides inside your posts or pages.
- There may not be a configuration page, but you may have to add some code to one of your theme's template files.

If you're unsure of what to do after you've uploaded and activated your plugin, be sure to read the README file that most likely came with the plugin or look at the FAQ on the plugin's website.

Many plugin authors accept donations. I strongly recommend giving donations to the authors of the plugins that you find useful. It helps to encourage everyone in the community to continue writing great plugins that everyone can use. Even if you can only donate a small amount, it will still count. Think how much time you saved thanks to the developer of your favorite plugin. If it's significant, maybe you should consider donating indeed.

If, for some reason, the auto-installation process has failed, then you will need to switch to the manual installation described in the previous section.

The must-have pack of plugins

Even though there are nearly 50,000 plugins available in the official directory, you surely don't need all of them on your WordPress site at the same time. There is a small set that we might call the "must-have pack." And, obviously, my list of must-have plugins can be different from the next guy's, so treat the following information more as guidance rather than as a written-in-stone necessity. That being said, if I am honest here, and despite the fact that some of my blogs feature more than 25 plugins, all working at the same time, the essential must-have list consists of only seven plugins. All these plugins handle a specific task geared toward making a WordPress site better and more functional.

Backing up

Backing up is probably the most important task for any website owner, and I'm saying this in all seriousness. For instance, can you imagine a situation in which you lose your whole site overnight with no ability to restore it? This might sound a bit hard to believe right now, but it does happen. If it's a personal blog you've been running, then it's not that tragic. But for a business website, it's a completely different story.

So, one of the main problems with backing up is that it's only effective if it's done regularly. In other words, you need to create backups often and keep them somewhere safe. While that's all fine, who has the time to do this manually? No one, honestly. That's why we'll be using a plugin that does its magic in the background without any supervision required on our part--introducing **UpdraftPlus**--a WordPress backup plugin, available at `https://wordpress.org/plugins/updraftplus/`:

This plugin allows you to handle website backups in an easy to grasp and hassle-free way. It connects with your remote storage account, such as Dropbox (but there are more possibilities here) and then backs up your site regularly on autopilot. It requires only minimal initial setup.

> If you don't have an account yet, you can sign up to Dropbox for free at `https://www.dropbox.com/`. As part of the free package, you get 2 GB disk space, which will be more than enough to keep your site backed up.

Here are the steps necessary to integrate UpdraftPlus with Dropbox. After installing and activating the plugin, navigate to **Settings | UpdraftPlus Backups** in your wp-admin, and then switch to the **Settings** tab. There, click on the Dropbox logo:

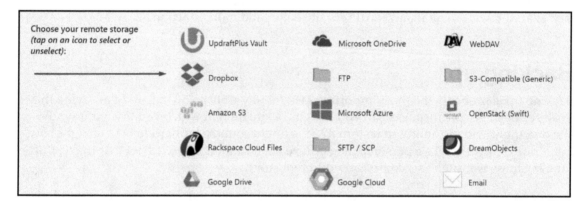

Right after clicking on the logo, scroll down and click on the main **Save Changes** button. This will reload the page and you'll see a notification that additional authorization with Dropbox is needed. Like so:

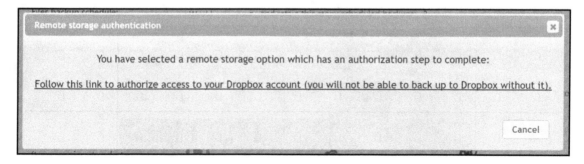

Just click on the link in the notification and you'll be taken to the Dropbox authorization page. To proceed, you'll need to log in to your Dropbox account and then confirm the authorization. After a couple of seconds, you will be redirected back to your site and your settings will be in place. At this stage, you have integrated the plugin with Dropbox. All that needs doing now is telling the plugin to back up your website automatically.

Go back to the **Settings** tab of the plugin. The two fields to pay attention to now are:

- **Files backup schedule**
- **Database backup schedule**

This depends on your personal preference, but for a website that doesn't publish multiple entries every day, setting the former to **Weekly** and the latter to **Daily** is going to be just fine. Like so:

With this plugin, you can also trigger backups manually (on top of the backup scheduling feature). Doing so is a good idea when you first install the plugin, just to check if everything's working fine and to have your initial backup done. You can start the backup in **Settings | UpdraftPlus Backups**. You will be presented with the following screen:

All you need to do is just click on the big **Backup Now** button.

Enabling Google Analytics

Google Analytics is a very popular site stats and analytics solution. It's free, easy to use for a beginner, and very powerful for anyone willing to get into it a little more deeply. In short, Google Analytics lets you in on a set of stats and data regarding the web traffic your site is getting, including things such as the exact number of visitors (daily, monthly, and so on), traffic sources, your most popular content, and a virtual myriad of other statistics. Google Analytics is available at `https://www.google.com/analytics/`.

To enable Google Analytics on your site, you have to sign up for a Google account first, then enable **Analytics**, then add your site in the control panel (all available on the official Google Analytics page, along with extensive tutorial documentation), and then take the tracking code that Google gives you and include it on your site. This last step is where the **Google Analytics for WordPress by MonsterInsights** plugin comes into play and makes the whole thing a lot simpler. You can get it at `https://wordpress.org/plugins/google-analytics-for-wordpress/.`:

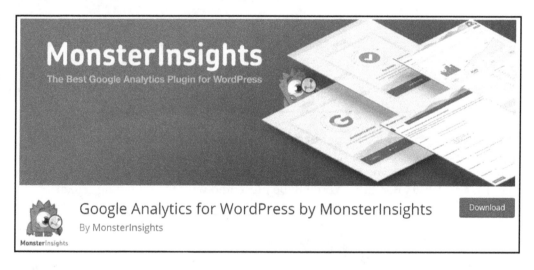

Once you download and activate it, proceed to **Insights** | **Settings** (in the wp-admin). Although the plugin has a lot of settings, the only thing you must do in order to make it work is to authenticate the plugin, to enable a connection with your Google Analytics account. Just click on the **Authenticate with your Google account** button:

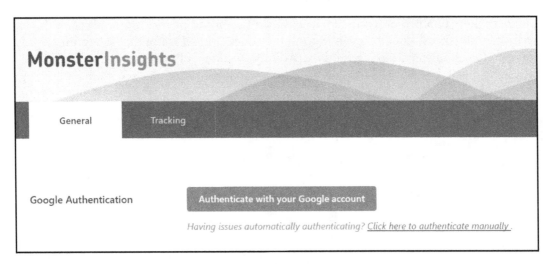

This will redirect you to a page on Google where you have to click on another button, **Grant access**, and then you'll be taken back to your wp-admin. Now, you can select what's called your *UA-profile* that you want to use for monitoring the site. If you're having problems with this semi-automatic way of authentication, you can simply input your Google Analytics code (called the UA code) manually. This code is visible in your profile at Google Analytics (usually starts with UA- and is followed by nine numbers).

Once you're done with the authentication procedure, your site is fully connected to Google Analytics and the traffic stats are being collected. After a while, you can navigate to your profile in Google Analytics and see how your site's been doing in terms of visitor popularity. Also, to get a more immediate indication of whether the tracking code has been set correctly or not, you can navigate to the **Real-Time** traffic section inside Google Analytics.

Caching

To be honest, caching is a pretty complicated concept. If you speak "engineering," then here's the definition: *in computer science, a cache is a component that transparently stores data so that future requests for that data can be served faster*. What it means in plain English is that if you have caching enabled on your site, it will load faster and be much more accessible for your audience/visitors. Luckily, even though the concept itself is not that straightforward, the plugin that enables you to "cache" is. Currently, the top of the line plugin is called **W3 Total Cache**, available at `https://wordpress.org/plugins/w3-total-cache/`.:

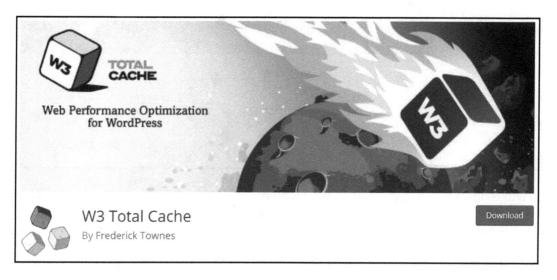

And, it's not just me recommending it. Actually, a number of major hosting companies and experts say that it provides *the* way to get your site optimized fast. More than that, the plugin is also in use on some major blogs around the web.

The installation procedure is the same as with any WordPress plugin. But right after you activate it, you'll see that the usage is quite different. For one, it's accessible through a completely new section in the left sidebar. It's labeled **Performance** and it's placed right below **Settings**. Less than a second after you click on it, you will realize that this plugin is a huge one. It could probably have a completely separate book written about it. So here, I will only provide a quick start guide, so to speak.

Go to **Performance** | **General Settings** and browse through the page. There are a number of checkboxes labeled **Enable**. Just to get started with the plugin, I advise you to enable (check the following checkbox) the following blocks:

- **Page Cache**
- **Database Cache**
- **Object Cache**
- **Browser Cache**

And, then, click on any of the **Save all settings** buttons. From now on, caching will be fully enabled on your site and your visitors should start experiencing performance improvements right away. Obviously, we've only touched on the possibilities and customizations that this plugin brings to the table, so I encourage you to give it a closer look in your spare time.

Search engine optimization

Search engine optimization (**SEO**) is one of the most popular topics online (at least among website owners). The simple truth is that working on your site's SEO, if done right, will raise its position in search engines (like Google) and will bring you more visitors on a daily basis. The concept is pretty simple in theory, but the work involved in order to achieve this can become a full-time job. If you're not interested in devoting a big chunk of your time to SEO, then at the very least get the **Yoast SEO** plugin, available at `https://wordpress.org/plugins/wordpress-seo/`, and have the basics handled. The plugin is very popular in the blogosphere, and it's in use on some of the most popular blogs out there:

Similar to the previous plugin, W3 Total Cache, this one has a custom section within the wp-admin too. It's visible right below **Settings** and it's called **SEO**. The best way to get the core how-to on this plugin is to go through the configuration wizard. You'll see the link leading to it right after visiting the plugin's section, **SEO,** in the wp-admin:

The wizard is really well made and it'll take you step by step through the whole configuration phase of the plugin, its most basic settings, and features. I really encourage you to spend a while optimizing your site with this plugin because this work will surely pay off in the long run, or maybe even much sooner:

There's a separate resource published by the author of the WordPress SEO plugin--Joost de Valk. It's where you should go to get a further in-depth information on how to set up the plugin and what else you can do to make your site SEO-friendly. You can find it at `https://yoast.com/wordpress-seo/`.

Securing your site

The issue of site security and hacker attacks is a really serious thing online these days. You might be thinking that no one will try to harm your site because you're not that popular yet, right? Well, the reality can be harsh in this case. Most hacker attacks are not about stealing your revenue or taking over your site as a whole. Usually, they are about including a small piece of code on your site that will link out to other external sites (most of the time either fraudulent sites or "naughty" content). The idea of such an attack is that you won't find out that it ever took place, which is the biggest danger.

Don't sweat though, there's a plugin that will help you with that--**Wordfence Security**, available at `https://wordpress.org/plugins/wordfence/`.

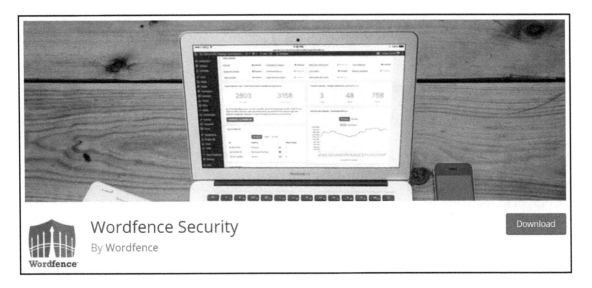

Getting started with this plugin requires only basic setting up. First of all, download and activate it (the usual procedure). Immediately afterward, you will see an invitation to take the tour and input your admin email to get notifications about your site's security, as shown in the following screenshot:

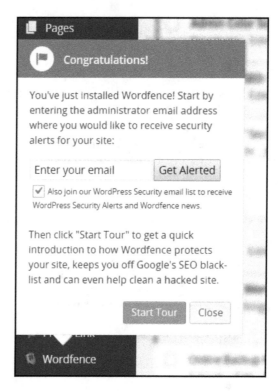

This tour, although short, will present all of the most important features to you and tell you how to work with the plugin effectively. For the most part, the plugin doesn't require any supervision, and thanks to the notification emails, you can just sit back, relax, and wait for the plugin to reach out to you, so to speak.

The best way to get started with the plugin is to go to **Wordfence | Scan** from the wp-admin, and then click on the big **START A WORDFENCE SCAN** button, as shown in the following screenshot:

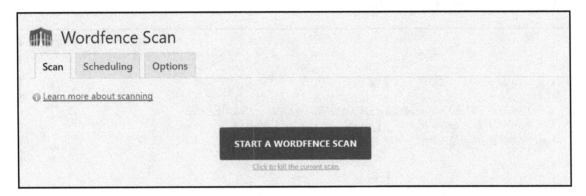

Right after doing so, you will see the scan running (inside the two blocks visible below the scan button you've just clicked on). When the scan is done and everything is okay, you will see a success message, as shown in the following screenshot:

Scan Summary

[Apr 26 18:43:26] Scanning comments for URLs on a domain blacklist	Secure.
[Apr 26 18:43:26] Scanning for weak passwords	Secure.
[Apr 26 18:43:27] Scanning DNS for unauthorized changes	Secure.
[Apr 26 18:43:27] Scanning to check available disk space	Secure.
[Apr 26 18:43:27] Scanning for old themes, plugins and core files	Secure.
[Apr 26 18:43:29] Scanning for admin users not created through WordPress	Secure.
[Apr 26 18:43:29] **Scan complete. Congratulations, no problems found.**	Scan Complete.

In case there are any problems, Wordfence will display them to you further down the page inside the **New Issues** block, as shown in the following screenshot, and will also give you tips on how to solve them. Unfortunately, or rather, *fortunately* I don't have a screenshot with actual problems inside to show you:

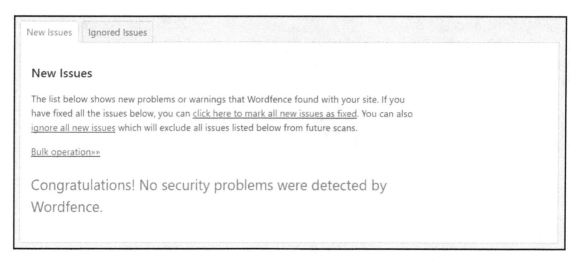

Apart from the basic scanning functionality, this plugin also gives you the ability to block certain IP addresses from accessing your site, improve your site's performance with caching, and even make your site inaccessible to whole countries (in case some geographical area causes you serious problems).

So, now your site is fully protected against various hacker attacks. As usual, there are a lot more settings available in this plugin. However, I wouldn't advise playing around with them without reading the official documentation first. This type of protection is a very powerful mechanism and it's easy to make a mess if you're not careful.

Social media integration

Social media has taken the online space by storm, and these days we can hardly imagine a website existing without at least some level of social media integration. The benefits of such integration are clearly visible. With a good social media WordPress plugin, you will be able to share your posts with friends and family on all of the most popular social platforms online. More than that, your readers will be able to do so too, effectively growing your audience and making your site more popular. Ultimately, publishing content that goes viral on social media can skyrocket your traffic and make your site visible to thousands of new people every week or even day.

So, the way we're going to make it easier for your readers (and you) to share your content is by displaying some social media buttons on your site, and more accurately, on each post and page that your site consists of.

The social media plugin by **GetSocial** is a great free solution that gives you the needed functionality. It's available at `https://wordpress.org/plugins/wp-share-buttons-analytics-by-getsocial/`:

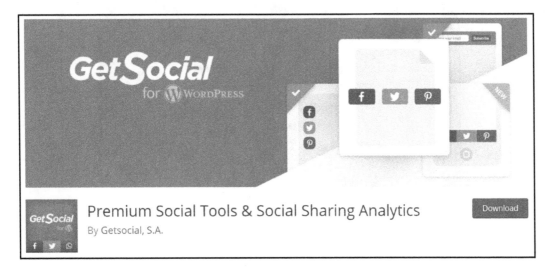

After installing and activating it, you will be presented with a handy getting started video that will take you through the important steps of setting up the plugin:

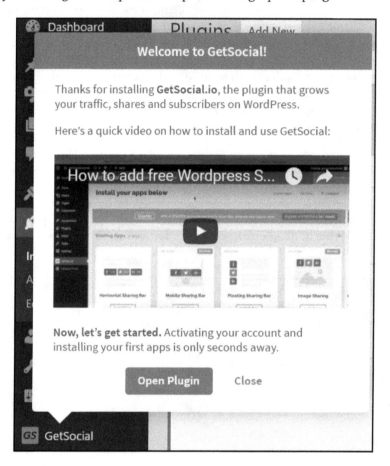

When you go to the plugin's section in the wp-admin by clicking on **GetSocial** in the main sidebar menu, you will see all the available social media integration options, like so:

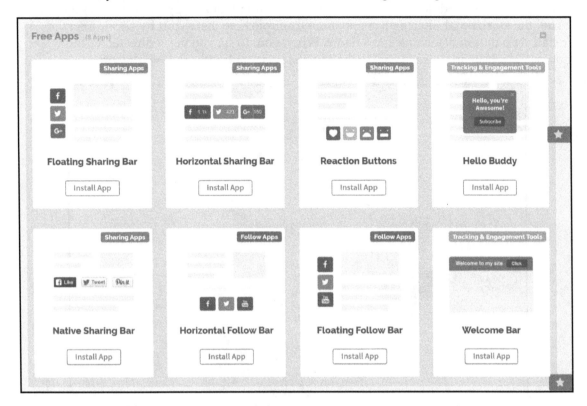

The complete list is impressive, and there are both free and paid options available. You don't need to invest any money to get the most basic and necessary features, though. To enable any of the modules, click on their corresponding **Install App** buttons. I'm going to install the **Horizontal Sharing Bar** app as an example here. Let's start by clicking on the **Install App** button below the app's name. When you do so, you get redirected to the GetSocial website in order to enable the specific social networks that you want:

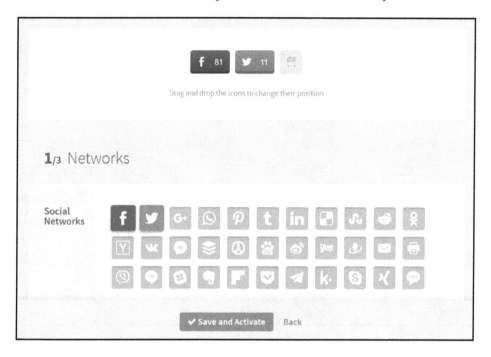

As you can see, the interface is really easy to grasp, lets you pick from a range of different social networks, and also gives you some basic customization options (like changing the size of the buttons, their position on the page, and whether or not you want the share counter to be displayed). When you're done experimenting with the settings, click on the **Save and Activate** button. At this stage, you have successfully enabled basic social media buttons on your website.

Here's what they look like on my *Daily Cooking* blog on a completely new post:

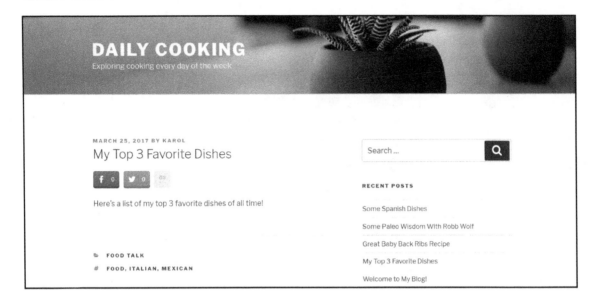

Jetpack

This mysterious name is exactly what one of the most popular plugins of today is called (it's being used by some mainstream blogs on the web, such as Tim Ferris's `http://www.fourhourworkweek.com/`). Jetpack, by the guys behind WordPress.com, offers a truly exceptional range of features and functionalities. The plugin consists of a number of modules that can be enabled or disabled one by one. This gives you full control over the features you want and don't want to use. Jetpack is available at `https://wordpress.org/plugins/jetpack/`:

After downloading and activating it, you'll see a new section in the wp-admin, but this time, it's right below **Dashboard**, as shown in the following screenshot:

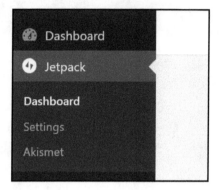

Inside, you can see all of the available modules and functionalities. First, you should navigate to **Jetpack | Settings** to enable or disable the modules you need/don't need. There are over 30 modules there, so you have a lot to choose from. Luckily, they've been grouped into a handful of categories:

- **Writing**: Everything that makes writing content easier
- **Sharing**: Some additional social media integration
- **Discussion**: Tools that help your readers discuss and interact with your content
- **Traffic**: Tools and settings that help you monitor the traffic that your website is getting
- **Security**: Backups, added security, and spam protection

I won't go over each of the modules here in detail because it would probably require a chapter of its own. Instead, I encourage you to click on the name of each module you'd like to look into and get all the info yourself. In general, each of the modules is quite user-friendly, so you shouldn't experience any trouble during installation or using them later on.

Summary

This chapter was all about expanding the features available on your site and making your content more attractive without the need to touch any source code. Basically, that's the whole idea behind plugins.

Some developers actually don't need plugins because they can code things on their own. However, for the rest of the world, plugins are what makes WordPress easy to use and attractive for everyone.

At this point, we know how to control the content of our WordPress site, so now it's about time to learn how to control the display. In the next chapter, we will start discussing themes.

6
Choosing and Installing Themes

One of the greatest advantages of using a **Content Management System** (**CMS**) for your website is that you are able to change the look and feel of your website without being knowledgeable about HTML and CSS. Almost every CMS allows users to customize the look of their website without having to worry about their content being changed. These managed looks are referred to as themes. On other platforms (for example, Blogger, Joomla!, Drupal, and so on), themes are sometimes called **templates** or **layouts**.

Thousands of WordPress themes are available for download free of cost, and thousands more are available at a pretty low cost. Some of the free themes are developed by members of the WordPress community and listed on WordPress's main website at `https://wordpress.org/themes/`, while others can be found across the web on independent sites.

But before you change the theme of your current website, you will want to know the following:

- Some basic factors about the theme you're considering
- How to find quality themes
- How to choose the theme that best suits your content and audience
- How to install a theme

In this chapter, we will discuss all of these topics. This chapter is a ground-up guide to using themes. And, in the next chapters, we will discuss the advanced topic of developing your own themes.

 If you are using WordPress.com to host your WordPress website, you cannot upload themes to your site. Instead, you have to choose from the hundred or so themes that WordPress.com makes available to you.

Finding themes

There are dozens of websites that offer WordPress themes for you to download and to implement on your own website. Many theme developers offer their themes for free, whereas some charge a small fee. Of course, if you cannot find a free theme that fits your needs, you can always hire a theme developer to create a customized theme for you, or you can be your own theme developer (see `Chapter 8`, *Developing Your Own Theme*).

WordPress Theme Directory

The first place you should always go to when looking for a theme is the official WordPress Theme Directory at `https://wordpress.org/themes/`. This is where everyone in the WordPress community uploads their free themes and tags them with keywords that describe the basic look, layout, and functions of their themes, as shown in the following screenshot:

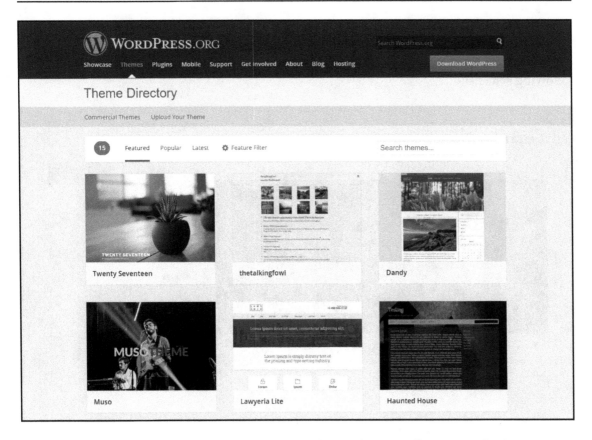

By looking at the list of popular themes on the right (in the preceding screenshot), you can see which themes are chosen most often. **Twenty Seventeen**, as you already know, is the default theme that WordPress uses automatically when you first install it.

To get a better idea of what a theme will look like, apart from what's offered by the thumbnail, just click on the title of the theme (in my case *Zerif Lite* at `https://wordpress.org/themes/zerif-lite`). You'll be taken to the theme's details page, as shown in the following screenshot:

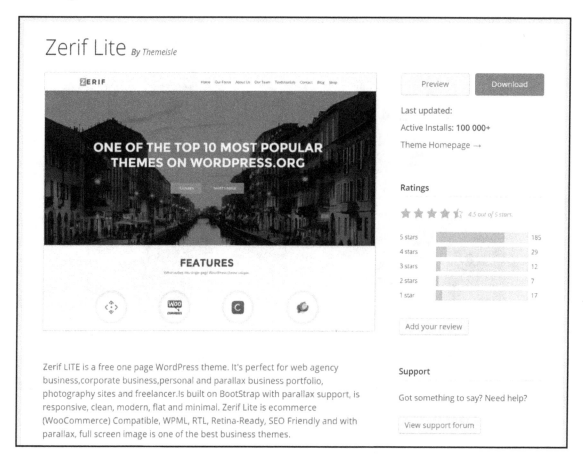

The preceding page shows you the theme's description, all of the tags that apply to it, the average rating given to it by other users, and some comments on the theme. If you click on the **Preview** button, you'll get to see the theme actually in action, as shown in the following screenshot:

As you browse through the Theme Directory, make sure to take note of any theme you find that you like; we'll discuss how to add it to your WordPress site later on in this chapter.

It's also worth pointing out that each theme in the official directory comes with its own **Support** section and user reviews section. You can view them by clicking on one of the links available in the right sidebar, as highlighted in the following screenshot:

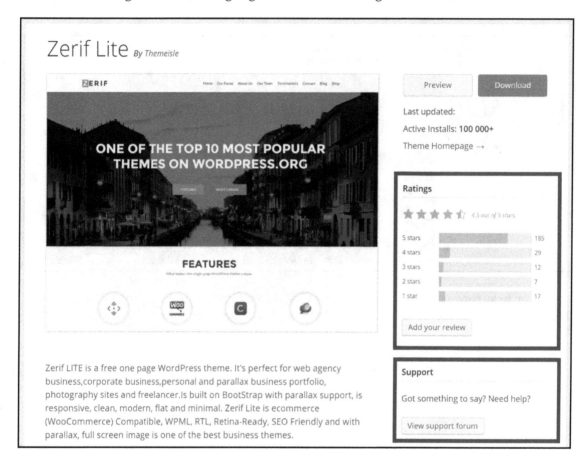

Main types of themes

As mentioned before, there are two main types of themes--**free themes** and **premium (paid) themes**. Also, if you don't consider price being a factor here, we can also divide themes into four additional groups--**standard themes, child themes, starter themes**, and **theme frameworks**.

- **Child themes**: We will discuss this in detail in the next chapters, so, for now, let's say that a child theme is a theme that inherits the functionality of another theme-- the parent.
- **Standard themes**: These are themes meant to work in their original form while allowing some basic customizations and tuning up (just like the default theme-- **Twenty Seventeen**).
- **Starter themes**: These are a relatively new concept in the WordPress world. In short, when using them, you are encouraged to modify the theme files directly, and effectively make them the foundation of the theme you're currently building like the name suggests, they provide a great starting point for your own theme to be built upon. They are a great solution for developers, but not so much for regular users who just want to download a great theme and be able to use it right out the box.
- **Theme frameworks**: These are somewhat similar to starter themes (they are meant to be used as the base for your custom theme development), but they usually deliver a larger range of various built-in features, plus they can be used straight out the box as a standalone theme (at least to some extent).

   In some way, the main difference between starter themes and theme frameworks is that when you get a starter theme, you must put work into it beforehand, in order to make the theme functional. While with frameworks, you get a functional theme right away, but then, you are expected to spend time tweaking its various elements to make it fit your site hand-in-glove. The thing with both theme frameworks and starter themes is that they are usually highly code-heavy products, which means that you can't really take full advantage of them if you don't possess any programming skill or don't have anyone on your payroll that does. This may not sound that clear right now, and that's okay. We will explain this concept some more in the next chapters.

The thing with both theme frameworks and starter themes is that they are usually highly code-heavy products, which means that you can't really take full advantage of them if you don't possess any programming skill or don't have anyone on your payroll that does. This may not sound that clear right now, and that's okay. We will explain this concept some more in the next chapters.

In the end, standard themes are what most bloggers and site owners work with during their WordPress journeys, especially if they don't need any advanced customizations or don't run purpose-specific websites (such as animated sites, interactive sites, and so on).

Finding more themes

If you can't find a theme in the directory that you like, you have other options. There are other sites with free themes, and also sites that sell themes for a price. Most commercial themes are offered at two or three price points:

- The first price is simply the cost of buying the theme for your own use and can be anywhere from $20 to $100. Such a license allows you to use the theme on a single site.
- The second price is the price you pay if you want to be able to use the theme on multiple sites (domains), or when you need the project graphics (for example, Photoshop documents) and other development files. In this case, it's usually from $60 to $200.
- The last price point, although not that popular nowadays, is the "exclusive license." You can get it if you want to be the only user of the theme. This can be anywhere from $500 to $1500, or even more.

Let's focus on free versus paid themes here. While every theme in the official directory is free, the rest of the internet is split in half on this. Some sites provide free themes exclusively, while others offer paid ones exclusively. There are also a number of distributors who sit in between. I, personally, don't advise getting any free themes from anywhere other than either the official directory or one of the respected theme stores (which offer some free themes as a promotional method).

The reason is simple. Only quality themes are allowed into the official directory, and I'm not just talking about the looks or the design. What matters apart from the design is also the code structure and code quality. There's no single theme that features any mysterious blocks of code (such as encrypted code or suspicious external links) that will ever find its way into the official directory. That's what ultimately makes the official directory one of the best sources of free WordPress themes on the internet.

When it comes to various free themes being released in theme stores, the story is quite similar. The "first league" of WordPress themes, so to speak, consists of respected, serious companies. So, even when they release a free theme, they can't afford it being low quality or lacking in any other way. Therefore, in most cases, they are safe to use as well.

The last thing we can witness online are hundreds, if not thousands, of free themes being released on random websites, promoted through paid advertising, "top themes" lists, advertorial articles, and so on. Let me say this again, I don't advise you to get any of those even if the designs are attractive. The fact is that you'll never know what sits on the inside and what security breaches can be taken advantage of to hack into such a theme. They are also almost never supported by their creators and there's no theme documentation or updates. In short, it is not worth it.

 If you want to learn more about why unknown-origin free themes are unsafe to use, feel free to visit the article at `http://newinternetorder.com/free-wordpress-themes-are-evil/`.

Finally, if you have some money you'd like to invest in your site and its quality, consider getting a full-blown premium theme or even a premium theme framework. As I mentioned earlier, the price range is around $20 to $100, depending on the manufacturer and the features the theme comes with.

You are welcome to check out any theme provider you wish. But just to make things quicker, the following is my go-to-first list of quality theme stores:

- **ThemeIsle**: `https://themeisle.com/`
- **Elegant Themes**: `https://www.elegantthemes.com/`
- **WPMU DEV**: `https://premium.wpmudev.org/`
- **ThemeForest**: `https://themeforest.net/category/wordpress`

Also, here's a separate list of the top WordPress theme stores on the web, based on sales and product quality: `https://www.codeinwp.com/blog/wordpress-theme-shop-directory-2016/`.

In general, most good commercial theme websites let you see a preview of the theme in action before you buy it. Some also let you customize the theme before downloading it. As with any other online shopping experience, do some research before buying to make sure you'll be getting a quality theme with decent support. There are plenty of badly coded themes out there and even themes with malicious code. Before buying a theme, verify the source of the theme and see if you can find feedback or reviews from anyone else who has purchased it.

To find even more websites that offer themes, just do a Google search for `WordPress themes` or `premium WordPress themes` and you'll get over 70 million hits. Also, keep in mind that you can choose a basic theme now and customize it, or create your own from scratch later, as you build skills by reading this book.

Some not-design-related theme basics

Let's take a quick look at some factors to consider when choosing and installing themes, just so that you'll be better informed.

The structure of a theme

A WordPress theme is actually a collection of files in a folder/directory. There are no special or unusual formats, just a few requirements for those files in the theme folder. The only requirements for a folder to be a valid WordPress theme are as follows:

- It should have a `style.css` file and an `index.php` file
- The `style.css` file must have the basic theme information in its initial lines

There are a number of additional files that you'll find in most theme folders. They are as follows:

- A `screenshot.png` file that is the little thumbnail that shows what the theme looks like
- An `images` folder where all images associated with the theme live
- A variety of files that are used for different purposes (for example, `functions.php`, `header.php`, `footer.php`, `page.php`, `single.php`, `archive.php`, and so on)

 To learn more about the structure of various theme files and their hierarchy, feel free to read the article at `https://codeinwp.com/blog/wordpress-theme-heirarchy/`.

You don't have to worry about these details now, but knowing them will help you identify what is going on inside the themes that you download. This will also be useful in the next chapters, where we will discuss making our own theme from scratch.

Also, don't worry if you download a theme and its directory structure looks very different from what's described here. Some theme developers decide to go with their own structure in order to provide some extra features and a more customizable environment. This is mostly the case with various theme frameworks and big premium themes that come with their pre-made child themes.

Factors to consider when choosing a theme

As you look through the themes available out there, you'll see that there is quite a variety in terms of look, feel, and layout options. To be honest, picking the perfect theme involves effort and some thought. A couple of years ago, there were just a handful of quality websites and stores where you could get your hands on some themes. Now, there are hundreds to thousands of them. All this results in a situation where there are multiple factors to consider when selecting a theme. It's best if you start with the following.

The purpose of the theme

As I've already mentioned multiple times in this chapter and the previous chapters, nowadays, WordPress is perfectly capable of running any kind of website, and this situation is reflected in the number of available themes. Therefore, the first question to answer is, *what do you need the theme for?*

Depending on the kind of site you're planning to launch, you should focus on different types of themes. The following are some of the popular possibilities:

- **Traditional blogs**: These are the ones where the content is presented in a reverse chronological order, with only several pages of static content.
- **Photo blogs**: These are very much like traditional blogs when it comes to the content organization, but in this case, the content consists mainly of photos. This is a popular type of blog among photographers and other creative individuals.
- **Video blogs**: These are much like photo blogs; except now, we're dealing with videos.
- **Small business websites and corporate websites**: Most small business sites don't feature a lot of "posts" like traditional blogs. They usually focus on static pages for providing the most important information about the business (such as contact data, offers, and so on). This type is most commonly used by local businesses such as restaurants, cafes, hotels, and other similar "physical" businesses. Corporate sites are very similar in nature, but are much bigger and feature much more content.

- **One-page micro-websites**: Some people know very well that they need only a minimal online presence, effectively treating their new website as a modern business card. In this case, a solution like a one-page site is perfect for them. In short, one-page sites are just what they sound like; they consist of only one page. However, due to clever design and structure of that page, the visitor can still get a rich experience browsing it.

- **Online magazines**: The main difference between traditional blogs and online magazines is that the latter features a lot more content, with usually as many as ten or more posts being published every day. This requires good content layout and clear presentation.

- **E-commerce stores**: Traditionally known as online stores or shops, an e-commerce store is every website that offers a shopping cart functionality and allows its visitors to buy a wide range of products, much like they'd do in a traditional store or supermarket.

- **Software/app websites**: These are websites devoted to promoting/selling a specific product. Nowadays, it's usually some kind of app or other piece of mobile software.

The trick when choosing a theme for your site is to understand its purpose and make your decision based not only on the appearance of the theme but also on the thing you need the theme for, its capabilities, as well as options for further customization. The easiest way to do this is to pay attention to the categories of themes on the site where you're looking for them. For instance, if you go to one of the popular theme stores such as the ones at `https://themeisle.com/wordpress-themes/` or `https://themeforest.net/category/wordpress`, you'll see that they feature great mechanisms for filtering themes by purpose. Here's how ThemeIsle does this:

Here's ThemeForest:

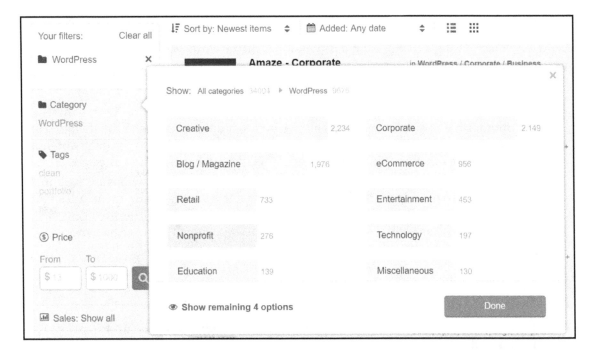

You can also do some research on the internet and notice what the standard is when it comes to the themes being used in your niche and for your type of site. For example, if you're thinking of launching a photo blog, check what sort of themes other photo blogs use--do they feature a lot of sidebars? How big are the photos they publish? Are there a lot of static pages? And so on. The idea is this--don't reinvent the wheel. If there's a significant number of sites that are similar to the one you're planning to launch, then you should always try learning from them and then making an educated decision when choosing your theme.

Theme licensing

If you're getting a theme from the official directory, then this part doesn't concern you.

However, when getting a theme from a professional theme store, you usually have two or more options regarding the license. As I've mentioned earlier, the price range is usually $20 to $100. Now, there are many licensing models, but the following two of them are the most popular web-wide:

- **Standard, one-site license**: This allows you to launch a site using the theme. It's the recommended choice if you're just searching for a theme for yourself and not to use it on other people's sites as well. This is the cheapest kind of license.
- **Developer license**: This is targeted at developers and people who want to launch more than one site with a theme. Additionally, the package usually includes PSD project files and other mid-development files (note that some one-site licenses include those as well). Developer licenses can be as much as two times more expensive than the standard, one-site licenses.

Up-to-date themes only

This is probably the most important parameter here. Your theme has to be up-to-date or it will fail to take advantage of the newest features in WordPress. The only bad news is that you can't know for sure whether a theme is a modern one or not. You can only rely on the details provided by the theme seller. But as bad as it sounds, it's actually not that big of a problem because big theme stores can't afford to lie in their marketing materials. So, whenever you see a message that the theme is compatible with WordPress version X.X, it's most likely true (provided you're getting a theme from a respected company).

Also, a good rule of thumb is to check when the last update took place. Depending on the theme store you're getting the theme from, this information can be displayed in various places, so I can't give you any specific advice on where to look for it. Nevertheless, if you're getting your theme from the official directory at `https://wordpress.org/themes/`, then you can find this detail in the right sidebar on every individual theme's page (labeled **Last Updated**).

Themes that are customizable

When considering a theme, make sure to find answers to the following questions:

- Are the sidebars flexible? Can I choose how many sidebars I want to display?
- Is it widget-ready?
- Does it support custom menus?
- Is it complex or simple? Which do I prefer?
- How flexible are the content and layout? Can I choose the column count and widths?
- Does it support the Customizer panel? Or does it offer a *Theme Settings* page where I can customize the layout, category display, homepage, and other options?

At this point in WordPress' development, I recommend rejecting any theme that does not support widgets and custom menus or does not deliver good customization features. The idea behind all this is that these days, a situation where you can use a theme right out of the box rarely happens, so having at least a couple of customization possibilities goes a very long way.

Themes with a responsive structure

This is one of the new parameters among modern themes. Back in the day, if you wanted to make your site mobile-friendly, you needed to get some plugins and additional mobile themes and then enable them to work at the same time. Now, with HTML5 and CSS3, you can use just one theme and be certain that it's going to look great on every possible device (from desktop computers to laptops, to mobile devices). The keyword to all this is *responsive design/structure*.

Whenever a theme developer indicates that their theme is responsive, it means that it's compatible with all the devices people use to access the internet these days. In a nutshell, whenever a theme is responsive, this fact will surely be mentioned on the official sales/download page.

Support, reviews, and documentation

This is especially important if you're getting a paid premium theme. Quite simply, since you're paying money, you naturally want to be sure that the product you're getting is a quality one that provides good customer service and well-designed functionality, hence the importance of documentation, reviews, and customer support. As simple as at.

I do admit that selecting a theme can take a while, especially if you have to remember about all of what we just covered, but this is work that will surely pay off. Let's not forget that you're going to be stuck with the theme you choose for at least a year or two (a common scenario), so you surely don't want to spend money on a low-quality product.

Installing and changing themes

Now that you've chosen the theme you want to use, you'll need to install it onto your WordPress website. You'll have the following two choices, as you did when adding new plugins:

- *If* the theme you want is in the WordPress Theme Directory, you can add the theme straight from within the wp-admin.
- *Else*, you'll have to download, extract, and then upload the theme by hand.

Adding a theme within the wp-admin

As mentioned in the preceding section, you can add a theme directly from within your wp-admin if you've chosen a theme from the WordPress Theme Directory, provided you're using a current enough version of WordPress. First, navigate to **Appearance**, and then click on the **Add New** button (visible at the top), as shown in the following screenshot:

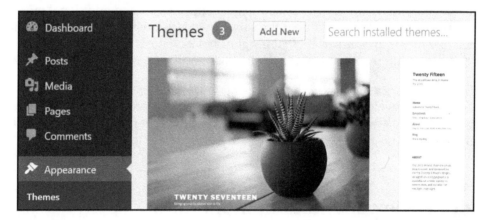

The screen that's going to appear will be very similar to the **Add New Plugins** screen. At the top, you'll see some familiar elements such as various sub-navigation links (**Featured**, **Popular**, **Latest**, **Favorites**, **Feature Filter**) along with a search box to the right. You can click on any theme displayed on the grid to see its details, along with a nice preview.

Using **Feature Filter** (the next screenshot), you can filter out some of the themes based on the functionality they have or don't have. The **Feature Filter** is a great way to find a theme that offers a specific range of functionalities that you require for the site you're currently building. For instance, you can choose to display themes featuring a responsive layout only. This will make sure that your website is going to look great on all devices, and that's including all desktop computers, as well as mobiles and tablets.

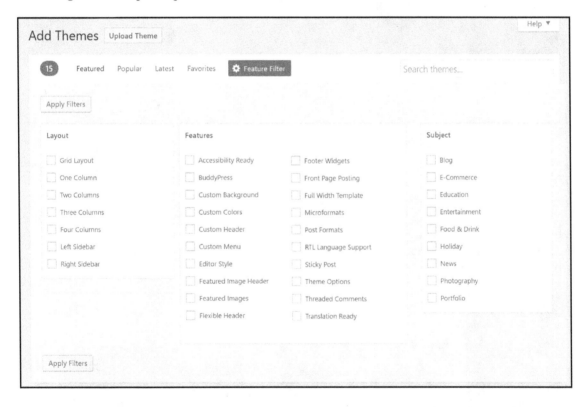

Now, I've already found a theme I like, so I won't bother with filtering and just put the name of the theme in the search box, as shown in the following screenshot:

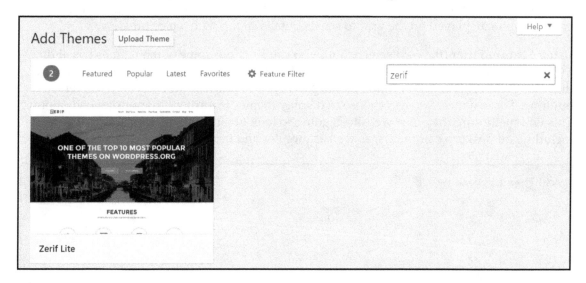

When I hover over the theme block, I will see additional links for details, preview, and installation. Clicking on **Preview** is a great way to see what the theme is most likely going to look like in action. Note that at this point, the theme preview will be the same as the preview on the **Theme Directory** page, rather than a preview of your own site's content. Until the theme is installed, you won't see a preview of your own site. If I click on **Install**, the theme will be downloaded and added to my collection of themes automatically (and will be visible in the **Appearance** section in the wp-admin), as shown in the following screenshot:

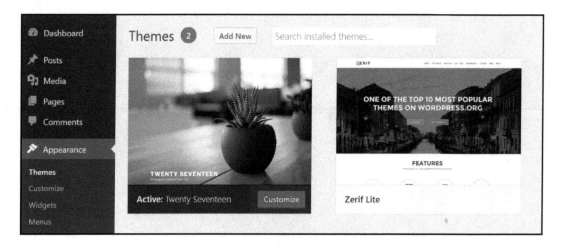

By clicking on the theme, I will see a larger block containing all the details, along with two more links to activate and see the live preview of the theme (which uses the content I currently have on my site), as shown in the following screenshot:

At this point, clicking on the **Activate** button will result in "turning the theme on" and using it as the new design on the website instead of **Twenty Seventeen** (which I'm using right now).

Downloading, extracting, and uploading

If you can't install a theme from within the wp-admin for whatever reason, you'll have to use the following procedure instead.

Additionally, due to the growing popularity of external theme sources such as various theme stores and independent developers, downloading and installing a theme manually becomes the default way of handling things, and gradually replaces the traditional approach of getting a theme from the official directory.

Therefore, to provide a good example when explaining the manual installation, I'm going to get a theme (a free one) and guide you through the process of having it installed. It doesn't matter where you get your themes from, the installation procedure always starts once you have the theme downloaded to your computer. When this is done, you'll see a ZIP file on your desktop (or in your `Downloads` folder).

The theme I'd like to try out is called *Underscores*, and it's a free starter theme available at `http://underscores.me/`.

Depending on the source of the theme, you might be required to either create a user account, make a purchase, sign up for a newsletter, and so on, in order to get the theme. Of course, sometimes, there's just a direct download link. Underscores uses a pretty straightforward model. All you need to do is input the name that you want to use for your theme in the field at `http://underscores.me/` (it can be whatever name you wish). After clicking on **GENERATE**, you'll get a ZIP download:

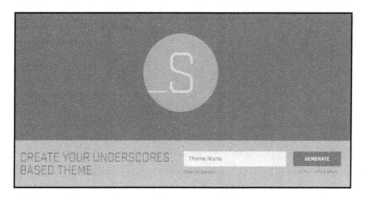

At this point, you can upload the ZIP file through the wp-admin by navigating to **Appearance | Themes** and clicking on the **Add New** button. There, you can click on the **Upload Theme** button, which will take you to the place where you can finally perform the manual installation, as shown in the following screenshot:

The only thing you need to do there is choose the ZIP file from your desktop and then click on the **Install Now** button. After a short while, you will be redirected to the success page where you will be able to activate your new theme.

If this doesn't work, continue with the following steps to extract and upload the theme files manually.

If you're using Mac, the ZIP file may have automatically been unzipped for you, in which case you'll see a folder on your desktop instead of the ZIP file, or in addition to the ZIP file. If not, then just do the extraction/unzipping manually so that you do have the theme folder on your desktop.

The following screenshot shows the file contents of the Underscores theme that I downloaded. Apart from the mandatory `style.css` file and the `index.php` file, it also has a number of other files that handle different tasks and take care of various aspects of the display and the functionality of the theme:

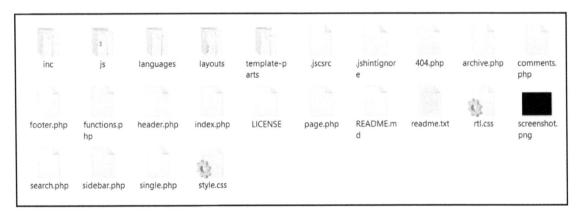

| inc | js | languages | layouts | template-p arts | .jscsrc | .jshintignor e | 404.php | archive.php | comments. php |

| footer.php | functions.p hp | header.php | index.php | LICENSE | page.php | README.m d | readme.txt | rtl.css | screenshot. png |

| search.php | sidebar.php | single.php | style.css |

Now, you need to upload the theme folder to your WordPress website. As you did in `Chapter 2`, *Getting Started with WordPress*, you need to start an FTP connection with your server. Once there, navigate to your WordPress website's installation folder. Next, go to the `wp-content` folder and then to the `themes` folder. You'll see one theme folder in here already named `twentyseventeen` (and possibly others as well). These are the themes that came pre-installed with WordPress. So, the only thing you have to do here is to upload the folder that you've just unzipped a minute ago so that it sits alongside the default `twentyseventeen` folder. And that's it!

At this point, when you go back to **Appearance** in your wp-admin, you will see the new theme waiting there. All that's left to do now is activating it and using it as the main design of your site.

Summary

This chapter described how to manage the basic look of your WordPress website. You learned where to find themes, why they are useful, what the basic differences between various themes are, how to select the perfect theme for your site, and how to install themes manually as well as through the wp-admin.

In the next chapter, you will learn how to customize existing WordPress themes--making your website look exactly how you want it to look.

7
Customizing Your Website Appearance/Design

At this stage, you already know how versatile WordPress is when it comes to the range of designs you can have on your site--all because of themes. However, just getting a theme and using it *as is* perhaps isn't the most optimized approach. So in this chapter, we're going to take it up a notch, you'll learn how to customize your theme.

We'll start by discussing how to manage navigation menus and work with the basic layout customization features to further enhance the capabilities of your entire website. Then, we'll talk about widgets and how to use them to make your sidebars even more functional and reader-friendly. Lastly, we'll cover the topic of WordPress Customizer, and what it can do for your overall website presentation.

Menus

Menus serve a very important role for any website's ease of navigation and helping readers find things. A classic website menu is one displayed near the top of the page, listing individual sub-pages that are part of the website. Those very often are pages like *About*, *Contact*, and so on. Under the hood, menus are just simple lists of links that point to different areas within your website.

It just so happens that WordPress handles menus in a very user-friendly way. As of WordPress 3.0, custom menus are now available within the wp-admin. This wasn't always the case, but these days, all modern themes support custom menus, and so does the default theme: Twenty Seventeen.

The **Custom Menus** feature lets you create menus with links to pages, category archives, and even arbitrary links to any URL (which also allows you to link to your individual posts). Then you can place your custom menu into your theme.

Adding a menu

Let's take a look at the menus management screen. To get there, just navigate to **Appearance | Menus**:

To create your first menu, enter a title (for example, Main) where it says **Menu Name**, and then click on **Create Menu**. After doing so, you can select individual *pages* from the panel on the left and click on the **Add to Menu** button to confirm:

If you want to add specific blog posts to the menu, you can do that too. Just click on the **Posts** heading in the panel and then pick the exact post you want to link too. To confirm, click on **Add to Menu**:

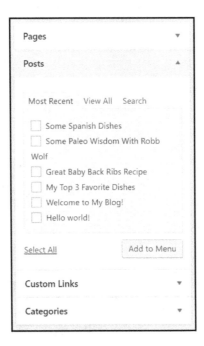

You can add some custom links to the menu as well. This can be done after clicking on the **Custom Links** heading on the left and then filling out the required link information. To confirm, click on **Add to Menu**:

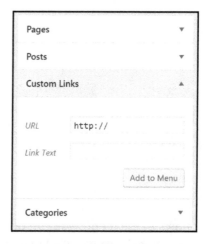

Next, you can add some category links. Click on the **Categories** heading on the left and then proceed to click on the checkboxes next to the categories you want to include. Click on **Add to Menu** to confirm:

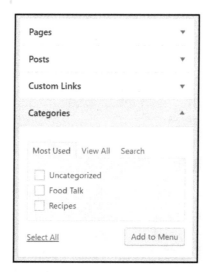

Finally, be sure to click on **Save Menu** in the upper-right corner. The following is what my new menu looks like now:

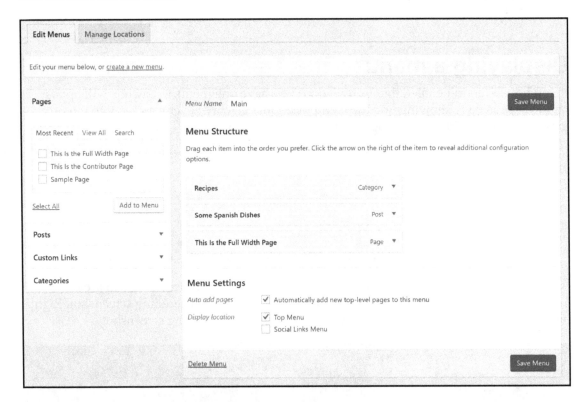

You can also drag items to the right to make them sub items of the item immediately above. For example, I'll drag one of my posts as a sub item under the **Recipes** category. Now, my menu looks like the following screenshot:

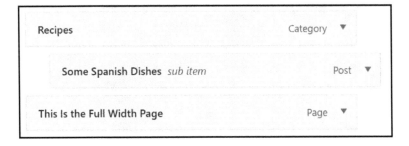

You can make more menus by clicking on the **create a new menu** link at the top and repeating the process. Now, you might ask: *I created my new menu, but how do I make it show up on my site?*

Displaying a menu

If you have a menu-enabled theme, then once you have one menu, a new box will appear on the **Menus** page showing you the menu locations. Twenty Seventeen has two menu locations, and they're named **Top Menu** and **Social Links Menu**:

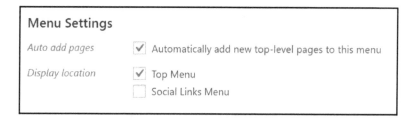

All you have to do to assign your newly created menu to the predefined menu area in Twenty Seventeen is to check one of the boxes, as shown in the preceding screenshot. Right now, my primary navigation on the website looks like the following screenshot:

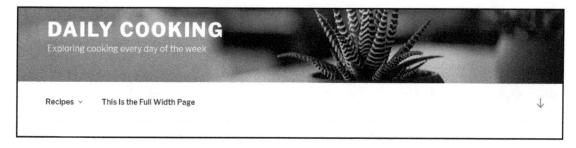

And when I click on the down arrow next to **Recipes**, I will also see my other post that was saved as a sub item, as shown in the next screenshot. Twenty Seventeen displays sub items in a rollover menu:

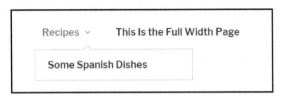

Widgets

Widgets are one of the native mechanisms in WordPress. Their main purpose is to provide us with an easy-to-use way of customizing the sidebars, footers, and headers of our site, with the addition of extra content. Even though the most common placement of widgets is indeed the sidebar, the only actual rule is that a widget can be displayed inside a widget area. And, a widget area can be anywhere a theme developer wants it to be. Common widgets contain the following:

- A monthly archive of blog posts
- A clickable list of pages
- A clickable list of recent posts
- A metadata box (containing log in/out links, RSS feed links, and other WordPress links)
- Recent comments posted on the blog
- A clickable list of categories
- A tag cloud
- A block of text and HTML
- A search box

These days, most themes are widget-enabled with one or more widget areas available for use. If I were to simplify this a bit, I'd say that widget areas behave like locations for menus. To control the widgets on your new website, navigate to **Appearance | Widgets**. Twenty Seventeen comes with three widget areas. They're called **Sidebar**, **Footer 1**, and **Footer 2**, as shown in the following screenshot:

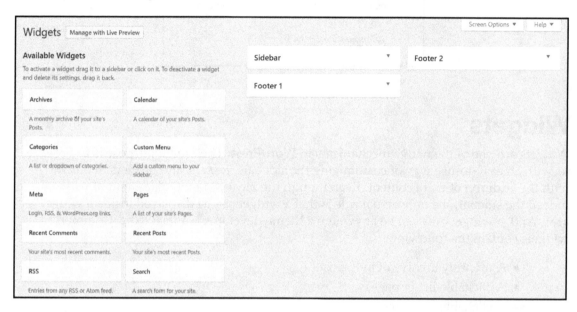

These widget areas appear in the right sidebar of the site and also the footer. The way you work with widgets is very simple. The only thing you have to do (on the **Appearance | Widgets** screen) is take any of the widgets visible on the left-hand side and drag and drop them into the right-hand area under any of the available widget areas. For example, let's take the **Custom Menu** block and drag it all the way to **Sidebar**. The result is as shown in the following screenshot:

Now, we can give this block a title and also use the dropdown to select the custom menu we want to include in this widget. Currently, there's only one menu that we created a while ago, **Main**. The following is what the site looks like with this custom menu placed in the right sidebar:

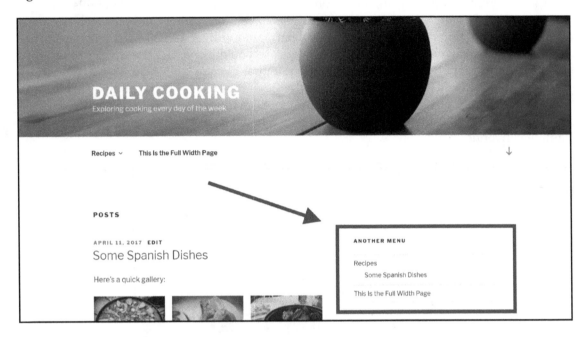

At this point, we have the main menu displayed two times on the site. There's one in the top area, and the second one is inside the right sidebar. As you can see, if you want to place your custom menu somewhere on the site, you have two ways of doing so. You can either assign it inside the **Appearance | Menus** section, or use it as a custom menu widget and place it in any widget area that your theme supports.

Enabling any other type of widget is very similar to the process described just now. All you need to do is drag the widget you like and drop it onto the area where you want to have it displayed. Then, once the widget is in place, you can adjust its settings and content.

When it comes to working in the **Appearance | Widgets** section, you can click on the little down arrow to the right of any widget to expand the details and see the options. You can drag a new widget in from the collection of available widgets on the left. You can drag existing widgets up and down to change their order. You can delete a widget by expanding it and then clicking on **Delete**.

Experiment with putting widgets into different widget areas and then refresh your blog to see what they look like. Always be sure to click on **Save** if you make any changes to a widget.

Also, at the bottom of the screen, there's one more section labeled **Inactive Widgets**, as shown in the following screenshot. Many widgets have their settings and parameters. Therefore, even if you don't want to display a particular widget on your site at the moment, but don't necessarily want to lose its settings (in case you'd like to use the widget again in the future), this section is where you should put it. Just like the label says, it's where you can drag your widgets to remove them from the sidebar but keep their settings. This is also where you will find any widgets that were previously active in a sidebar, but that got deactivated automatically after switching to a theme that didn't use the same sidebar naming convention.

The WordPress Customizer

Yet another feature in WordPress that's highly dependent on your theme is the **Customize Your Site** module. If you still have the welcome box enabled in your Dashboard's screen settings, you can access this module by clicking on the big **Customize Your Site** button, as shown in the following screenshot:

Another way of accessing this module is by visiting `http://yoursite.com/wp-admin/customize.php`. This is what you'll see (provided you're working with the default theme):

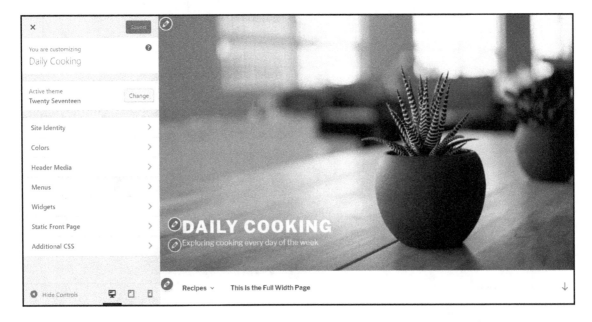

By going through the individual tabs on the left, you can adjust various aspects of your site--some that we've already talked about in this chapter, as well as some that are completely new. We're going to look through them here. The available customizations are as follows:

- **Site Identity**
- **Colors**
- **Header Media**
- **Menus**
- **Widgets**

- **Static Front Page**
- **Additional CSS**

The best thing about this module is that it provides a live preview, which makes editing the basic aspects of your design much quicker. When you're done, you can click on either the **X** button or the **Save & Publish** button that are visible in the top left corner:

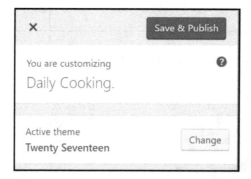

Before we get into the individual sections of the Customizer, let's have a glance at those curious-looking pencil icons in various parts of the interface. You can see an example in the next screenshot:

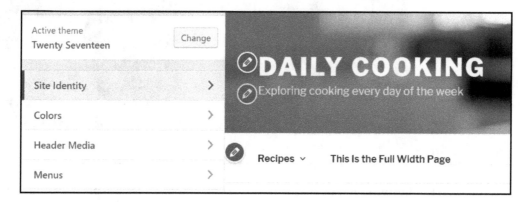

In a nutshell, those are shortcut icons. Meaning, they get displayed next to specific interface elements that can be edited within the Customizer. So instead of you having to search for a given customization in the left sidebar, you can simply click on the shortcut icon corresponding to it, and you will be immediately taken to the correct options panel. For example, if you click on the site's title, you will be taken to the exact section where you can edit it as shown in the following screenshot:

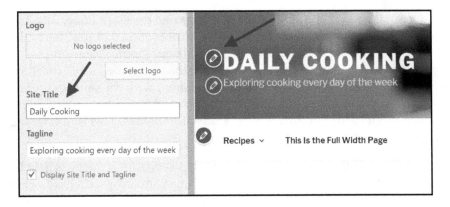

We'll explore the options one by one as we go through the Customizer.

Site identity

Site Identity is the first block that's available in the Customizer's sidebar:

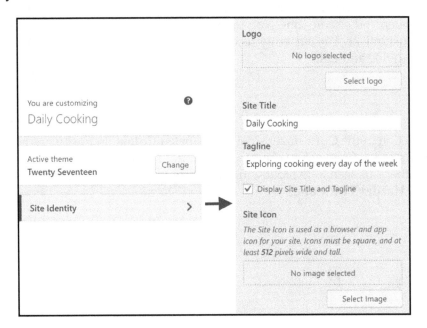

When you click on it, you will be able to adjust things like the site's **Logo**, **Site Title**, **Tagline**, and **Site Icon**. What needs to be said here, however, is that the effect all those options have on your site depends greatly on your current theme. For example, one theme will display the **Logo** in a completely different place than the other, same for the **Site Title**, and so on. It's therefore always a good idea to experiment with the settings there and find out on your own what effect they have. Under the hood, the options we're dealing with here are just standard input fields and image/media selection panels. This is everything that we already covered in the previous chapters of this book

The one element that usually works the same for most WordPress theme is **Site Icon**. A site icon is this small icon that's visible in the corner of your web browser window. For instance, if you go to this book's publisher's website, at `https://www.packtpub.com/`, you will see the site icon presented in the following screenshot:

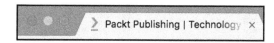

Overall, site icons are a nice way of giving your website some visual representation in the visitor's web browser, so that they can identify it more easily when having a handful of browser tabs open at the same time. You can pick your site icon easily by selecting it through the Customizer. The currently recommended image dimensions for the icon are at least 512 pixels wide and tall.

Colors

The second section in the Customizer sidebar is labeled **Colors**. In it, you can pick one of the current theme's pre-defined color schemes for the site. The Twenty Seventeen theme has three options there, as seen in the following screenshot. Plus, there's also an additional setting for the **Header Text Color**.

Changing from **Light** to **Dark** switches the site design from white background colors to near-black ones. If you click on **Custom**, you get to use a color picker to adjust some of the colors used in the design in a more freehand way. Lastly, the **Header Text Color** setting changes the color of your site's title/headline as shown in the following screenshot:

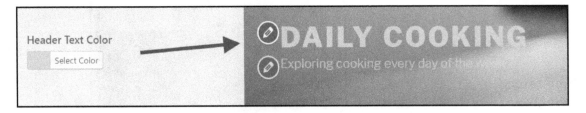

Header Media

Header Media is the next section in the Customizer sidebar. Again, the functionality I'm about to describe is highly dependent upon your current theme. Not all themes support header functionality, and even the ones that do, can provide you with different sets of features related to this topic. However, most modern themes these days do support header customizations in some form. So, learning a few things about this feature will surely come in handy to you sooner than later.

If you're starting your WordPress adventure with the default theme, Twenty Seventeen, then the **Header Media** section of the Customizer offers you some interesting options. Refer to the following screenshot:

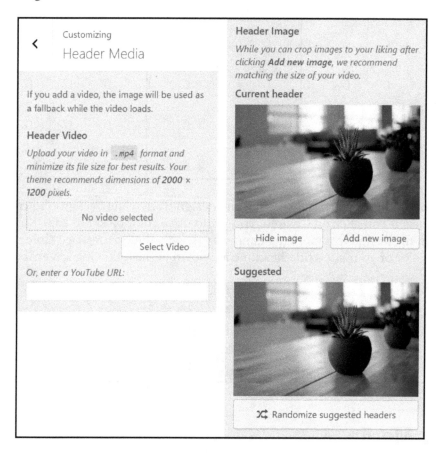

Most themes will allow you to select any image to be placed inside the header, and sometimes even a video - like Twenty Seventeen does. Twenty Seventeen also has some specific requirements for the header image (actually, most themes have, and Twenty Seventeen is only an example of that). The suggested size is 2000 pixels wide by 1200 pixels tall, but you don't have to worry all that much about this because WordPress also provides some handy image editing tools. All you have to do here is use the **Choose image** or **Add new image** button and select one of the pictures from your **Media Library**, or upload a new one. WordPress will immediately redirect you to the aforementioned image editing tools, where you can adjust and crop your image, as shown next:

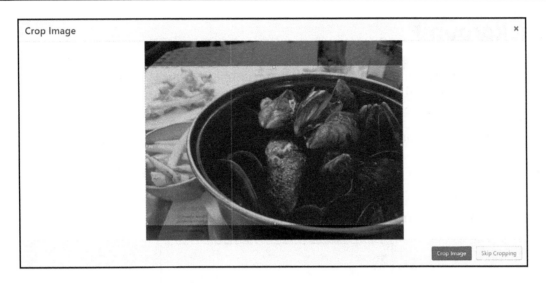

After clicking on the **Crop Image** button and then **Save & Publish**, we're done with setting up the header image. Here's what my site looks like now:

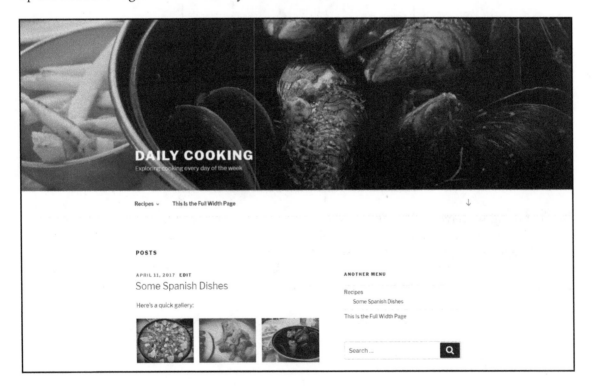

Background

Some WordPress themes allow you to adjust not only the header but the whole background of the site as well. Meaning, you can place whatever image in the background of the whole site, and make it sit there at all times. This works kind of like a desktop wallpaper, but for your WordPress website.

Although the current default theme, Twenty Seventeen, doesn't offer this functionality, this is still a very common feature to find in other themes, so let's discuss it here using another theme as our example, Twenty Fifteen, the former default theme in WordPress.

If you use that theme, and you go to the Customizer, you will see a new section in the sidebar called **Background Image** as shown in the following screenshot:

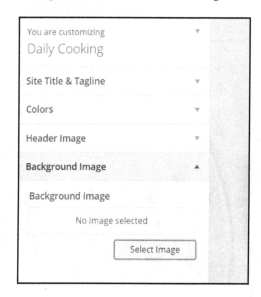

The first thing we have to do is select an image we want to place in the background of our whole site. Let me say that again, our whole site. Right after selecting an image (just click on **Select Image** visible in the preceding screenshot), the preview block will get refreshed, and you will be able to see what your background looks like at the moment. Immediately, there are some new options visible at the bottom of the options block:

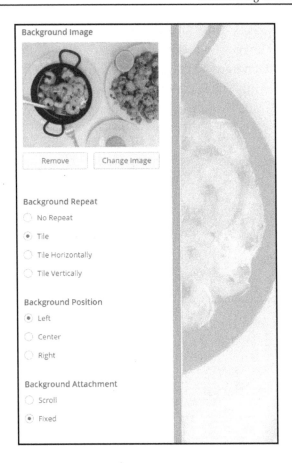

The various options are as follows:

- **Background Repeat**: This can be **No Repeat**, **Tile**, **Tile Horizontally**, or **Tile Vertically**:
  - **No Repeat**: This means that your background image will be displayed only once, and after the visitor scrolls down, they will simply *run out* of the background image.
  - **Tile**: This is the most popular setting and actually the default one as well. This means that WordPress will repeat your image in both dimensions (width and height). No matter what part of your site the visitor is browsing, the background image will always be visible.
  - **Tile Horizontally**: This tiles your image horizontally.
  - **Tile Vertically**: This tiles your image vertically.

- **Background Position**: This can be **Left, Center,** or **Right**. This decides whether the background image should be aligned to the left, center, or right.
- **Background Attachment**: This can be either **Scroll** or **Fixed**:
    - **Scroll**: Your image scrolls along with the content.
    - **Fixed**: Your image remains in a fixed position. In other words, it stands still in the background at all times.

I encourage you to play around with these settings for a while when adjusting your site. In the meantime, you can see the exact settings I've selected in the preceding screenshot.

Widgets

Even though we did discuss widgets earlier in this chapter, the Customizer offers you an alternative way of working with them. You can do it in the section called **Widgets**:

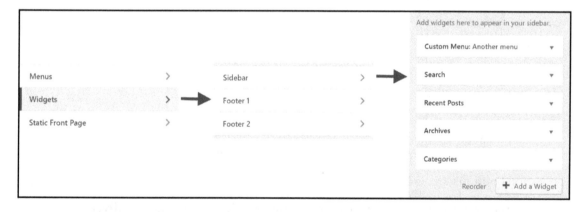

Once you click on it, in the next step, you will see all the widget areas currently available in your theme (the middle section in the preceding screenshot). Then, once you click on any of them, you will see all the individual widgets that are assigned to that given area (the far right section in the preceding screenshot). All those widgets can be easily edited much like we did earlier in this chapter, the methodology is the same. Also, you can add new widgets by clicking on the + **Add a Widget** button.

Static Front Page

Static Front Page is the name of the next section in the Customizer. Once you navigate there, you will be able to change the main settings of what page gets displayed when a visitor comes to your home page, the main address of your website. You can set a couple of things in the **Static Front Page** section:

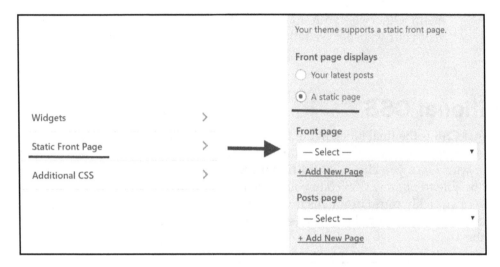

Once you go there, you will be able to choose between the default setting of **Your latest posts** (in this mode, the homepage is just a classic listing of your latest blog posts; this is the default setting that you're probably used to) and a new setting labeled **A static page**. That second one gives you the possibility to set whatever page you wish as the homepage of your website. You can either select an existing page from the dropdown list under **Front page** or create a new page by clicking on the **+ Add New Page** link.

For example, a good idea would be to simply create a new page and call it *HOME* or something else that's equally intuitive. Once you create this new homepage, you will then be able to come back to the standard editing panel for pages (in wp-admin under **Pages**) and treat the new home page like any other page on your site, put whatever content you wish to it, and so on.

Apart from the **Front page**, there's also another block here, labeled **Posts page**. If you change your home page to a static one, it's always a good idea to assign a new **Posts page** as well. Since the classic listing of your latest posts will no longer be displayed on the home page, the new **Posts page** is meant to handle this task from now on. Much like with the home page, you can select an existing page to serve as the new posts page, or create a new one.

In this case, however, it's actually more convenient to create a completely new page rather than pick an existing one. You can call yours BLOG or another similar name that conveys the page's purpose. What's interesting about this page is that you don't need to edit it manually or place any content on it. WordPress will populate this page with content on its own, so the only thing you need to do is just create it, and that's it.

 If you do create a new **Posts page**, don't forget to link it from your main menu. Otherwise your audience will have no way of finding it when they visit your website. We talked about menus earlier in this chapter.

Additional CSS

Additional CSS is the final block in the Customizer. This one can be handy if you want to include some custom changes into your current theme, changes that can't be achieved in any other way. Once you click on **Additional CSS**, you will see a text input block where you will be able to put any CSS code you wish. Be careful here, though. Working with raw CSS code can quickly cause problems if you're not sure what you're doing. Overall, this section is meant for advanced theme customizations. Take a look at the following screenshot:

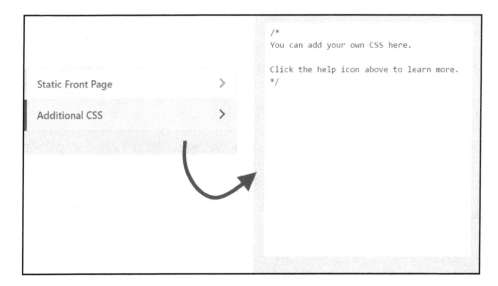

Last but not least, there are four interesting icons sitting in the bottom-left corner of the Customizer window. As seen in the following screenshot:

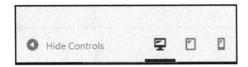

From the left, they are--the **Hide Controls** button (it hides the whole Customizer sidebar to give you a bigger canvas when adjusting your website), the desktop view icon, the tablet view icon, and the mobile view icon. Those final three icons are particularly important here. These days, more people tend to browse the web on their mobile devices than on classic desktop computers. Because of that, it's crucially important for you to make sure that your website displays properly on those devices. These three icons--the desktop view icon, the tablet view icon, the mobile view icon, allow you to do just that. When you click on any of them, the whole Customizer window will change in size to emulate the display mode on tablets and mobile devices. Switching back and forth between the modes, you can make sure that your site looks great on all devices. I really encourage you to experiment with this when adjusting your site's design.

Summary

In this chapter, you learned the basics of theme customization. You now know about menus, widgets, header and background settings, how to work with the WordPress Customizer, and more. At this stage, you know how to pick a great WordPress theme for your website and then how to customize it to fit your needs 100%.

In the next chapter, you will learn, step by step, how to build your own theme from scratch.

8
Developing Your Own Theme

At this point, you know how to find themes on the web and install them for use on your WordPress website. But, there's a lot more that WordPress has to offer, particularly in the theme development department. So, in this chapter, you'll learn how to turn your own design into a fully functional WordPress theme that you'll then be able to use on your site. You'll also learn how to convert your theme folder into a ZIP file that can be shared with other WordPress users on the web.

All you will need before we get started are the following:

- Your own design
- The ability to slice and dice your design to turn it into HTML

We'll start out with tips on slicing and dicing so that your HTML and CSS files are as WordPress-friendly as possible, and then cover the steps for turning that HTML build into a fully functional theme. Note that I assume you are already comfortable writing and working with HTML and CSS. You don't need to be familiar with PHP, because I'll be walking you through all of the PHP code.

 This chapter covers only the very basics of theme creation. This topic actually deserves a whole book, and it has one! I highly recommend the book *WordPress Theme Development: Beginner's Guide, Rachel McCollin and Tessa Blakeley Silver, Packt Publishing*. This book covers everything you could possibly want to know about creating your own theme in detail, including details such as choosing a color scheme, considering typography, writing the best CSS, and laying out your HTML using rapid design comping. If this chapter leaves you wanting more, go there!

Setting up your design

Just about any design in the world can be turned into a WordPress theme. However, there are some general guidelines you can follow--both regarding the design and the HTML/CSS build of your theme--that will make your job a lot easier.

Designing your theme to be WordPress-friendly

While you can design your blog any way you want, a good starting point would be with one of the standard blog layouts.

Note that, while these standard layouts have a differing number of columns, they all have these essential parts:

- Header
- Main column
- Side column(s)
- Footer

WordPress expects your theme to follow this pattern, and so, it provides functions that make your work easier. As you're designing your first blog theme, I suggest including these parts. Also, a build that stays within the same general design patterns of WordPress themes will most easily accommodate the existing plugins and widgets.

That being said, a common situation in the WordPress world is to build custom homepages or landing pages (purpose-specific pages, mostly commercial) that feature completely different designs. Therefore, you might stumble upon websites that don't look like they're built with WordPress at first glance. Also, many modern theme frameworks give us the possibility to create such custom home pages, as well as other custom page templates. This is all part of the trend to make WordPress capable of running any kind of website.

In this chapter, you're going to learn how to build a basic WordPress theme that offers a classic blog layout. Here's what the final product is going to look like:

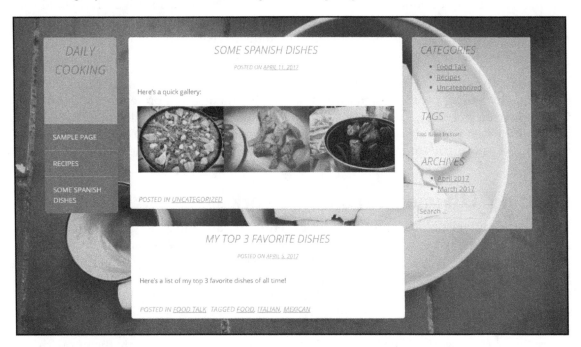

The HTML structure of the design is built on top of the **_S** starter theme (which is read as Underscores, `http://underscores.me/`), and the visual elements are all done through CSS, with only minimal modifications to the original HTML structure.

Three paths of theme development

Essentially, there are three paths you can follow when developing your new theme. You can either work from the ground up, by building the HTML structure and the functional structure of the theme by hand. Or, you can work on top of an existing theme framework, where you only have to adapt your design to work on the structure provided by the framework itself. Or, you can go for a solution that sits somewhere in between. All of these paths have their pros and cons though, as always.

Building a theme from the ground up

The main advantage of building a theme from the ground up is the massive educational value of this path. When you're developing a theme from scratch, you're learning the basics of theme construction and function. This kind of knowledge goes a long way for your future projects in WordPress.

On the other hand, it's also the longest of the three paths. In a professional production environment (among people designing and developing themes as a profession), creating themes from scratch is a highly time-consuming approach, making it quite ineffective. And it's not that much about adapting the design (which must always be done with theme frameworks as well); it's more about building the core functionality of the theme.

Building a theme with a framework

The main advantage of this approach is its time efficiency and the quality of the final result. For instance, if you're building a theme from scratch, you have to make sure to keep your theme up-to-date long after the development process has been finished. The thing is that WordPress gets updated very frequently (around once every 50 days), and many features change their purpose over time and get completely erased or replaced with new ones. In such a scenario, only modern themes that are kept up-to-date can take full advantage of these features. Updating your theme will obviously take a massive amount of work. This is where theme frameworks come into play. In essence, theme frameworks are themes with a very minimalist design and no visually complicated aspects.

The purpose of frameworks is to make them the base of any future theme by acting as the parent theme. So, the fact that the framework itself has no design allows every creator to introduce almost any design imaginable, while taking full advantage of the features and constructions provided inside the framework. Now, the strength of quality frameworks is that they get updated almost as frequently as WordPress plugins. In short, if you're using a framework, you don't have to worry about your theme going out-of-date. Whenever there's an update available, you can simply perform it and forget about the whole thing.

This brings me to the main disadvantage of using theme frameworks. Most of the time, theme frameworks are big and complex pieces of web software (PHP scripts). So, if you want to be able to use them effectively, you'll have to spend a significant amount of time learning the framework. On top of this, if you decide to switch to a different framework later down the road, you'll have to learn it all over again (frameworks are usually very different from each other). As you can see, reaping the benefits of using frameworks has its price.

Here are some of the popular theme frameworks (both paid and free ones):

- **Gantry** (free): `http://gantry.org/`
- **Hybrid** (free): `https://themehybrid.com/hybrid-core`
- **Genesis** (paid): `https://my.studiopress.com/themes/genesis/`
- **Headway** (paid): `http://headwaythemes.com/`
- **Thesis** (paid): `http://diythemes.com/`
- Some frameworks listed by WordPress: `https://codex.wordpress.org/Theme_Frameworks`

Building a theme with a starter theme

Finally, there's also a third solution, one that's somewhere in the middle of building a theme from the ground up and using a framework. What I'm talking about is using a starter theme.

A starter theme, like the one we'll be using in this chapter to create the base of our HTML structure, is a great solution to make sure that the theme you're building has the right scaffolding and that it's up-to-date with modern practices and optimized to be used for a WordPress site. Apart from this, the starter theme leaves you all the freedom in the world to adjust your creation however you wish (you have almost the same freedom as you do with from-the-ground-up theme building).

In other words, a starter theme provides us with the best of both worlds, that is, starting from scratch and using a framework. You can learn the basic structure of WordPress themes this way, and at the same time, we don't need to worry about making any silly mistakes because the core of the task is being handled by the starter theme itself.

So, in short, going with a starter theme is what we're going to do here. The main idea is to use it to learn the craft and get to know all the basic structures and mechanisms sitting inside WordPress. Your journey with theme development starts once you have a graphic design prepared in Photoshop or some other similar tool. You can also take the code bundle for this chapter and work with the design from there. Either way, the next step is to turn it into some HTML code.

Converting your design into code

The next step toward turning your ideal design into a WordPress theme is to slice images out of your design and write HTML and CSS files that put it all together. For the purpose of this chapter, I assume that you already know basically how to do this. We'll cover some pointers on how to do your slicing and dicing in a way that will fit best into WordPress.

Let's get down to business and take a look at the HTML structure that was generated (by the _S starter theme) for the purpose of the theme we're building here. Just to remind you, the starter theme can be generated at `http://underscores.me/`.

Examining the HTML structure

The following is the very basic layout of the HTML file for my food blog design; I'm showing it here just to give you a general understanding of what we're going to be working on:

```
<!DOCTYPE html>
<html lang="en-US">
<head>
<meta charset="UTF-8">
<meta name="viewport" content="width=device-width, initial-
scale=1">
<link rel="profile" href="http://gmpg.org/xfn/11">
<link rel="stylesheet" id="open-sans-css"
  href="//fonts.googleapis.com/css?family=Open+Sans%3A300italic
  %2C400italic%2C600italic%2C300%2C400%2C600&subset=latin%2
  Clatin-ext&ver=4.0.1" type="text/css" media="all" />
<!-- embedding Google Fonts -->
<link rel="stylesheet" id="daily-cooking-custom-style-css"
  href="style.css" type="text/css" media="all" />
<!-- embedding the style sheet for the design -->
<title>Daily Cooking</title>
</head>

<body>
<div id="page">
  <header id="masthead" class="site-header" role="banner">
    <div class="site-branding">
      <h1 class="site-title">Daily Cooking</h1>
    </div>
    <nav id="site-navigation" class="main-navigation"
    role="navigation">
      <!-- placeholder for site navigation -->
    </nav>
```

```
    </header>

    <div id="content" class="site-content">
      <div id="primary" class="content-area">
      <main id="main"  class="site-main" role="main">
      <article>
        <header class="entry-header">
          <h1 class="entry-title">Hello world!</h1>
        </header>

        <div class="entry-content">
          <p>Welcome!</p>
          <!-- main content block -->
        </div>

        <footer class="entry-footer">
          <!-- footer of the content block -->
        </footer>
      </article>
      </main></div>

      <div id="secondary" role="complementary">
        <!-- sidebar -->
      </div>
    </div>

    <footer class="site-footer" role="contentinfo">
      <!-- main footer of the page -->
    </footer>
  </div>
</body>
</html>
```

You can see that I've separated out these major parts:

- The header is in an HTML5 `<header>` tag.
- As part of it, there's the main site navigation, also an HTML5 tag `<nav>`
- Next, we have the main content block, `<div id="content" class="site-content">`; each individual post will be displayed inside separate HTML5 `<article>` tags.

- After this, we have a section that handles the sidebar, `<div id="secondary" role="complementary">`. The sidebar is set with the `role="complementary"` attribute. Roles are one of the relatively new HTML parameters. Essentially, a role attribute describes the role that the element plays in the context of the document. In this case, the sidebar is complementary to the main content (and if you pay close attention, you'll notice that the main part, that is, the content, is indeed set to `role="main"`). In general, such attributes are meant to explain the purpose of elements in the HTML structure.
- Finally, there's the footer using the `<footer>` tag. Keep in mind that this is HTML5 and it may not work on older web browsers.

Now that I've got my basic layout, I'm going to add a few more HTML elements to flesh it out a bit, including more information in `<head>` as well as in the main content box, plus some additional CSS. Then, I'll fill up the sidebar, header, content, and footer.

Examining the CSS

Generally, a very good practice in web development is to start your CSS design by resetting all the default styles used by various web browsers. The main issue, and the reason why this is an important step, is that most popular web browsers, or should I say every single one of them, have their own default set of CSS styles. And, if you want your theme to look exactly the same in every browser, you have to start your work by resetting these styles, whatever they might actually be. The good thing about this is that you don't have to do it by hand. You can just use one of the reset scripts available on the internet. Keep in mind that every piece of code that's listed in this chapter is also available in the official code bundle that came with your book. So, what we're doing first is just having the following CSS at the beginning of our new `style.css` file:

```
/* setting up the basic elements - starter setup */
html, body, div, span, applet, object, iframe,
h1, h2, h3, h4, h5, h6, p, blockquote, pre,
a, abbr, acronym, address, big, cite, code,
del, dfn, em, font, ins, kbd, q, s, samp,
small, strike, strong, sub, sup, tt, var,
dl, dt, dd, ol, ul, li,
fieldset, form, label, legend,
table, caption, tbody, tfoot, thead, tr, th, td {
  border: 0;
  font-family: inherit;
  font-size: 100%;
  font-style: inherit;
  font-weight: inherit;
  margin: 0;
```

```
  outline: 0;
  padding: 0;
  vertical-align: baseline;
}

html {
  font-size: 62.5%;
  overflow-y: scroll;
  -webkit-text-size-adjust: 100%;
  -ms-text-size-adjust: 100%;
  box-sizing: border-box;
}
*, *:before, *:after {
  box-sizing: inherit;
}

body {
  background: #fff;
}

/* resetting the basic content blocks */
article, aside, details, figcaption, figure, footer, header, main,
  nav, section {
  display: block;
}

/* resetting the lists */
ol, ul {
  list-style: none;
}

table {
  border-collapse: separate;
  border-spacing: 0;
}
caption, th, td {
  font-weight: normal;
  text-align: left;
}

blockquote:before, blockquote:after, q:before, q:after {
  content: "";
}
blockquote, q {
  quotes: " "";
}

a:focus {
```

```
    outline: thin dotted;
  }
  a:hover, a:active {
    outline: 0;
  }
  a img {
    border: 0;
  }
```

Let's now take a look at the actual CSS--the things that build our design and not just reset it. First, we'll review the CSS that displays everything you see in the design. Note that I've got styles for all of the key elements such as header, sidebar, main content area, and footer.

Also, note that this is just the scaffolding, so to speak. It only indicates the individual areas of the final CSS style sheet. Talking about CSS isn't the main thing we're focusing on in this book. Therefore, I'm including the complete version of the aforementioned code bundle, and right now, I'm only presenting the individual areas of the CSS. This is just to make the whole thing easier to grasp once you look at the complete style sheet. To be honest, the final CSS isn't actually that complex from a CSS design point of view, but it is quite lengthy. Here's the simplified version.

Let's start with the typography settings and various standard content elements. I'm not showcasing the individual styles here, as they are kind of basic and don't have a huge role in our WordPress site structure:

```
/*---------
Typography
-----------*/

body, button, input, select, textarea {}
h1, h2, h3, h4, h5, h6 {}
h1 a, h2 a, h3 a, h4 a, h5 a, h6 a {}
p {}
b, strong {}
dfn, cite, em, i {}
blockquote {}
address {}
pre {}
code, kbd, tt, var {}
abbr, acronym {}
mark, ins {}
sup, sub {}
small {}
big {}


/*--------
Elements
```

```
---------*/

hr {}
ul, ol {}
dt {}
dd {}
img {}
figure {}
table {}
button, input, select, textarea {}
```

What follows next is a set of rules that will take care of the alignment, general design structure, the headers, and other typical HTML elements:

```
.site-header {
  width: 15%;
  float: left;
  height: auto;
  background: #279090;
  margin-right: 2.5%;
  border-radius: 6px;
}

#page {
  width: 1160px;
  margin: 0 auto;
  margin-top: 50px;
  position: relative;
  overflow: auto;
}

#primary {
  width: 56%;
  float: left;
}

/* Navigation */
.main-navigation {
  clear: both;
  display: block
  float: left;
  width: 100%;
}

/* Alignments */
.alignleft {
  display: inline;
  float: left;
```

```
    margin-right: 1.5em;
}
.alignright {
  display: inline;
  float: right;
  margin-left: 1.5em;
}
.aligncenter {
  clear: both;
  display: block;
  margin: 0 auto;
}
```

The center part of the site structure is where the posts and pages will be displayed. The code for it is as follows:

```
.site-content .page, .site-content .post {
  margin-bottom: 40px;
  background-color: white;
  border-radius: 6px;
}

.entry-header h1.entry-title {
  text-align: center;
}

.site-content .entry-content {
  padding: 10px 20px;
}
```

The code for the main sidebar is this:

```
#secondary {
  width: 24.5%;
  float: left;
  height: auto;
  margin-left: 2%;
  opacity: 0.6;
  background-color: white;
  border-radius: 3px;
  padding: 0 10px;
}
```

And finally, the code for the footer is as follows:

```
.site-footer {
   float: right;
   padding: 20px;
}
```

Inside this style sheet, you will find many specific classes that aren't just my own creations but rather come from WordPress itself. Here's what I mean; when WordPress spits out items that include page lists, category lists, archive lists, images, and galleries, it gives many of these items a particular class name. If you know these class names, you can prepare your style sheet to take advantage of them. This is one more reason why we're using a starter theme here. With it, we don't have to worry about any of this.

 To learn more about this, feel free to check out `https://css-tricks.com/` `back-basics-wordpress-css-understanding-native-classes/` for an in-depth post on one of the top websites about CSS on the web.

For example, when you add an image to a post or page, WordPress gives you the option to have it to the right or left, or at the center of the text. Depending on what you choose, WordPress will give the image the `alignleft`, `alignright`, or `aligncenter` class. These classes, for example, are handled in the *Alignments* section of our CSS style sheet. Another thing is that, when you add an image with a caption, WordPress gives it the `wp-caption` class. This particular thing is handled in the *Captions* section of the style sheet we're using. WordPress uses many other classes that you can take advantage of when building your style sheet. I've listed a few of them in `Chapter 13`, *Creating a Non-blog Website Part Two - E-Commerce Websites and Custom Content Elements*.

Now that you've got your HTML and CSS lined up, you're ready for the next step: turning the HTML build into a WordPress theme.

Converting your build into a theme

You'll be turning your HTML build into a theme, which is composed of a number of template files and other scripts. We are going to first dig into the inner workings of a theme, so as to get familiar with how it's put together. Then, we'll actually turn the HTML build into a theme folder that WordPress can use. Finally, we'll include WordPress functions that spit out content. As I mentioned in an earlier chapter, doing development for your WordPress website in a local environment can make the whole process much smoother. Consider getting a server up and running on your home computer using WAMP, MAMP, or some other way to install Apache and MySQL.

Creating the theme folder

The first step to turning your HTML build into a theme is to create your theme folder and give it everything it needs to be recognized as a theme by WordPress. Let's look at an overview of the steps and then take them one by one:

1. Name your folder and create backup copies of your build files
2. Prepare the essential files
3. Add a screenshot of your theme named `screenshot.png`
4. Upload your folder
5. Activate your theme

Let's take these steps one by one now.

Name your folder and create backup copies of your build files

You'll want to give your build folder a sensible name. I'm naming my theme **Daily Cooking Custom**. I'll name the folder `daily-cooking-custom`. Now, I suggest creating backup copies of your HTML and CSS files. As you'll eventually be breaking up your build into template files, you can easily lose track of where your code came from. By keeping a copy of your original build, you'll be able to go back to it for reference.

Prepare the essential files

WordPress has only the following two requirements to recognize your folder as a theme:

- A file called `index.php`
- A file called `style.css`

Just rename your main design's HTML file as `index.php`, and this takes care of the first requirement. To satisfy the second requirement, your style sheet needs to have an introductory comment that describes the basic information for the whole theme: title, author, and so on. Also, it has to be at the very top of the style sheet. I've added this comment to my `style.css` file:

```
/*
Theme Name: Daily Cooking Custom
Theme URI: http://newinternetorder.com/
Author: Karol K
```

```
Author URI: http://karol.cc/
Description: Daily Cooking Custom is a custom theme created for the buyers
of "WordPress Complete"
Version: 1.0
License: GNU General Public License v2 or later
License URI: http://www.gnu.org/licenses/gpl-2.0.html
Text Domain: daily-cooking-custom
Tags: brown, orange, tan, white, yellow, two-columns, right-sidebar,
flexible-width, custom-header, custom-menu, translation-ready
*/
```

The preceding structure has been created on the basis of the template available at `https://codex.wordpress.org/Theme_Development#Theme_Stylesheet`. Whenever you're creating a new theme, it's always good to check the currently recommended template beforehand. When you add this comment section to your style sheet, just replace all of the details with those that are relevant to your theme.

Add a screenshot

Remember when you first learned how to activate a new theme that there were thumbnail versions of the themes in your **Appearance** tab? You'll want a thumbnail of your own design. It should be a PNG file with the name `screenshot.png`. Just do the following:

1. Flatten a copy of your design in Photoshop.
2. Change the image width to 1200px and the height to 900px.
3. Save it for the web as a PNG-8 file.

The preceding requirements (1200px by 900px) are the current ones at the time of writing. To get the latest guidelines at any point in time, revisit the official codex at `https://codex.wordpress.org/Theme_Development#Screenshot`.

file screenshot.png and save it in your build folder

This is all it takes to have the screenshot enabled and allow WordPress to recognize it when it loads your theme.

Upload your folder

Using your FTP software, upload your template folder to `wp-content/themes/` in your WordPress build. It will share the themes folder with `twentyseventeen` and any other theme you've added as you installed WordPress. In the following screenshot, you can see my `daily-cooking-custom` theme living in the `themes` folder:

Activate your theme

You've got the absolute basic necessities in there now, so you can activate your theme (although it won't look like much yet). Log in to your wp-admin and navigate to **Appearance**. There, you'll see your theme waiting for you. As you can see, I've created a nice screenshot for my theme, with the name of the theme on it for easier identification:

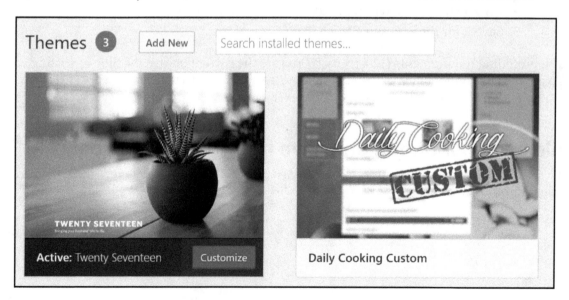

At this point, you can activate your new theme and continue working on it to include WordPress-generated content and make it into a full-fledged WordPress theme in general. Don't be alarmed if the theme doesn't look perfectly right after activation though. There's still a lot of work to do. This is another good reason to have a development server. You wouldn't want to have this incomplete theme active on a live site while you finish the final pieces in the background.

Note that not every theme installation goes as expected, and sometimes, you have to deal with an error. In most cases, WordPress will let you know what went wrong through a notification. Every once in a while, however, the activation can end up in a critical error and your whole site can go blank. If that happens, simply rename the new theme's folder or delete it completely. This will force WordPress to switch to the default theme, and things should get back to normal. From there, you can start looking for the issue that caused the crash in the first place.

Speaking of final pieces, your theme is now ready to have all of the WordPress content added, so let's do just that!

How to create basic WordPress content

Right now, your `index.php` file is your only theme file. We'll be breaking it up into template files a bit later. First, we need to include WordPress functions that will spit out your actual content into your theme.

The functions.php file

, the `functions.php` file is meant to set up your theme and provide some helper functions and settings to make usage of the theme easier. Apart from this, the functions file also has many other applications that we're not going to be discussing here, as they are beyond the scope of this book. In essence, `functions.php` is a kind of file that allows you to perform a very wide scope of modifications. Even though there is a set of standard things that should always be taken care of when dealing with a functions file, no one restricts you from doing virtually anything you wish. For instance, you can create a classic PHP function such as `my_function_name()` and then call it from within one of your template files (such as `index.php`) through `<?php my_function_name(); ?>`, but this is just one of the possible scenarios.

Although this isn't a requirement, it's always good to start your functions file with the following lines of code (just as a good reference point):

```php
<?php
/**
 * Daily Cooking Custom functions and definitions.
 *
 * @package Daily Cooking Custom
 */
```

The preceding lines of code provide the essential information about the theme.

Next in line is the `$content_width` variable. Here's how to use it:

```php
if(!isset($content_width))
   $content_width = 610; //pixels
```

This parameter is often overlooked by many theme developers, despite the fact that it can mean a lot to the final form of the theme. It's simply the maximum width of the content area allowed in your theme (in pixels). For example, if you ever upload a picture that massively exceeds this value, it will always be scaled down to prevent messing up your site's layout. The exact value you should set depends on your CSS and design. The value `610` in the preceding example is just that, an example.

The next part in our `functions.php` file is the setup of the default features that the theme is going to enable:

```php
if(!function_exists('daily_cooking_custom_setup')) :
function daily_cooking_custom_setup() {

  //Make theme available for translation.
  //Translations can be filed in the /languages/ folder.
  load_theme_textdomain('daily-cooking-custom',
  get_template_directory().'/languages');

  //Adds RSS feed links to <head> for posts and comments.
  add_theme_support('automatic-feed-links');

  //Let WordPress manage the document title.
  add_theme_support('title-tag');

  //This theme uses wp_nav_menu() in one location.
  register_nav_menus(array(
    'primary' => __('Primary Menu', 'daily-cooking-custom'),
  ));

  //Switch default core markup for search form, comment form,
```

```
//and comments to output valid HTML5.
add_theme_support('html5', array(
  'search-form', 'comment-form', 'comment-list', 'gallery', 'caption',
));

//Enable support for Post Formats.
add_theme_support('post-formats', array(
  'aside', 'image', 'video', 'quote', 'link',
));

//Set up the WordPress core custom background feature.
add_theme_support('custom-background', apply_filters(
  'daily_cooking_custom_custom_background_args', array(
  'default-color' => 'ffffff',
  'default-image' => '',
)));

}
endif; //daily_cooking_custom_setup
add_action('after_setup_theme', 'daily_cooking_custom_setup');
```

The preceding function, `daily_cooking_custom_setup()`, is going to be executed at just the right time, triggered by the `after_setup_theme` action called at the end to set up the basic features of our theme properly. Most of the code is pretty self-explanatory due to the comments, but there's just one thing I'd like to mention individually, which is this part (registering the menu):

```
register_nav_menus(array(
  'primary' => __('Primary Menu', 'daily-cooking-custom'),
));
```

This is a small piece of code that will let us assign any custom menu to appear as the primary menu later on. It is also what we'll use to set in our new theme. In addition, the preceding function allows you to register even more menu areas if you wish so, and all you'd have to do is add the following line: `'secondary' => 'Secondary Menu'`.

Next, let's enable our style sheet CSS file to load with our theme, or more accurately, to be *enqueued* and then load in precisely at the right moment. Here's how to do so:

```
function daily_cooking_custom_scripts() {
  wp_enqueue_style('daily-cooking-custom-style', get_stylesheet_uri());
}
add_action('wp_enqueue_scripts', 'daily_cooking_custom_scripts');
```

As you can see, there's only one style sheet here. It is enabled by the very first line in the function.

Nowadays, the preceding code is the best practice for including various CSS styles and JS scripts into our themes. You can still go with the traditional (alternative) approach by placing `<link rel="stylesheet" href="<?php bloginfo('stylesheet_url'); ?>" type="text/css" media="screen" />` inside the header section of your design, but it will lower the performance of your site as CSS styles and various JS scripts tend to take a long time to load. So, it's always better to deal with them through the modern `wp_enqueue_scripts` handle.

The preceding code closes our first template-like `functions.php` file. Later, we will add new lines to it to make it even more functional. Now, the interesting part is that there is no closing PHP tag in the functions file (no `?>`). This is not a typo. It's intentional. Since most of the file is pure PHP, we don't need this tag. The complete file is as follows:

```php
<?php
/**
 * Daily Cooking Custom functions and definitions
 *
 * @package Daily Cooking Custom
 */

if(!isset($content_width))
  $content_width = 610; //pixels

if(!function_exists('daily_cooking_custom_setup')) :
function daily_cooking_custom_setup() {

  //Make theme available for translation.
  //Translations can be filed in the /languages/ folder.
  load_theme_textdomain('daily-cooking-custom',
  get_template_directory().'/languages');

  //Adds RSS feed links to <head> for posts and comments.
  add_theme_support('automatic-feed-links');

  //Let WordPress manage the document title.
  add_theme_support('title-tag');

  //This theme uses wp_nav_menu() in one location.
  register_nav_menus(array(
    'primary' => __('Primary Menu', 'daily-cooking-custom'),
  ));

  //Switch default core markup for search form, comment form,
  //and comments to output valid HTML5.
  add_theme_support('html5', array(
    'search-form', 'comment-form', 'comment-list', 'gallery', 'caption',
```

```
));

//Enable support for Post Formats.
add_theme_support('post-formats', array(
  'aside', 'image', 'video', 'quote', 'link',
));

//Set up the WordPress core custom background feature.
add_theme_support('custom-background', apply_filters(
  'daily_cooking_custom_custom_background_args', array(
  'default-color' => 'ffffff',
  'default-image' => '',
)));

}
endif; //daily_cooking_custom_setup
add_action('after_setup_theme', 'daily_cooking_custom_setup');

function daily_cooking_custom_scripts() {
  wp_enqueue_style('daily-cooking-custom-style', get_stylesheet_uri());
}
add_action('wp_enqueue_scripts', 'daily_cooking_custom_scripts');
```

Just to remind you, this whole functions.php file can be found inside the code bundle for this chapter.

The <head> tag

Okay, let's move on to our index.php file and the things we can do inside of it. In the following section of the chapter, we're going to be altering specific lines of code from the original HTML structure.

First, we'll set up the <head></head> section of your HTML file. Let's start with charset and the device width parameter. Simply, here are the two lines to begin with right after the opening <head> tag:

```
<meta charset="<?php bloginfo('charset'); ?>">
<meta name="viewport" content="width=device-width, initial-scale=1">
```

The first one holds the character set that your blog uses. The other defines the width of the viewport used. Here, it's set to the width of the device being used (this allows everyone to view the site correctly, including desktop computer users, iPad users, and Android phone users).

Next, you need to add another important chunk of code--first, to put header tags into your theme for the pingback URL; second, other miscellaneous WordPress stuff. Add the following lines in your `<head>` section:

```
<link rel="profile" href="http://gmpg.org/xfn/11">
<link rel="pingback" href="<?php bloginfo('pingback_url'); ?>">
```

Finally, add the following line right before the closing `</head>` tag (it takes care of displaying your site's title and enabling a number of WordPress-specific functionalities):

```
<?php wp_head(); ?>
```

Now, add the `body_class()` function to the body tag, so it looks like this:

```
<body <?php body_class() ?>>
```

Your header now looks something like this:

```
<!DOCTYPE html>
<html <?php language_attributes(); ?>>
<head>
<meta charset="<?php bloginfo('charset'); ?>">
<meta name="viewport" content="width=device-width, initial-scale=1">
<link rel="profile" href="http://gmpg.org/xfn/11">
<link rel="pingback" href="<?php bloginfo('pingback_url'); ?>">
<?php wp_head(); ?>
</head>

<body <?php body_class(); ?>>
```

The header and footer

It's time to start adding some content. Here, we'll take care of things such as displaying a link to the blog's home page, displaying the blog's title, displaying the tagline, and displaying the main navigation. All these operations are pretty simple, so let's just take a look at the lines of code that take care of them. Then, we'll put these lines of code in just the right place within our HTML structure.

First, we have the code that displays the site's main URL:

```
<?php echo esc_url(home_url('/')); ?>
```

Next, the code that displays the site's title is as follows:

```
<?php bloginfo('name'); ?>
```

Here's the code for displaying the tagline:

```
<?php bloginfo('description'); ?>
```

The preceding two lines pull information from where you set the blog name and description in wp-admin, and you can simply change them from the **Settings** | **General** page.

Lastly, displaying the main navigation is done through the following code:

```
<?php wp_nav_menu(array('theme_location' => 'primary')); ?>
```

The `wp_nav_menu()` function is a built-in way of displaying the navigation menu. It will take care of the proper HTML structure of the menu and all its elements. In other words, you don't have to worry about anything else other than using this one line of code.

Now, the part of your HTML that describes the header looks like what the following listing presents. As you can see, additionally, we're linking the logo to the home page, a standard practice in modern website design:

```
<div id="page" class="hfeed site">
  <a class="skip-link screen-reader-text" href="#content">
  <?php _e( 'Skip to content', 'daily-cooking-custom' ); ?></a>

  <header id="masthead" class="site-header" role="banner">

    <div class="site-branding">
      <h1 class="site-title"><a href="<?php echo
        esc_url(home_url('/')); ?>"
        rel="home"><?php bloginfo('name');?></a></h1>
      <h2 class="site-description"><?php bloginfo('description');?>
      </h2>
    </div><!-- .site-branding -->

    <nav id="site-navigation" class="main-navigation"
      role="navigation">
      <button class="menu-toggle" aria-controls="menu"
        aria-expanded="false">
      <?php _e( 'Primary Menu', 'daily-cooking-custom' ); ?></button>
      <?php wp_nav_menu(array('theme_location' => 'primary')); ?>
    </nav><!-- #site-navigation -->

  </header><!-- #masthead -->

  <div id="content" class="site-content">
```

Are you wondering why you should bother with some of this when you could have just typed your blog title, URL, and a description of the theme? One reason is that, if you ever want to change your blog's title, you can just do it in one quick step in wp-admin and it will change all over your site. The other reason is that, if you want to share your theme with others, you'll need to give them the ability to easily change the name through their own wp-admin panels. Keep in mind that anything, anything at all, that will change from site to site based on the site's purpose and content, should not be hardcoded into the theme, but should be dynamically generated.

Now, when I refresh the site, there's the actual blog title in the header:

The two links visible in the header are live links coming from one of my custom menus. Just to tie things up, I'm going to add some code to my footer to display the *proudly powered by WordPress message,* and to include the `wp_footer()` function/hook that's often used by many plugins in one way or another, so every theme should feature it. The code for my footer section now looks like the following:

```
</div><!-- #content -->

<footer id="colophon" class="site-footer" role="contentinfo">
  <div class="site-info">
    <a href="<?php echo esc_url( __( 'http://wordpress.org/',
      'daily-cooking-custom' ) ); ?>">
    <?php printf( __( 'Proudly powered by %s', 'daily-cooking-custom' ),
      'WordPress' );?></a>
    <span class="sep"> | </span>
    <?php printf( __( 'Theme: %1$s by %2$s.', 'daily-cooking-custom' ),
      'Daily Cooking Custom', '<a href="http://karol.cc/" rel="designer">
      Karol K.</a>, and
      <a href="http://underscores.me/" rel="designer">_S</a>' ); ?>
  </div><!-- .site-info -->
</footer><!-- #colophon -->

</div><!-- #page -->

<?php wp_footer(); ?>

</body>
</html>
```

One thing you might have noticed inside the previous listing is the mysterious function `__()`. It's a native WordPress function that retrieves the translated string corresponding to the parameters given in the function. It's a feature meant for the internationalization of your site. More details about the function can be found at `https://codex.wordpress.org/Function_Reference/_2`.

The sidebar

Now we can move along to adding WordPress-generated content in the sidebar. Essentially, this part of our work is pretty simple. All we have to do is include some WordPress functions that will handle displaying various bits of dynamic content. In this case, it is the categories, tags, and archives.

Starting at the top, include the following piece of code in the sidebar area:

```
<div id="secondary" class="widget-area" role="complementary">
  <?php if(is_active_sidebar('sidebar-1')) dynamic_sidebar('sidebar-1' );
?>
</div><!-- #secondary -->
```

This code takes care of displaying whatever widgets have been assigned to that particular widget area. Placing widgets in the sidebar of your HTML structure is the easiest and probably the most usable way of widget-enabling your theme. Also, WordPress will take care of actually displaying everything properly, so you don't have to worry about any weird-looking elements on your site. For instance, every menu is displayed as an `<ul>` list, and every menu element is inside `<li>`. This is as in tune with the standards as it can be.

Main column – the loop

The most important part of the WordPress code comes next. It's called the loop, and it's an essential part of your theme. The loop's job is to display your posts in a reverse chronological order, choosing only those posts that are appropriate. You need to put all of your other post tags inside the loop. The basic loop text, which has to surround your post information, is displayed using the following code:

```
<?php if (have_posts()) : ?>
<?php while (have_posts()) : the_post(); ?>
  <?php get_template_part('content', get_post_format()); ?>
<?php endwhile; else: ?>
  <?php get_template_part('content', 'none'); ?>
<?php endif; ?>
```

The `get_template_part()` function call that's right in the middle fetches another file that contains the rest of the loop, but for now, let's just focus on the main section here.

There are two basic parts of the loop:

- Individual post information
- What to do if there are no appropriate posts

The first part is handled by a standard PHP `while` loop that goes through every post and, for each element, calls the appropriate `content-[TYPE].php` file. The second part is similar, as it calls the `content-none.php` file if there are no posts that can be displayed. The use of these various `content-[TYPE].php` files is currently the standard for handling the different types of content that WordPress displays. It's a lot more effective and clear than working with the individual `if` or `switch` clauses.

So, in order to get started with this, let's create a basic `content.php` file that will serve the role of a placeholder for the default type of content. In this file, let's place the following code that handles the loop:

```
<article id="post-<?php the_ID(); ?>" <?php post_class(); ?>>

<header class="entry-header">
  <?php the_title(sprintf('<h1 class="entry-title">
  <a href="%s" rel="bookmark">', esc_url(get_permalink())), '</a></h1>');
  ?>

  <?php if('post' == get_post_type()) : ?>
  <div class="entry-meta">
    <?php daily_cooking_custom_posted_on(); ?>
  </div>
  <?php endif; ?>
</header>

<div class="entry-content">
  <?php
  the_content(sprintf(__('Continue reading %s <span class="meta-nav">&rarr;
  </span>', 'daily-cooking-custom'), the_title('<span class="screen-reader-
  text">"', '"</span>', false)));

  wp_link_pages(array('before' => '<div class="page-links">' . __('Pages:',
  'daily-cooking-custom'), 'after'  => '</div>'));
  ?>
</div>

<footer class="entry-footer">
  <?php daily_cooking_custom_entry_footer(); ?>
```

```
</footer>

</article><!-- #post-## -->
```

If you give it a closer look, you'll notice that it's very similar to the static HTML version I shared earlier in this chapter. The only difference is that instead of the dummy text, there are calls to specific WordPress functions and custom-made functions that we'll discuss in a minute.

Let's take it from the top; the file starts with these two lines:

```
<article id="post-<?php the_ID(); ?>" <?php post_class(); ?>>
  <header class="entry-header">
```

This is just some standard HTML and basic WordPress function calls to display proper element IDs and CSS classes. For instance, the the_ID() function displays the ID of the post. Next, we have the following line:

```
<?php the_title(sprintf('<h1 class="entry-title"><a href="%s"
rel="bookmark">', esc_url(get_permalink())), '</a></h1>'); ?>
```

It displays the link and the title of the current content element (usually a post), instead of using the dummy text. The the_title() function takes three parameters (all optional). Right here, we're using just two. The first one defines the text to place before the title (in this case, we're making a sprintf() function call), and the second one defines the text to place after the title. Right below this line, there's a piece of code that displays various types of meta information about the current content element:

```
<?php if('post' == get_post_type()) : ?>
<div class="entry-meta">
  <?php daily_cooking_custom_posted_on(); ?>
</div>
<?php endif; ?>
```

If what we're dealing with is a standard post, a custom function is called to display the details. This way of handling things, through an additional function, makes everything much clearer in comparison to placing the code right there. Here's what the function looks like (we can place it in our main functions.php file, or inside a new file in a separate subdirectory called inc, indicating that it holds additional functions):

```
function daily_cooking_custom_posted_on() {
  $time_string = '<time class="entry-date published updated"
  datetime="%1$s">%2$s</time>';
  if ( get_the_time( 'U' ) !== get_the_modified_time( 'U' ) ) {
    $time_string = '<time class="entry-date published"
    datetime="%1$s">%2$s</time><time class="updated"
```

```
      datetime="%3$s">%4$s</time>';
  }

  $time_string = sprintf( $time_string,
    esc_attr( get_the_date( 'c' ) ),
    esc_html( get_the_date() ),
    esc_attr( get_the_modified_date( 'c' ) ),
    esc_html( get_the_modified_date() )
  );

  $posted_on = sprintf(
    _x( 'Posted on %s', 'post date', 'daily-cooking-custom' ),
    '<a href="' . esc_url( get_permalink() ) . '" rel="bookmark">'
    . $time_string . '</a>'
  );

  $byline = sprintf(
    _x( 'by %s', 'post author', 'daily-cooking-custom' ),
    '<span class="author vcard"><a class="url fn n" href="' .
    esc_url( get_author_posts_url( get_the_author_meta( 'ID' ) )
    ) . '">' . esc_html( get_the_author() ) . '</a></span>'
  );

  echo '<span class="posted-on">' . $posted_on . '</span><span
  class="byline"> ' . $byline . '</span>';
}
```

As you can see, this is quite a long function, but the thing to remember is that it's just meant to display the date of when the post was published and the byline of the author. Also, there are language functions (_e() and _x()) used here to fetch translated data from the database. You can learn more about these functions at https://codex.wordpress.org/Function_Reference/_e and https://codex.wordpress.org/Function_Reference/_x.

Going back to our content.php file, we have the following:

```
<div class="entry-content">
  <?php
  the_content(sprintf(
    __('Continue reading %s <span class="meta-nav">&rarr;</span>',
    'daily-cooking-custom'),
    the_title('<span class="screen-reader-text">"', '"</span>', false)
  ));

  wp_link_pages(array(
    'before' => '<div class="page-links">' . __('Pages:', 'daily-
    cooking-custom'),
    'after'  => '</div>',
```

```
  ));
  ?>
</div>
```

The first part (`the_content()`) takes care of displaying the contents of the current post, along with a `Continue reading` link. This is actually the most important part of the whole file. Next, the second part (`wp_link_pages()`) is meant to display page links for paginated posts (WordPress allows you to divide your content into individual subpages; this can be useful when dealing with an overly long piece of text). Finally, we have the code for the footer section of the entry:

```
<footer class="entry-footer">
  <?php daily_cooking_custom_entry_footer(); ?>
</footer>
```

There's another call to a custom-made function there. Here's what the function looks like:

```
function daily_cooking_custom_entry_footer() {
  // Hide category and tag text for pages.
  if ( 'post' == get_post_type() ) {
    $categories_list = get_the_category_list( __( ', ',
     'daily-cooking-custom' ) );
    if ( $categories_list && daily_cooking_custom_categorized_blog() ) {
      printf( '<span class="cat-links">' . __( 'Posted in %1$s',
        'daily-cooking-custom' ) . '</span>', $categories_list );
    }

    $tags_list = get_the_tag_list( '', __( ', ', 'daily-cooking-custom'
      ) );
    if ( $tags_list ) {
      printf( '<span class="tags-links">' . __( 'Tagged %1$s',
        'daily-cooking-custom' ) . '</span>', $tags_list );
    }
  }

  if ( ! is_single() && ! post_password_required() &&
  (comments_open() || get_comments_number() ) ) {
    echo '<span class="comments-link">';
    comments_popup_link(__('Leave a comment', 'daily-cooking-custom'),
      __('1 Comment', 'daily-cooking-custom'), __('% Comments',
    'daily-cooking-custom'));
    echo '</span>';
  }

  edit_post_link( __( 'Edit', 'daily-cooking-custom' ),
    '<span class="edit-link">', '</span>' );
}
```

All this code handles the post details such as the categories and tags, and the comment links (which other visitors can click to submit their own opinion about the post). One interesting thing I'd like to point out here is the call to the `comments_popup_link()` function:

```
comments_popup_link(__('Leave a comment', 'daily-cooking-custom'), __('1
Comment', 'daily-cooking-custom'), __('% Comments', 'daily-cooking-
custom'));
```

Here, you can see that there are three arguments passed, separated by commas:

- The first option tells WordPress the text that it has to display when there are no comments.
- The second option tells WordPress the text that it has to display when there is just one comment.
- The third option tells WordPress the text that it has to display for more than one comment. The percent symbol (%) gets replaced with the actual number of existing comments.

I'm happy to say that this is it when it comes to a basic understanding of the loop. Of course, its structure allows you to do many more things and include many custom features. But for now, we are good with what we have here. Once you save your `index.php` and reload your website, you will see your new theme in action.

 This version of the `index.php` file is available in the code bundle for this chapter--inside a sub folder labeled `phase 2`. Our theme files will go through a couple of phases before we have the final version (phase 1 was the raw HTML).

Later in the chapter, I will show you how to create a custom page template, which will take advantage of the loop and use it for a slightly different purpose.

Creating template files within your theme

You've now got a functional basic template for your theme. It works great on the main blog page and successfully loads content for anything you can click on in your site. However, we want slightly different templates for other types of content on our site. For example, a single post page needs to have a comment form where visitors can post comments; the page doesn't need to show the date, category, or tags; and the category page should show the category name.

Before we can create other templates, we need to break up the main `index.php` file into parts so that these different templates can share the common elements. I've mentioned many times the importance of the header, sidebar, and footer. We're going to break them up now. First, let's take a quick look at how it works.

Understanding the WordPress theme structure

Usually, WordPress themes are composed of a number of template files. This allows the different parts of the site (such as the frontend, blog archive, pages, single posts, and search results) to have different purposes. Breaking the `index.php` file into template files allows us to not only share some common parts of the design, but also to have different code in different parts. As I mentioned earlier, we'll soon be breaking up the four main pieces of the design (header, sidebar, main column, and footer) so that WordPress can make good use of them. That's because while the header and footer are probably shared by all pages, the content in the main column will be different. Also, you may want the sidebar on some pages, but not on others. We'll first create these template files and then move on to other, more optional template files.

Breaking it up

We're going to break up the `index.php` file by removing some of the code into three new files:

- `header.php`
- `footer.php`
- `sidebar.php`

The header.php file

First, cut out the entire top of your `index.php` file. This means cutting the `doctype` declaration, the `<head>` tag, any miscellaneous opening tags, and the `<header>` tag. In my case, I'm cutting out all the way from this initial line:

```
<!DOCTYPE html>
```

I'm cutting through to, and including, these lines:

```
</header><!-- #masthead -->
<div id="content" class="site-content">
```

Then, paste this text into a new file named `header.php` that you created within your `theme` folder.

Now, at the very top of the `index.php` file (that is, where you just cut the header text from) write in the following line of WordPress PHP code:

```
<?php get_header(); ?>
```

This is a WordPress function that includes the `header.php` file you just created. If you save everything and reload your website now, nothing should change. The important part here is to make sure that the call to the preceding PHP function sits right at the very top of your `index.php` file.

The footer.php file

Next, we will create the footer file. To create this, first cut out all of the text at the very bottom of the `index.php` file from the following code:

```
</div><!-- #content -->
<footer id="colophon" class="site-footer" role="contentinfo">
```

Cut all the way through to the `</html>` tag. Paste the text you just cut into a new `footer.php` file that you create within your theme folder.

Now, at the very bottom of the `index.php` file (from where you just cut the footer text), write in the following line of WordPress PHP code:

```
<?php get_footer(); ?>
```

This is a special WordPress function that includes the `footer.php` file you just created. Again, you should save everything and reload your website to make sure nothing changes.

The sidebar.php file

There is just one more essential template file to create. For this one, cut out the entire `div` element containing your sidebar. In my case, it's the following text:

```
<div id="secondary" class="widget-area" role="complementary">
  <?php if(is_active_sidebar('sidebar-1')) dynamic_sidebar('sidebar-1' );
?>
</div>
```

Paste this text into a new file in your theme folder named `sidebar.php`.

Now, in `index.php`, add this function in the place you just cut your sidebar from:

```php
<?php get_sidebar(); ?>
```

This will include the sidebar. In the case of my design, I want the sidebar on every page. So, it's not crucial for it to be a separate file. I could have included it in the `footer.php` file. However, in some templates, including the default template that came with your WordPress installation, the designer prefers to not include the sidebar in some views such as the page view and single posts.

Your four template files

You've now got four template files in your theme folder, namely `header.php`, `footer.php`, `sidebar.php`, and the now-much-shorter `index.php`. By the way, my `index.php` file now has only a handful of WordPress functions and the loop. The following is the entire file:

```php
<?php get_header(); ?>

    <div id="primary" class="content-area">
        <main id="main" class="site-main" role="main">

    <?php if (have_posts()) : ?>

        <?php /* Start the Loop */ ?>
        <?php while (have_posts()) : the_post(); ?>

            <?php
            get_template_part('content', get_post_format());
            ?>

        <?php endwhile; ?>

        <?php daily_cooking_custom_paging_nav(); ?>

    <?php else : ?>

        <?php get_template_part('content', 'none'); ?>

    <?php endif; ?>

        </main><!-- #main -->
    </div><!-- #primary -->
```

```
<?php get_sidebar(); ?>
<?php get_footer(); ?>
```

This whole cutting-and-pasting process to create these four files was just to set the scene for the real goal of making alternative template files.

 This version of the `index.php` file, as well as `header.php`, `footer.php`, and `sidebar.php`, is available in the code bundle for this chapter - inside a subfolder labeled phase 3.

Archive template

WordPress is now using the `index.php` template file for every view on your site. Let's make a new file--one that will be used when viewing a monthly archive, category archive, or tag archive.

 To learn even more about how WordPress utilizes different files to display its content, feel free to read the guide at `https://www.codeinwp.com/blog/wordpress-theme-heirarchy/`.

To create your archive template, make a copy of `index.php` and name this copy `archive.php`. Now, navigate to a monthly archive on the site by clicking on one of the month names in the sidebar. At this point, it looks exactly like the main listing, the one handled by `index.php`.

Let's make one change to the archive template. I'd like it to display a message that lets users know what type of archive page they are on. Currently, the archive looks the same as the main index listing, and this isn't the most optimized situation. To fix it, just add this code below the `<?php if (have_posts()) : ?>` line:

```
<header class="page-header">
  <?php
  the_archive_title('<h1 class="page-title">', '</h1>');
  the_archive_description('<div class="taxonomy-description">', '</div>');
  ?>
</header>
```

Now, when I click on a month, category, or tag, I see a new heading at the top of the page that lets me know where I am:

This version of the `archive.php` file is available in the code bundle for this chapter, inside a sub folder labeled `phase 4`.

Single template

The next template we need to create is the single post view. To view a single post, you can usually just click on the post title. Right now, the single post looks like the site's front page (because it's using `index.php`) - except with just one post.

To get started, again make a copy of `index.php`, and name the copy `single.php`. This is the template that WordPress will look for first when it's serving a single post. If it doesn't find `single.php`, it'll use `index.php`.

Without further delay, here's my `single.php` file. You should notice that the file features almost exactly the same elements as the `index.php`. The only difference is that the `get_template_part()` function call fetches a different element. In this case, it's single.

```php
<?php get_header(); ?>

  <div id="primary" class="content-area">
    <main id="main" class="site-main" role="main">

    <?php while (have_posts()) : the_post(); ?>

      <?php get_template_part('content', 'single'); ?>

      <?php daily_cooking_custom_post_nav(); ?>

      <?php
      if (comments_open() || get_comments_number())
        comments_template();
      ?>

    <?php endwhile; // end of the loop. ?>
```

```
     </main><!-- #main -->
   </div><!-- #primary -->

<?php get_sidebar(); ?>
<?php get_footer(); ?>
```

The aforementioned `get_template_part('content', 'single')` call will fetch the `content-single.php` file. Here's what the file looks like:

```
<article id="post-<?php the_ID(); ?>" <?php post_class(); ?>>
  <header class="entry-header">
    <?php the_title('<h1 class="entry-title">', '</h1>'); ?>

    <div class="entry-meta">
      <?php daily_cooking_custom_posted_on(); ?>
    </div>
  </header>

  <div class="entry-content">
    <?php the_content(); ?>
    <?php
      wp_link_pages( array(
        'before' => '<div class="page-links">' . __( 'Pages:',
        'daily-cooking-custom' ),
        'after'  => '</div>',
      ) );
    ?>
  </div>

  <footer class="entry-footer">
    <?php daily_cooking_custom_entry_footer(); ?>
  </footer>
</article><!-- #post-## -->
```

This file's structure is almost exactly the same as the one we've discussed a couple of pages ago - `content.php`. Also, the following are three specific things that are worth pointing out:

- The presence of the `<article>` tag. The individual post's content is displayed inside this tag.
- The call to the `the_content()` function. This time, we're displaying the whole content of the post, not just the excerpt.
- The call to the `comments_template()` function in `single.php`. It displays the comment form and the individual comments that have been submitted for this post.

These versions of the `single.php` file and the `content-single.php` file are available in the code bundle for this chapter, inside a sub folder labeled `phase 4`.

Page template

The last template we're going to create is for the static page view. On my food blog site, this would be the sample page, for example. The easiest way to go about this is to start with the `single.php` file this time. So, just make a copy of this file and name it `page.php`. Now, we'll be simplifying the file so that only the essential information about a given page is displayed. In the end, this is what my `page.php` file looks like:

```php
<?php get_header(); ?>

    <div id="primary" class="content-area">
    <main id="main" class="site-main" role="main">

      <?php while (have_posts()) : the_post(); ?>

        <?php get_template_part('content', 'page'); ?>

      <?php endwhile; // end of the loop. ?>

    </main><!-- #main -->
    </div><!-- #primary -->

<?php get_sidebar(); ?>
<?php get_footer(); ?>
```

I did just a few modifications here. They are as follows:

- I changed the last parameter of the `get_template_part()` function to page, instead of single
- I erased the call to `daily_cooking_custom_post_nav()`, which handled the display of post navigation
- I erased the whole block of code that handled the comments. We don't need those on pages

Next, we need a custom `content-page.php` file. The easiest way to build it is to make a copy of the `content-single.php` file and tune it up a bit. Here's my final `content-page.php` file:

```php
<article id="post-<?php the_ID(); ?>" <?php post_class(); ?>>
  <header class="entry-header">
    <?php the_title('<h1 class="entry-title">', '</h1>'); ?>
  </header>

  <div class="entry-content">
    <?php the_content(); ?>
    <?php
      wp_link_pages(array(
        'before' => '<div class="page-links">' . __( 'Pages:',
        'daily-cooking-custom' ),
        'after'  => '</div>',
      ));
    ?>
  </div>

  <footer class="entry-footer">
  </footer>
</article><!-- #post-## -->
```

Here's what I did here in terms of simplifying:

- I got rid of the whole code displaying metadata.
- I erased the entry footer, which was meant to display categories and tags. We don't use those with WordPress pages.

Now, my sample page looks much cleaner:

 These versions of the `page.php` file and the `content-page.php` file are available in the code bundle for this chapter, inside a sub folder labeled `phase 4`.

Generated classes for body and post

As you're modifying your theme to make accommodations for different types of pages, you should also know about the CSS classes that WordPress will put into your theme. If you look carefully at the code we've been using, you'll see these two functions:

- `body_class()`: For example, in the `header.php` file, the exact line is `<body <?php body_class(); ?>>`
- `post_class()`: For example, in the `content-page.php` file, the exact line is `<article id="post-<?php the_ID(); ?>" <?php post_class(); ?>>`

The `body_class()` function adds a whole bunch of classes to the body tag, depending on the page you're viewing. For example, the main page of my site has the following class in the body:

```
<body class=" home blog custom-background">
```

My **Some Spanish Dishes** single post page's body tag looks like the following:

```
<body class=" single single-post postid-41 single-format-standard custom-background">
```

If I wanted to style anything differently on different pages, I could do it largely with CSS, without having to create another template.

The `post_class()` function does something similar with the individual post's `div`, giving it different classes depending on the characteristics of the post itself. For example, my **Some Spanish Dishes** post's tag has the following class:

```
<article id="post-41" class="post-41 post type-post status-publish format-standard hentry category-uncategorized">
```

Further, my sample page post tag has the following class:

```
<article id="post-2" class="post-2 page type-page status-publish hentry">
```

Using these classes in my style sheet, I could style every post differently depending on its category, tag, post type, and so on. Keep this in mind as you design your next theme. This becomes extremely important when working with theme frameworks further down the road. Although modifications inside PHP files are allowed, most of the time, you can customize the design of your whole site just by working in the CSS and tweaking various classes (both the native ones in WordPress and the new ones that the framework uses). Situations, where a whole new site working on a theme framework gets built purely in the CSS files are not uncommon.

Other WordPress templates

In addition to `archive.php`, `single.php`, and `page.php`, there are a number of other standard template files that WordPress looks for before using `index.php` for particular views. We're not going to create these files here, but you should feel free to experiment on your own WordPress installation. To learn about the complete file hierarchy for WordPress themes, feel free to visit `https://www.codeinwp.com/blog/wordpress-theme-heirarchy/` (yes there's a typo in *hierarchy*, they've made a small mistake here). There's a great graph there that presents the hierarchy visually. It's very easy to follow and does a much better job at explaining this than I would do here through just words. In addition, when you browse the official code bundle for this chapter, you'll see that many additional files have been created and are actually available inside the bundle. We're not covering them here, however, as it would probably be too much information at this point.

Learning more
You can also find a detailed flowchart of the template hierarchy at `https:/ /developer.wordpress.org/themes/basics/template-hierarchy/`.

In this chapter, we've experimented with the uses of quite a number of WordPress template tags. In `Chapter 13`, *Creating a Non-Blog Website Part Two - E-Commerce Websites and Custom Content Elements*, I have listed more of the most useful template tags.

Next, we'll explore making custom templates for pages.

Creating and using a custom page template

WordPress allows you to create custom templates. These can only be used for pages (not for posts). A custom template allows you to display content differently or easily use built-in WordPress functions within a template.

Just to give you a good example of what custom page templates are and how they can benefit your site (no matter what theme you're using), let's create a custom version of the archives template. This is also what we will use to create a custom archives page that should be much more useful to our readers than the standard one. Here's what the archives look like on my blog right now:

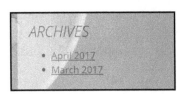

There are just a couple of small links in the sidebar that redirect visitors to a standard monthly archive. Of course, later on, when there are more posts on your site, there will be many more links shown (exactly one link for each month of your site's existence).

Now, as far as the idea of *archives* goes, I have to admit, somewhat reluctantly, that WordPress was never good at this. One of the few problems with the platform as a web publishing solution was the fact that posts usually have very short life spans. Whenever you publish a post, it sits on the front page for a while and then it vanishes in the archives never to be seen again, irrespective of whether it's still relevant or not. In the end, it's really hard for a new visitor to find these old posts on your site.

One of the few chances you have at reviving those old posts is mastering the art of SEO and driving some new traffic to your old posts through your SEO efforts only (it's the most popular solution). But luckily, it's not the only way around to fix this issue. Again, custom page templates are an interesting remedy here.

In the preceding screenshot, you can see that the default version of the archives is just a sidebar widget with some links to the individual months. The problem with such content organization is that it provides a rather bad user experience. Archives, in general, are not about listing everything in one place; they are about providing a hub where the visitor can go and find a specific piece of content. For example, think about how archives work in your local library. This is what you want to eventually have on your site as well. So, what we're going to do here is say no to the traditional archives template in WordPress and create a custom page template to handle archives manually. Then, we're going to link to this archive from one of the menus. Here's how to do it.

On our new archives page, we want to achieve the following things:

- Display a piece of custom text. For instance, as a form of introduction or a notification message explaining what's in the archives.
- Display a categories archive--a list of all the categories in use on the site.
- Display a tag cloud--a form of tag archive where all of the tags in use on the site are displayed one after the other (inline, not in a list format), and the font size increases for the tags that have been used more often than others.
- Display a list of the 15 latest posts, or whatever another number you wish.
- Display a monthly archives block. The fact that it's displayed at the bottom is not accidental, as this block is not particularly useful for a typical visitor.

To do this, we need to create a template. The following are the steps we'll take:

1. Create the template file. Make a copy of `page.php` within your theme and give it a new name. I like to prepend all of my custom template files with `tmpl_` so that they are sorted separately from all the WordPress template files that I will create. I'll name this file `tmpl_archives.php`. In order for WordPress to be able to identify this file as a template file, we need to add a specially styled comment to the top of the page (just as we did with `style.css`). The comment needs to be formatted as follows:

```php
<?php
/* Template Name: Blog Archives Custom */
?>
```

In the wp-admin panel, the template will be identified by this template name, so make sure the name signals to you for what the template is used.

2. Add WordPress functions. This is a crucial part of the process, but thankfully not a complicated one at this stage. Look over your new template file and find the occurrence of this line:

```php
<?php get_template_part('content', 'page'); ?>
```

3. Now, erase it and put this in its place:

```php
<?php get_template_part('content', 'tmpl_archives'); ?>
```

This is the result we're after; the middle part of your `tmpl_archives.php` file should now look like the following:

```php
<?php while (have_posts()) : the_post(); ?>
  <?php get_template_part( 'content', 'tmpl_archives' ); ?>
<?php endwhile; // end of the loop. ?>
```

4. Next, create a completely new file called `content-tmpl_archives.php` and put the following code in it:

```php
<article id="post-<?php the_ID(); ?>" <?php post_class(); ?>>
  <header class="entry-header">
    <?php the_title('<h1 class="entry-title">', '</h1>'); ?>
  </header>

  <div class="entry-content">
    <?php the_content(); ?>

    <div style="float: left; width: 50%;">
      <h2>Categories</h2>
      <ul>
      <?php wp_list_categories('orderby=name&title_li='); ?>
      </ul>
    </div>
    <div style="float: left; width: 50%;">
      <h2>Tags</h2>
      <?php wp_tag_cloud('smallest=8&largest=20'); ?>
    </div>
    <div style="clear: both;"></div><!-- clears float -->

    <?php
    $show_many_last_posts = 15;
    echo '<h2>Last '.$show_many_last_posts.' Posts</h2>';
    $my_query = new WP_Query('post_type=post&nopaging=1');
```

```
        if($my_query->have_posts()) {
          echo '<ul>';
          $counter = 1;
          while($my_query->have_posts() &&
            $counter<=$how_many_last_posts)
          {
            $my_query->the_post();?>
            <li><a href="<?php the_permalink() ?>"
              rel="bookmark" title="Permanent Link to <?php
              the_title_attribute(); ?>"><?php the_title();
              ?></a></li>
            <?php
            $counter++;
          }
          echo '</ul>';
          wp_reset_postdata();
        }
        ?>

      <h2>By Month</h2>
        <p><?php wp_get_archives('type=monthly&
          format=custom&after= |');
        ?></p>
      </div>

      <footer class="entry-footer">
      </footer>
    </article><!-- #post-## -->
```

The preceding code includes some additional functionality on our new archives template. Actually, because we are creating a custom template, we can add any of the WordPress functions we discovered earlier in the chapter, as well as any other WordPress function in existence (see Chapter 13, *Creating a Non-Blog Website Part 2 - E-Commerce Websites and Custom Content Elements*).

What we did here is the following. Here are some of the more interesting parts of the code. Starting with the following:

```
<div style="float: left; width: 50%;">
  <h2>Categories</h2>
  <ul>
  <?php wp_list_categories('orderby=name'); ?>
  </ul>
</div>
```

It's about adding a complete list of categories that are present on the site. The `div` elements are responsible for displaying this block on the left side and allowing the next block, tags, to be placed next to it (it's a more effective way of achieving such an effect than using HTML tables because it's a more cross-device-friendly approach).

The next part of the code is the following:

```
<div style="float: left; width: 50%;">
  <h2>Tags</h2>
  <?php wp_tag_cloud('smallest=8&largest=20'); ?>
</div>
<div style="clear: both;"></div><!-- clears float -->
```

It has a very similar purpose, only this time we're displaying the aforementioned tag cloud. The last div element visible here is meant to clear the `float` parameter used in the previous `div` elements.

Next, we have the part responsible for displaying the latest posts:

```
<?php
$how_many_last_posts = 15;
echo '<h2>Last '.$how_many_last_posts.' Posts</h2>';
$my_query = new WP_Query('post_type=post&nopaging=1');
if($my_query->have_posts()) {
  echo '<ul>';
  $counter = 1;
  while($my_query->have_posts() && $counter<=$how_many_last_posts) {
    $my_query->the_post();
    ?>
    <li><a href="<?php the_permalink() ?>" rel="bookmark"
      title="Permanent Link to <?php the_title_attribute();
      ?>"><?php the_title(); ?></a></li>
    <?php
    $counter++;
  }
  echo '</ul>';
  wp_reset_postdata();
}
?>
```

Currently, the code displays 15 latest posts, but this can be adjusted if you just change the value of the `$how_many_last_posts` variable.

Finally, there's the block that displays a traditional monthly archive, where every month is represented as a standard link:

```
<h2>By Month</h2>
<p><?php wp_get_archives('type=monthly&format=custom&after=
   |'); ?></p>
```

At this point, you can save the file and proceed to the next step which is to apply the template to a page.

Leave your HTML editor and log in to your wp-admin. You need to edit or create the page in which you want to use this template. In this case, I will create a page and name it **Archives**.

On the **Edit Page** screen, look for the **Template** menu within the **Page Attributes** box (on the right, by default):

Change it from **Default Template** to **Blog Archives Custom**, and click on **Update** (Note that you can also change a page's template using **Quick Edit** in **Pages | Edit Page**). Now, in order to see the page somewhere, you have to add it to one of the menus. We already covered this in Chapter 4, *Pages, Media, Importing/Exporting Content*, so I'm sure you can get it done quickly. Once you have this handled, you can return to the frontend of your website and click on the **Archives** page. However, because your site is not that content-heavy at this point, you won't get a staggering effect, but there's still a nice presentation of the most recent posts:

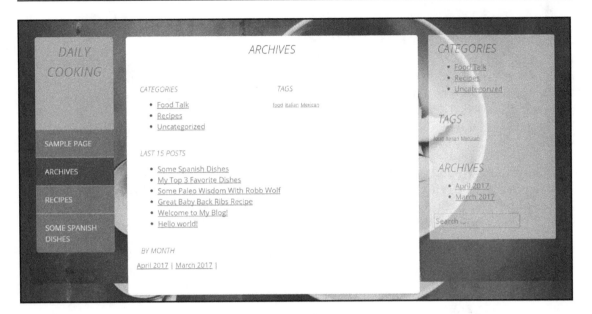

There is no limit to the number of custom templates you can make in your WordPress theme.

 These versions of the `tmpl_archives.php` file and the `content-tmpl_archives.php` file are available in the code bundle for this chapter, inside a subfolder labeled `phase 5`.

Making your theme widget-friendly

If you want to be able to use widgets in your theme, you will need to make your theme widget-friendly (also known as *widgetizing* your theme). Widgetizing is actually pretty easy, and to be honest with you, we already took care of that when constructing our sidebar. I didn't discuss much back then, but now let's go back to this topic and explain how widgetizing works.

Going back to our sidebar

Back in the old days, it was very common for a WordPress site to use statically placed content blocks in the sidebar. In other words, the only way to place dynamic content in the sidebar of our sites was to use handmade code that would fetch whatever data we wanted and then display it. This solution wasn't very usable for the everyday user who might not be familiar with the PHP source code. So, a better solution needed to be found. Hence, widgets.

Widgets give us the ability to set the sidebars in a way so that they fetch the data that's been set in **Appearance | Widgets**. Therefore, the only thing the user has to do is go to **Appearance | Widgets** and pick whatever type of content they want to feature in the sidebar (or any other widget area for that matter; it can be in the footer as well).

Just to give you an example of old versus new, here's what a standard piece of code might look like that handles displaying blog archives the old way (this can be placed in `sidebar.php`):

```
<div id="secondary" class="widget-area" role="complementary">
  <aside>
    <h1>Archives</h1>
    <ul>
      <?php wp_get_archives(); ?>
    </ul>
  </aside>
</div><!-- #secondary -->
```

However, this code is not customizable in any way, so a much better solution to display the archives is to use the code that we already have in our `sidebar.php`, which is as follows:

```
<div id="secondary" class="widget-area" role="complementary">
  <?php if(is_active_sidebar('sidebar-1')) dynamic_sidebar(
    'sidebar-1' ); ?>
</div><!-- #secondary -->
```

And then, just assign a new `Archives` widget to this sidebar in the **Appearance | Widgets** section of wp-admin.

Working with the functions.php file

Okay. So right now, let's examine how all this actually works. As I said earlier, the functions.php file can contain many different elements, so now, it's about time to focus on how to actually enable dynamic sidebars, also known as widgets. So, in the functions.php file, we place the following code:

```
function daily_cooking_custom_widgets_init() {
  register_sidebar(array(
    'name'          => __('Sidebar', 'daily-cooking-custom'),
    'id'            => 'sidebar-1',
    'description'   => '',
    'before_widget' => '<aside id="%1$s" class="widget %2$s">',
    'after_widget'  => '</aside>',
    'before_title'  => '<h1 class="widget-title">',
    'after_title'   => '</h1>',
  ));
}
add_action('widgets_init', 'daily_cooking_custom_widgets_init');
```

In this code, I'm using one new function to register a new widget area. As you can see, the widget area is simply called Sidebar (the name parameter).

Now, the final add_action('widgets_init', 'daily_cooking_custom_widgets_init') function call is what actually registers the widget areas (it's the most important line of code here; it lets WordPress know when to enable the widget areas).

Adding some widgets

At this point, your theme is ready for widgets! You can now go to wp-admin, navigate to **Appearance | Widgets**, and add widgets. For example, as you can see in the following screenshot, I've added three widgets to one of the widget areas:

Be sure to click on **Save**, and then return to your website and reload the page. The default items you had placed in the sidebar will have been replaced with widgets, as shown in the following screenshot:

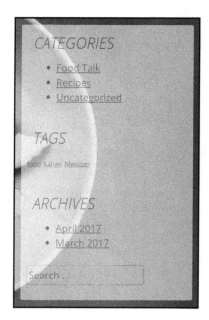

Additional widgetizing options

What we just covered is the simplest way to widgetize a theme. There are actually a lot of other possibilities that you could utilize when adding the code to your `sidebar.php` and `functions.php` pages. For example, there are options that allow you to do the following:

- Widgetize more than one sidebar, giving each a name
- Widgetize a part of your sidebar, but leave in some default items
- Widgetize the footer
- Customize the search form widget, and much more

 Learning more
To learn about the variety of options available and how to take advantage of them, take a look at the Codex at `https://codex.wordpress.org/Widgetizing_Themes`.

Enabling a menu in your theme

The good news I have for you right now is that menus are already enabled in the structure of the theme we're creating here. Because we used the `wp_nav_menu()` function in the header of the site (in the `header.php` file), if the user creates a menu in **Appearance | Menus** and then assigns it to the area indicated as **Primary Menu**, it will show up on the site.

Menu Settings

Auto add pages	☐ Automatically add new top-level pages to this menu
Display location	☑ Primary Menu

If you want to have more than one navigation menu in your theme, you can register multiple navigation menu locations, let the user create multiple menus and choose which menu goes in which location. To learn more about this, check out the Codex at `https://codex.wordpress.org/Navigation_Menus`.

Learning more

The `wp_nav_menu()` function is quite powerful and can take a number of parameters that will let you control the classes and IDs, the name of the menu, and more. Take a look here: `https://developer.wordpress.org/reference/functions/wp_nav_menu/`.

Making your theme editable in the WordPress Customizer

--also known as the Customize API, is a relatively recent addition to the WordPress ecosystem. In short, it's a framework meant for live-previewing any changes that the user makes to their website. The Customizer's interface allows for the modifcation of various aspects of the theme's and website's appearance, starting from the name of the site, the tagline, all the way to the colors used, layouts, widgets, menus, and more. We talked about the Customizer from the user's point of view back in `Chapter 7`, *Customizing Your Website Appearance/Design*.

Now from a developer's perspective, when you're building your own WordPress theme, there are a couple of things that you should do in order to make your theme compatible with the Customizer. Luckily, the starter theme that we're using in this chapter as the foundation of our theme, the _S theme, already comes with some basic Customizer integrations. Let's go over them one by one, and at the same time see how we can expand our theme's functionality further.

First, let's look at the following line of code. It should be placed at the end of your `functions.php` file:

```
require get_template_directory() . '/inc/customizer.php';
```

This definition simply includes an additional file that takes care of the Customizer integration itself. Even though we could do everything right in the `functions.php` file, having the Customizer handled in a separate file makes for a theme structure that's easier to grasp.

That new `customizer.php` file is where we're going to add all of our new code. The core of the Customizer integration is done via the `customize_register` hook. It allows us to define new Customizer panels, sections (the main elements of navigation within the Customizer), settings (the data that our theme can accept) and controls (the visual UI elements that allow us to tweak our settings).

In order to register all of our new Customizer elements, we can use the following function:

```
function daily_cooking_custom_customize_register( $wp_customize )
  { /* */ }
add_action( 'customize_register', 'daily_cooking_custom_customize_register'
);
```

Within that function is where creating new sections, settings and controls are done. However, as you'll notice, we already have this function in the `customizer.php` file created. This is, again, a result of building our theme on top of the _S starter theme. We've opted for such an approach since it allows us to get started with theme development a lot quicker than building things from scratch.

Our current `daily_cooking_custom_customize_register()` function already features the following lines:

```
$wp_customize->get_setting( 'blogname' )->transport = 'postMessage';
$wp_customize->get_setting( 'blogdescription' )->transport = 'postMessage';
```

This code capitalizes on some Customizer abilities that are available for WordPress themes by default. Namely, those two enable us to modify the title and blog description.

Now it's time to add something new to the Customizer. Firstly, adding a new section is very simple. Let's start by including the following function call inside our main `daily_cooking_custom_customize_register()` function:

```
$wp_customize->add_section();
```

The function can take two arguments: the first one is the identifier for your new section, and the other is an array of additional options. Here's what we're going to do:

```
$wp_customize->add_section( 'menu_bar_colors' , array(
  'title' => 'Menu Bar Colors',
  'priority' => 30) );
```

This creates a new section titled `Menu Bar Colors` and identified by `menu_bar_colors`. Now let's add a new setting. Settings provide a way to communicate with WordPress and let it know that we're using a value that the user can modify. New settings can be added via the `$wp_customize->add_setting()` function call. We can handle this like so:

```
$wp_customize->add_setting( 'menu_bar_color1' , array(
  'default' => '#69CACA') );
$wp_customize->add_setting( 'menu_bar_color2' , array(
  'default' => '#279090') );
```

As you can see, I'm adding not one, but two new *settings*.

Once the settings are in place, the last elements of the puzzle are some new controls. Controls tie the two together, they let WordPress know which sections work with which settings. This is done via the `$wp_customize->add_control()` function call. Here's what we can do:

```
$wp_customize->add_control( new WP_Customize_Color_Control( $wp_customize,
'menu_bar_color1', array(
  'label' => 'Menu Bar Color 1',
  'section' => 'menu_bar_colors',
  'settings' => 'menu_bar_color1') ) );
$wp_customize->add_control( new WP_Customize_Color_Control( $wp_customize,
'menu_bar_color2', array(
  'label' => 'Menu Bar Color 2',
  'section' => 'menu_bar_colors',
  'settings' => 'menu_bar_color2') ) );
```

As you can see, each of our settings gets its own *control*. At this stage, when you save the file and go to your Customizer (**Appearance** | **Customize**), you'll see the new section in the sidebar. Inside it, you'll also see that the elements are all operational. Albeit, they don't have much impact on the appearance of the theme yet. We'll handle that next. Take a look at the following screenshot:

The first thing we need to do now is alter the CSS of the theme based on what the user has set in the Customizer. To make that happen, let's add the following code at the end of the `customizer.php` file:

```php
function daily_cooking_customizer_menu_css()
{
  ?>
  <style type="text/css">
  .site-header .site-branding { background: <?php echo
    get_theme_mod('menu_bar_color1', '#69CACA'); ?>; }
  .main-navigation ul li { border-bottom: 1px solid <?php echo
    get_theme_mod('menu_bar_color1', '#69CACA'); ?>; }
  .site-header { background: <?php echo
    get_theme_mod('menu_bar_color2',
    '#279090'); ?>; }
  </style>
  <?php
}
add_action( 'wp_head', 'daily_cooking_customizer_menu_css');
```

This new function hooks up to `wp_head` and alters the CSS of the website. The most important instructions in it are those three inline PHP echo blocks. Here's one of them:

```php
echo get_theme_mod('menu_bar_color1', '#69CACA');
```

The `get_theme_mod()` function allows you to grab the current theme's settings and indicate the name of the specific setting that you need in the first parameter (the second one is the default value). When you save your file now, the new color selection options should be fully enabled. Refer to the following screenshot:

We have only scratched the surface here in terms of what's possible in the Customizer, but it still gives you a good overview, and also proves that the Customizer is actually a very developer-friendly environment to work in. In the end, you shouldn't be scared of it. Always try putting as many of your theme's settings as possible in the Customizer module. The end user will thank you for it.

want to learn more about how to work with the Customizer and uncover some of its other features (such as working with JS files for dynamic live previews, for example), then don't hesitate to visit either of these resources:

`https://codex.wordpress.org/Theme_Customization_API` and `https://developer.wordpress.org/themes/customize-api/`

Creating a child theme

If you've found an existing theme or theme framework that you like and you just want to adjust it a bit to fit your requirements hand-in-glove, you can create a child theme on top of this existing theme. A child theme uses the parent theme as a starting point and, without changing the theme itself, alters just the bits you want to alter.

As a matter of fact, using child themes is the recommended way of making modifications to any theme. The rule of thumb is simple--if you want to change anything at all about a stock theme (either inside the source code, graphics, or template files), do it through a new child theme.

In plain English, a child theme inherits the functionality and features of the parent theme. The biggest value of creating child themes is that you can introduce any bells and whistles you wish without altering the structure of the parent theme. I know that this sounds like some additional work, because if you just want to change a couple of lines of code, then it's always going to be quicker to do it directly within the theme. However, taking the longer *child theme* way has its benefits.

The main one is that if you were to modify the original theme directly, all your modifications would vanish the minute you updated the theme. However, if you're using child themes, you can take full advantage of any update that the original theme's authors release. Let me say this again: preserving your modifications after performing a theme update is impossible unless you're using a child theme.

Another benefit of working with child themes is that you have a very clear view of the modifications that you've introduced into your theme. Basically, every new thing that you're implementing through a child theme has to be placed in a new file, so even when you come back to review your child theme after a while, you can still easily identify every piece of your work.

The final benefit, actually, there's probably a lot more of them, but the final one on this short list is that it's very easy to revert every modification you've introduced through a child theme. In short, if something is causing any serious problems and you have to fix your site quickly (you know, in an emergency), then you can simply delete the files responsible. If you were modifying your original theme directly, going through every file individually would surely take much more time and would make any sort of quick recovery very difficult to achieve.

Let's take a quick look at how to make a child theme.

Creating the new theme folder

Just to make things easier to understand here, we'll take the theme that we've been creating in this chapter and build a child theme for it. The starting point is really simple. Create a new folder in `wp-content/themes/` and name it `daily-cooking-child`.

Creating the style sheet

The only file you need to start with in this folder is the style sheet (`style.css`). The style sheet needs the usual header, plus a new line:

```
/*
Theme Name: Daily Cooking Child Theme
Description: Child theme for the Daily Cooking Custom theme.
Theme URI: http://newinternetorder.com/
Author: Karol K
Author URI: http://karol.cc/
Template: daily-cooking-custom
*/
```

The key line in that code is `Template: daily-cooking-custom`. This instructs WordPress that your new theme is a child theme of `daily-cooking-custom`. Just to emphasize, that one line is really crucial. Then, to make your child theme start out with the CSS from the parent theme, add the following code below the comment:

```
@import url("../daily-cooking-custom/style.css");
```

If you don't use the preceding line, your child theme will begin its existence on a blank style sheet. In most cases, this is not a desirable scenario.

Using your child theme

That's it! Your new theme now shows up on the **Appearance** page (the new child theme doesn't have a screenshot icon yet), as shown in the following screenshot:

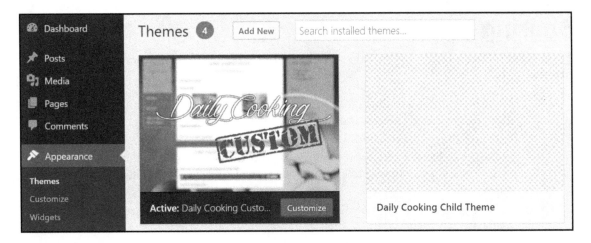

Granted, the theme is not really useful at this point, but it does exist and we can use it as the base for further modifications. By default, it will use all of the main theme's styles, template files, functions, and everything else. If you activate it, it will present your site as if you were using your main theme.

If you want to change anything, do so in your child theme's folder. You will override the main theme's original template file if you create a new template file (for example, `single.php`, `index.php`, and `archive.php`). The `functions.php` file works a little differently, however. If you create a new `functions.php` file, it will be executed in addition to the main theme's original `functions.php` file. In fact, your new file will be loaded first, right before the original one. If you want to override a specific function in the original `functions.php` file, just create a function with the same name. You can also create completely new functions that are not present in the parent theme.

Like I said, every other template file you create inside the child theme (such as `page.php` and `single.php`) will override its namesake, so it's the perfect method to include a new, slightly different design or some new features. Apart from replacing the existing template files, you can add new ones that are not present in the parent (including custom page templates).

In the end, the whole topic of child themes is quite an easy one to grasp once you spend a little while trying out different things and checking how your site reacts to the things you include in the child theme.

Learning more
The WordPress Codex has a page devoted to learning about child themes at `https://codex.wordpress.org/Child_Themes`.

Sharing your theme

If you want to turn your template into a package that other people can use, you just have to take the following steps:

1. Make sure you have the rights to redistribute images, icons, photos, and so on, that you included in your theme.

2. Remove all unnecessary files from your theme's folder. Be sure you don't have backup versions or old copies of any of your files. If you do delete any file, be sure to retest your theme to ensure you didn't accidentally delete something important.

3. Make sure the comment at the top of the `style.css` file is complete and accurate.

4. Create a `Readme.txt` file. This is a good place to let future users know what version of WordPress your theme is compatible with and if it has any special features or requirements.

5. Zip the folder and post your theme's ZIP file on your own website for people to download, or submit it directly to the WordPress **Theme Directory** at `https://wordpress.org/themes/`. Keep in mind, though, that the review process there tends to take a while. So be ready for a 3-6 month wait before you see your theme online.

Even though the preceding looks like a standard step-by-step process, it's actually nothing like it. To be honest, your theme has to be a really quality one if it's to be allowed into the directory. For example, every theme undergoes a human review, which often results in your theme not passing it. In this case, you just have to make the requested changes, resubmit your work, and keep trying until you get in.

Then, there's also the issue of licensing. By default, WordPress is available under the GNU **General Public License** (**GPL**). In plain English, this means that WordPress (the platform) is free and every derivative work that is built on top of it has to be filed under GPL too--this includes themes. In short, every piece of PHP code you find inside WordPress, various themes, or plugins is GPL (that includes premium themes and plugins). When it comes to artwork and CSS, GPL might not apply. If you want to learn more about the GPL licensing, it's best if you go straight to the official statement at `https://wordpress.org/news/2009/07/themes-are-gpl-too/`.

Now, apart from the official directory, you can share your theme through other channels. First of all, you have to decide whether you want your theme to be available for free or not. In the case of the former, you can reach out to some popular blogs about WordPress and WordPress design and simply let them know that you have a theme you'd like to share. Most of the time (if the theme looks attractive), they will have no problem notifying their community that there's a cool new free theme.

If you want to make your theme a premium one, you can go to **ThemeForest** (http:// themeforest.net/) and try submitting it there. The only challenge is that your theme must really be a quality one.

I'm not forcing you to share your theme with the community right away, but once you build some expertise and build your themes to be really cool and useful, you really should reach out to the community and share your work.

Finally, if you're interested in making an impact with your new theme in the community, consider launching a website dedicated to your theme. This website will be a place where you can publish a demo version, deliver some documentation, and provide support forums and other things to deliver a great user experience.

 The final versions of all the theme files (including the child theme) are available in the code bundle for this chapter, inside a sub folder labeled `final`.

Summary

You have now crossed to the other side of the WordPress themes world--you have learned how to make your own theme. With just basic HTML and CSS abilities, you can create a design and turn it into a fully functional WordPress theme.

In this chapter, we saw how to turn your HTML build into a basic theme, create WordPress templates to influence the display of a variety of views on your site, create custom templates to be applied to pages within your site, make your new theme widget-ready, create a child theme, make the theme compatible with the WordPress Customizer, and share your theme with everyone in the WordPress community.

In the next chapter, we'll discuss the topics of social media integration, podcasting, and HTTPS. This information will allow you to expand your blogging habits and make your work more diverse and more noticeable on the web.

9
Social Media Integration, Podcasting, and HTTPS

Social media has grown a lot in importance over the last couple of years. Basically, if you don't have your profile on at least a couple of the most popular social networks, then you might as well not exist at all, right? Well, no matter if you agree with that or not, this certainly rings true for your website. In other words, if you hope to attract any kind of audience and somehow convince them to keep coming back to your website, you absolutely have to, *have to!* integrate it with social media.

Luckily, WordPress lets you do so in more or less an easy to grasp way. Even though social media integration is not a built-in feature per se, it can still be enabled via different plugins or other mechanisms. In this chapter, you will learn all about these. We'll cover things such as how to enable simple social media share buttons on your website, how to work with social media APIs and integrations, how to publish your blog content to social media automatically, and more.

But wait, that's not all! We're also going to cover podcasting (which for some site owners is an important element of their online presence), and a relatively new topic in the WordPress realm--HTTPS, which is all about making your website more secure by adding an additional level of encryption to the browser-website communication. An important thing worth pointing out here is that Google now expects all websites to have HTTPS encryption enabled. If your website fails to comply, Google might decide to lower your search engine rankings, and thus make your website less visible compared to your competition.

Integrating social media

We've briefly mentioned the topic of social media integration in `Chapter 5`, *Plugins - What They Are and Why You Need Them*, when discussing the plugins that are worth having on your WordPress site. So now, let's take a moment to expand upon this and list some more ways in which you can make your site social media friendly, and also see why you'd want to do that in the first place.

Let's start with the *why*. In this day and age, social media is one of the main drivers of traffic for many sites. Even if you just want to share your content with friends and family, or you have some serious business plans regarding your site, you need to have at least some level of social media integration.

Even if you only install simple social media share buttons, you will effectively encourage your visitors to pass on your content to their followers, thus expanding your reach and making your content more popular.

Making your blog social media friendly

There are a handful of ways to make your site social media friendly. The most common approaches are as follows:

- Social media share buttons, which allow your visitors to share your content with their friends and followers
- Social media APIs integration, which makes your content look better on social media (design-wise)
- Automatic content distribution to social media
- Social media metrics tracking

Let's discuss these one by one.

Setting up social media share buttons

This is something we talked about in Chapter 5, *Plugins - What They Are and Why You Need Them*, when discussing plugins. There are hundreds of social media plugins available out there that allow you to display a basic set of social media buttons on your site. The one I advise you to use is called **GetSocial** (available at https://wordpress.org/plugins/wp-share-buttons-analytics-by-getsocial/). Its main advantage is that it allows you to display buttons for all of the most popular social media networks, and you can also choose where and how you want those buttons displayed.

You can find a full description, plus a tutorial on how to set everything up, in Chapter 5, *Plugins - What They Are and Why You Need Them*.

Setting up social media APIs integration

The next step worth taking to make your content appear more attractive on social media is to integrate it with some social media APIs; particularly, that of Twitter. What exactly their API is and how it works isn't very relevant to the WordPress discussion we're having here. So instead, let's just focus on what the outcome of integrating your site with this API is.

Here's what a standard tweet mentioning a website usually looks like (notice the overall design, not the text contents):

Here's a different tweet, mentioning an article from a site that has Twitter's (Twitter Cards) API enabled:

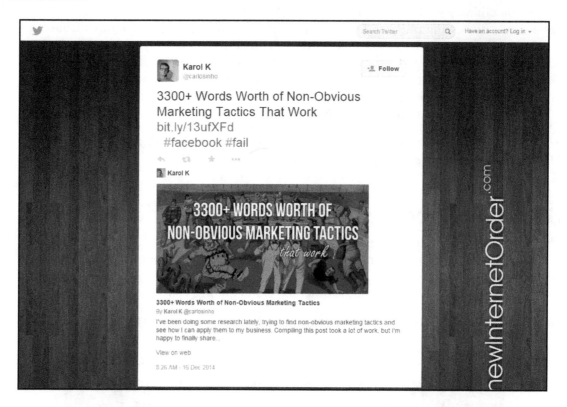

This looks much better. Luckily, having this level of Twitter integration is quite easy. All you need is a plugin called **JM Twitter Cards** (available at `https://wordpress.org/plugins/jm-twitter-cards/`). After installing and activating it, you will be guided through the process of setting everything up and approving your site with Twitter (mandatory step).

Setting up automatic content distribution to social media

The idea behind automatic social media distribution of your content is that you don't have to remember to do so manually whenever you publish a new post. Instead of copying and pasting the URL address of your new post by hand to each individual social media platform, you can have this done automatically.

This can be done in many ways, but let's discuss the two most usable ones, the Jetpack and Revive Old Post plugins.

The Jetpack plugin

The Jetpack plugin is available at `https://wordpress.org/plugins/jetpack/`. We talked about the Jetpack plugin and its many modules in Chapter 5, *Plugins - What They Are and Why You Need Them*. One of those modules can be found by navigating to the **Jetpack** | **Settings** section of the wp-admin and then to the **Sharing** tab:

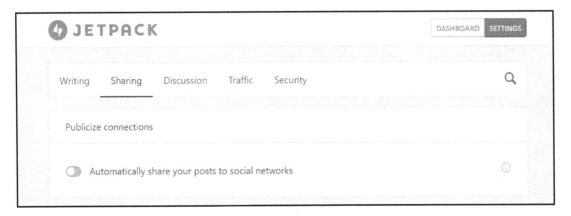

There, you will be able to enable the feature labeled **Automatically share your posts to social networks** (visible in the preceding screenshot).

After doing so, click on the new link that's going to appear, labeled **Connect your social media accounts**. This will allow you to integrate one of the six available social media platforms:

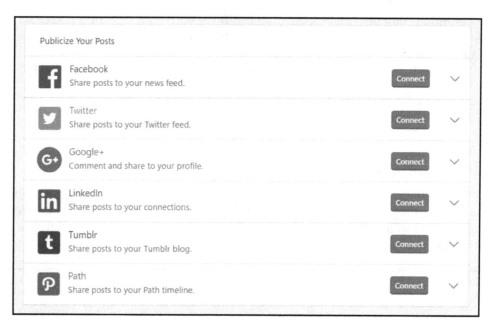

After going through the process of authorizing the plugin with each service, your site will be fully capable of posting each of your new posts to social media automatically.

The Revive Old Post plugin

The **Revive Old Post** plugin is available at `https://wordpress.org/plugins/tweet-old-post/`. While the Jetpack plugin takes the newest posts on your site and distributes them to your various social media accounts, the Revive Old Post plugin does the same with your archived posts, ultimately giving them a new life. Hence the name, Revive Old Post.

After downloading and activating this plugin, go to the section in the wp-admin called **Revive Old Post**. Then, switch to the **Accounts** tab. There, you can enable the plugin to work with your social media accounts by clicking on the authorization buttons:

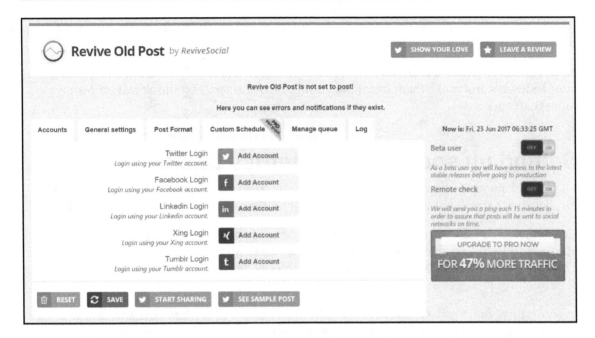

Then, go to the **General settings** tab and handle the time intervals and other details of how you want the plugin to work with your social media accounts. When you're done, just click on the **SAVE** button:

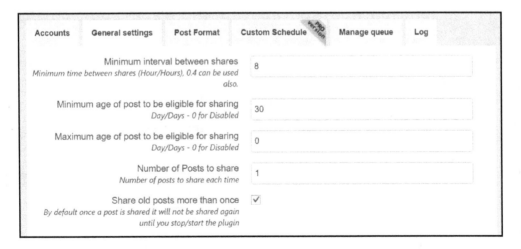

At this point, the plugin will start operating automatically and distribute random archived posts to your social media accounts.

Note that it's probably a good idea not to share things too often if you don't want to anger your followers and make them unfollow you. For that reason, I wouldn't advise posting more than once a day.

Setting up social media metrics tracking

The final element in our social media integration puzzle is setting up some kind of tracking mechanism that will tell us how popular our content is on social media (in terms of shares).

Granted, you can do this manually by going to each of your posts and checking their share numbers individually. However, there's a quicker method, and it involves another plugin. This one is called **Social Metrics Tracker,** and you can get it at `https://wordpress.org/ plugins/social-metrics-tracker/`.

In short, this plugin collects social share data from a number of platforms and displays it to you in a single readable dashboard view. After you install and activate the plugin, you'll need to give it a couple of minutes to crawl through your social media accounts and get the data. Soon after that, you will be able to visit the plugin's dashboard by going to the **Social Metrics** section in the wp-admin:

For some web hosts and setups, this plugin might end up consuming too much of the server's resources. If this happens, consider activating it only occasionally to check your results and then deactivate it again. Doing this even once a week will still give you a great overview of how well your content is performing on social media.

This ends our short guide on how to integrate your WordPress site with social media. I'll admit that we're just scratching the surface here and that there's a lot more that can be done. There are new social media plugins being released literally every week, and describing every single one of them would fill a book on its own. That being said, the methods described here are more than enough to make your WordPress site social media friendly and enable you to share your content effectively with your friends, family, and audience.

Podcasting

Podcasting has become very popular in the last couple of years. Right now, there are thousands of podcasts available on the web, touching upon any topic or niche imaginable. Basically, a podcast is like a radio show or program, but run on the internet entirely. Under the hood, however, a podcast is just an audio recording. It can be episodic or serial, depending on your preference and the way you want to have it made. The main idea with podcasts is that people can subscribe to them and they are notified whenever a new episode is available. Basically, your subscribers, instead of reading your posts on their computers, can listen to your content through their headphones at any time.

Adding a podcast to your WordPress blog is rather easy. From a technical point of view, the "subscription" mechanism of a podcast is handled by **Really Simple Syndication (RSS)** feeds. RSS is web technology that allows you to deliver (or consume) content structured in an XML format. RSS feeds are usually organized with the most recent information at the top. The way WordPress works with RSS feeds by default is that it enables feeds for your most recent posts, as well as for the most recent comments. Whoever wants to stay up to date with your content can use one of the popular feed aggregators and connect it to your site's RSS feed. For example, **Feedly** (`http://feedly.com`) is a popular such solution nowadays.

Using RSS feeds is also how podcast distribution is handled in WordPress. While generating your blog's RSS feeds, WordPress automatically adds all the required tags if an audio file is linked within that post. These tags are read by podcast clients/tools (like iTunes). Therefore, all you have to do is make a post, and WordPress will do the rest for you.

Creating a podcast

For basic podcasting, there are just two steps you need to take:

1. Record.
2. Post.

Let's look at these steps in detail.

Recording yourself

Using any commercial or free software, you can record your voice, a conversation, music, or anything else you'd like to podcast, and then save it as an MP3 file. You may also find that you need to do some editing afterward.

Some examples of good software to consider using are as follows:

- I recommend using **Audacity**, which is a free, cross-platform sound recorder and editor. You can download Audacity from `https://sourceforge.net/projects/audacity/`. You may have to do a bit of extra fiddling around to get the MP3 part working, so pay attention to the additional instructions at that point. If you don't want to learn the basics of audio compression and equalization, then you may also want to use a leveling tool such as the **Levelator**, which can be found at `http://www.conversationsnetwork.org/levelator/`. Although it has not been updated since the end of 2012, it still works well if you want to level the volume in a simple audio file.
- Alternatively, you can use **OBS Studio** `https://obsproject.com/download`. It's another cross-platform solution, it's open source, and some users find it superior to the other tools in the market.
- If you are working on a Mac and want some free software, take a look at **Garage Band**. It comes with the OS, so it will already be installed on your computer.
- If you want to examine some advanced pieces of audio software, called **digital audio workstation** (**DAW**), used by professional podcast producers and musicians, then look into **Sonar X2**, **Studio One**, **Logic**, or **ProTools**.

To learn more about the basics of audio recording and production for podcasters, which will make your podcasts sound professional, feel free to check this in-depth tutorial at `http://www.hongkiat.com/blog/audio-production-for-podcasters/`.

Making a post

Now that you've created an MP3 file and it's sitting on your computer, you're ready to make a WordPress post that will be the home for the first episode of your podcast:

1. In the wp-admin, click on **New Post** in the top menu. Enter some initial text into your post if you want to provide a description for the episode. Also, at this point, add a new category called **Podcast** to your blog.

2. Just so you can learn the basics of including media files, let's upload your media file via the Media Manager. Later on in this chapter, I will explain why this is not always the most effective approach. However, for now, you're here to learn. Start by clicking on the **Add Media** button, and drag and drop your MP3 file. If all goes well, your file will be on the server shortly (remember that audio files are bigger than images, so uploading will always take a little longer).

3. Next, insert the MP3 file into your post. This is the options screen:

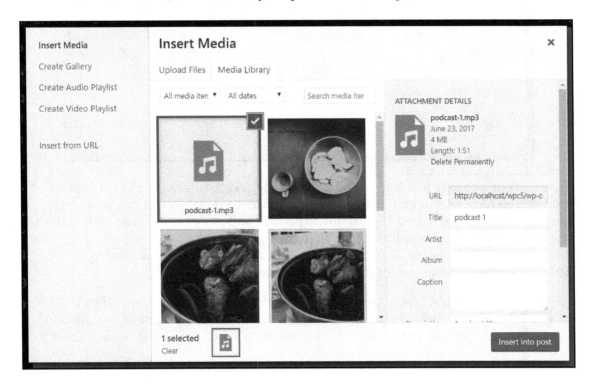

4. WordPress gives you three main possibilities under the **Embed or Link** section. The default one is **Embed Media Player**. If you select it, WordPress will display your audio file inside an interactive player (as shown in the following screenshot). However, here we're going to select the second option, namely **Link to Media File**:

5. Click on **Insert into Post**.
6. Make any other changes or additions you want, and publish the post; you're done! The final result is visible in the following screenshot (it's just a standard link):

PODCAST EPISODE #1

POSTED ON <u>JUNE 23, 2017</u>

This is the first episode of the podcast: <u>Podcast Episode #1</u>

POSTED IN <u>PODCAST</u>

That's it! Your website's RSS feed can now be used by podcast clients to pick up your podcast. You can use your own podcast client to subscribe right away. If you are using iTunes, navigate to **Advanced** | **Subscribe to podcast** and paste the RSS feed URL of the new podcast category you've just set (for example, `http://yoursite.com/category/podcast/feed/`). At this point, you (and your visitors) can enjoy the new podcast you've just created.

 This is just how you can add your podcast to your own iTunes. If you want to make the podcast searchable via iTunes for the public, you need to go through the submission process described at `https://itunespartner.apple.com/en/podcasts/overview`.

Podcasting plugins

You have just learned that it's quite easy to add a podcast to your WordPress website. However, if you want additional features, you may want to use a podcasting plugin. Some additional features could be as follows:

- Automatic feed generation and configurable RSS feeds to optimize your podcast even further for clients such as iTunes, Google Play, or Stitcher
- A preview of what your podcast will look like in iTunes
- Download statistics and tracking the number of listeners you're getting
- Automatic inclusion of a player within your post on your website
- New custom post types to handle your podcasts in a more specialized way
- Running multiple podcasts from the same site
- Shortcodes for displaying your podcast episode lists, single episodes and playlists
- Easy settings to host your episodes on another server

There are quite a number of podcast-related plugins available in the WordPress plugin repository. The three most popular ones are as follows:

- **PowerPress Podcasting plugin by Blubrry** (https://wordpress.org/plugins/powerpress/)
- **Seriously Simple Podcasting** (https://wordpress.org/plugins/seriously-simple-podcasting/)
- **Podlove Podcast Publisher** (https://wordpress.org/plugins/podlove-podcasting-plugin-for-wordpress/)

 For an in-depth guide on how to use the PowerPress plugin (which is my favorite one from the preceding list) and how to configure it correctly, watch this 30-minute video tutorial by Pat Flynn at https://www.youtube.com/watch?v=Ei67QMWD4MA#!. Through this tutorial, you'll learn how to optimize your podcast and set it up properly so that it can be picked up by iTunes and then shared across the community.

There are hundreds of other similar plugins available. You can find them by looking at all the plugins tagged podcasting (https://wordpress.org/plugins/tags/podcasting) in the official plugin directory at WordPress.org. Don't forget to read the plugin descriptions and user reviews to decide which of these might be the best match for you.

Using a service to host audio files for free

As I mentioned earlier, the old-school approach of uploading your podcast straight to your blog has its flaws, which doesn't make it the most effective way to handle things these days. First of all, if you want to host the media file on your main server (the one where your website is hosted), you can quickly encounter serious bandwidth problems, especially if your podcast becomes popular. Also, there's a problem with the maximum upload size in WordPress. Depending on your web host, you might not be able to upload files larger than 2 MB, 8 MB, or 16 MB (you can contact your web host's support to clarify this for you). This is what the problem looks like in the uploader:

Therefore, if you anticipate having a large number of subscribers, or if you plan to produce such a large volume that you'll run out of space on your own server, you can use an external hosting service that will host your audio files, either for a fee or free of cost. Some options to consider are as follows:

- **Libsyn**: This company provides effective and affordable podcast hosting. Go to: `https://www.libsyn.com/`.
- **Blubrry**: Another great host for podcasts. What makes their offer particularly interesting is that they integrate with WordPress very well. They even have their own plugin, which I mentioned earlier in this chapter. Go to `https://create.blubrry.com/resources/podcast-media-hosting/`.
- **PodBean**: This company offers free podcast hosting for a period of time. Go to: `https://podbean.com/`.

Working with each of the companies mentioned is slightly different. However, the main thing you always need to do is upload your media file to your chosen company's servers rather than to your own media library in WordPress. In return, you'll get a direct URL pointing to your podcast file, which you can then use however you wish. For instance, you can insert that URL into your WordPress post using one of the plugins mentioned earlier.

HTTPS - what, why, and how

Surprisingly, the story with HTTPS starts somewhere else--it starts with HTTP. As you possibly know, **HTTP** stands for **Hypertext Transfer Protocol**, which is a web protocol through which information is sent online between the user's web browser and the website they're trying to visit. HTTP defines the structure of that data and the way it's being sent. This topic is highly technical and we certainly don't need to understand it from top to bottom just for the purpose of what we're discussing in this chapter.

Overall, the current way in which HTTP is implemented doesn't allow for very secure connections. For the most part, with HTTP, the data is being transmitted in plain text, which means that if someone were to intercept the communication, they would be able to see everything that's being transmitted. Now, this may not seem like much of a problem at first, but imagine what could happen when dealing with sensitive information. For example, when you're submitting your credit card info at some checkout, you really don't want it to be intercepted by anyone. Unfortunately, HTTP doesn't give you any sort of protection in that area. This is where HTTPS comes into play.

What is HTTPS

HTTPS, which stands for **Secure Hypertext Transfer Protocol**, is basically an upgraded version of HTTP. Under the hood, the main mechanisms that make it work are kind of the same, but instead of using its own layer protocol for sending data, HTTPS uses additional protocols, secure ones, called **Secure Sockets Layer** (**SSL**) and **Transport Layer Security** (**TLS**). SSL encrypts the information that's being sent, which means that even if someone intercepts it, they won't be able to decode it anyway. The true meaning of that data is not visible without the encryption/decryption key.

How do you know if a website has HTTPS? Finding that out is very simple. Basically, your web browser will let you know. When you're visiting a website that has HTTPS enabled (and properly integrated), you'll see a green padlock icon next to the website's address. Additionally, you should also see `https://` in the address bar. Here's an example from PayPal:

Why HTTPS is important for a modern WordPress site

While HTTPS is not a requirement per se, it's still a great step towards a safer web overall. Every website that supports HTTPS is simply safer to use, and especially when dealing with any sort of user input. Quite naturally, people are not happy about submitting their personal information anywhere, and particularly if they're not sure whether this information is going to be taken care of properly. These days, we're constantly hearing about hacks and security breaches even at some of the most respectable web properties. With that in the picture, the public becomes more concerned with data security and privacy every year.

With that said, modern WordPress sites need to embrace the idea to the fullest. There really is no downside to having HTTPS enabled on your website, and the process of doing it is not too difficult either. Add to that, in 2014, Google announced that HTTPS was officially a ranking factor for Google search. What this means is that you have a better chance of getting your website ranked, and thus found by potential visitors, if you have HTTPS integrated.

How to set up HTTPS

Setting up HTTPS on WordPress is a two-part process. First, you need to have an SSL certificate assigned to you, which you can then use on the site. Second, you need to integrate that SSL with your WordPress site.

Let's start with getting the SSL certificate itself. The thing with those is that they often come with a price tag. A good certificate can cost you anywhere from a couple of dollars to as much as $600 per year. This probably doesn't sound too attractive, but lucky for everyone, there are also good, free SSL options out there. Particularly, one of them. It's called **Let's Encrypt** (https://letsencrypt.org/). Let's Encrypt is a free, automated, and open **Certificate Authority** (**CA**). It has been found to popularize SSLs and make them affordable for all websites, thus increasing the number of sites worldwide with encrypted connections.

The way you can get started with Let's Encrypt highly depends on the web host where your WordPress website is hosted. Usually, at least with most hosts, you can enable a Let's Encrypt certificate straight from your hosting control panel. Showing the exact steps of how that's done would be difficult to do since each host has their own control panel and their own way of letting you enable a Let's Encrypt certificate. Therefore, the first step is to actually contact your host and ask them to help you enable the certificate.

Before you do that though, you can consult the official documentation at Let's Encrypt and make sure that your host does indeed support Let's Encrypt certificates. This documentation can be found at `https://community.letsencrypt.org/t/web-hosting-who-support-lets-encrypt/6920`.

After you go through with your host's process, which shouldn't be too complicated, honestly, you can now finish up the integration in your WordPress dashboard.

In order to make your site fully integrated, you're going to need an additional plugin. This plugin is called **Really Simple SSL** (`https://wordpress.org/plugins/really-simple-ssl/`) and it's going to do two main things for you:

- It will update the URL of your site to HTTPS and overwrite the previous settings in the WordPress database
- It will add a permanent 301 redirect to your non-HTTPS URLs so that all your visitors, as well as search engines, will be forwarded to the new HTTPS versions of your content (posts and pages)

The plugin is very simple to use. All you need to do is install and activate it, and then you can go to the plugin's settings in **Settings | SSL**. Once there, just click on the main **Go ahead, activate SSL!** button:

Almost ready to migrate to SSL!
Some things can't be done automatically. Before you migrate, please check for:

- Http references in your .css and .js files: change any http:// into //
- Images, stylesheets or scripts from a domain without an ssl certificate: remove them or move to your own server.

You can also let the automatic scan of the pro version handle this for you, and get premium support and increased security with HSTS included. check out Really Simple SSL Premium

`Go ahead, activate SSL!`

The plugin will then work its magic in the background, and once it's done, it will log you out of the admin panel. This is normal, you don't need to be worried here. When you try logging back in, you'll notice that you've been redirected to the HTTPS version of the admin panel. Just to make sure that everything is working, you can try visiting your website at `http://YOURSITE.com` and see if you get automatically redirected to `https://YOURSITE.com`. At this stage, your WordPress site is fully integrated with HTTPS.

Summary

There was a lot going on in this chapter. First, we focused on social media integration--the bread and butter of all modern websites. Next, there was the topic of podcasting and a brief guide to getting started (how to configure your feeds, what plugins to use, and so on). Finally, we talked about HTTPS and SSL certificates--what those things are, their importance for your website's security (and the security of your visitors' personal information), and how to enable them.

In the next chapter, we'll discuss the topic of developing your own plugins and widgets-- what the basics are and how to get your head around them. We'll also introduce you to the REST API.

10
Developing Plugins, Widgets, and an Introduction to the REST API

In Chapter 5, *Plugins - What They Are and Why You Need Them*, you learned how to install plugins. Plugins are essentially a way to add to or extend WordPress' built-in functionalities. There are thousands of useful plugins (at the time of writing, the official counter at https://wordpress.org/plugins/ shows over 51,000 plugins) available from the online WordPress community, and they perform all different kinds of functions. In the earlier chapters, we installed plugins that catch spam, back up your site, give you basic SEO features, and more. You can also get plugins that manage your podcasts, track your stats, translate your content into other languages, and much more.

Sometimes, however, you'll find yourself in a situation where the plugin you need just doesn't exist. Luckily, it's quite easy to write a plugin for WordPress that you can use on your own site and share with the larger community if you want to. All you need is some basic PHP knowledge, and you can write any plugin you want.

This chapter is divided into three major parts:

- In the first part, we'll create two plugins using an easy-to-follow step-by-step process
- In the second part, we'll create a widget using the built-in WordPress widget class
- In the third part, you will learn what shortcodes are and how to use them

Plugins

In this section, we'll create a plugin via a simple step-by-step process. We'll first see what the essential requirements are, then try out and test the plugin, and then briefly discuss the PHP code involved. With that said, you should already have a basic PHP background going into this chapter.

Building plugins from scratch

First of all, you're here to learn about WordPress, so in this particular case, we will indeed build things from scratch. This is always the best approach to get an in-depth look into how a particular technology works.

However, later on, once you're working with WordPress on a regular basis managing your own or other people's websites, I actually advise you to always look for an already existing plugin before deciding to write a new one yourself. As I mentioned earlier, there are around 51,000 plugins in the official directory alone, not to mention all the premium plugins available all over the web. In short, if you need some functionality, most likely, *there's a plugin for it*, so you can just go out and get it.

Why is this the recommended approach? If I'm correct, you've chosen to use WordPress because you wanted to make your site as functional as possible with the least amount of effort possible. Following this line of thought, using an existing plugin simply requires much less effort than building one. Also, many existing plugins are already used by thousands of other people and have large communities supporting them. Choosing a quality plugin is, therefore, a lot safer path to take.

I feel that I should emphasize this clearly because experience tells me that many young WordPress developers tend to press their peers to create things from scratch just for the heck of it despite the fact that there are other and better solutions available.

Moreover, remember that everything that's a derivative work based on WordPress is available under GPL. So, there's nothing standing in your way to take an existing plugin, building upon it, making it better, and then re-sharing your version with the world. That way, we all win and there's no redundant work.

But before we can do that, you indeed must learn the craft by constructing something of our own from start to finish. Onward then!

Plugin code requirements

Just as there were requirements for a theme, there are requirements for a plugin. At the very least, your plugin must satisfy the following:

- It must be placed in the `wp-content/plugins` folder (inside the root folder of WordPress)
- It must have a PHP file with a unique name (not used by any other plugin in the main `wp-content/plugins` folder)
- It must have a specially structured comment at the top of the file (see `https://codex.wordpress.org/File_Header`)

That's it. Then, of course, you must have some functions or processing code, but WordPress will recognize any file that meets these requirements as a plugin.

If your plugin is a simple one, then you can just place a unique PHP file straight in your `wp-content/plugins` folder, so it can sit next to the default **Hello Dolly** plugin that WordPress comes with. However, a much better practice is to create a subfolder (again, unique) and place your PHP file there. It makes the `wp-content/plugins` folder seem much more organized. Plus, you never know when your plugin is going to need some additional files (it's always easier to simply add new files to a previously existing `plugin` folder than to restructure the plugin from scratch).

Basic plugin - adding link icons

As a demonstration, we will create a simple plugin that adds icons to document links within WordPress. For example, in Chapter 9, *Social Media Integration, Podcasting, and HTTPS*, we added a link to an MP3 file. It looks like the following now:

PODCAST EPISODE #1

POSTED ON *JUNE 23, 2017*

This is the first episode of the podcast: Podcast Episode #1

POSTED IN *PODCAST*

Once this plugin is complete, the link will look like the following instead:

To accomplish this, we have to do the following:

1. Provide images of the icons that will be used.
2. Have a PHP function that identifies the links to documents and adds a special CSS class to them.
3. Have a style sheet that creates the CSS classes for displaying the icons.
4. Tell WordPress that whenever it prints the content of a post (that is, using the `the_content()` function), it has to run the PHP function first.
5. Tell WordPress to include the new styles in the `<head>` tag.

Keep this list in mind as we move forward. Once all these five requirements are met, the plugin will be done. So, let's get started!

Naming and organizing the plugin files

Every plugin should have a unique name so that it does not come into conflict with any other plugin in the WordPress universe. When choosing a name for your plugin and the PHP file, be sure to choose something unique. You may even want to do a Google search for the name you choose in order to be sure that someone else isn't already using it.

Apart from the main plugin file itself, your plugin can contain any number of other files and subfolders. If the situation calls for it, you can even use media files like audio and videos to go along with your plugin. Of course, additional CSS or JS files (or even full libraries) are allowed as well.

In this case, as my plugin will be composed of multiple files (a PHP file, a style sheet, and some image files), I'm going to create a folder to house my plugin. I'll name the plugin Add Document Type Styles New and place it in a folder called add_doctype_styles_new. The PHP file, doctype_styles_new.php, will live in this folder. I've also collected a number of document type icons (provided by http://www.freepik.com/ via http://www. flaticon.com/).

The folder I created for my plugin now looks like this:

 It is best practice to also create folders like images, css, and js inside your plugin's folder if what you're building will consist of more files.

Now that I've got the images in my folder, I've taken care of the *first* requirement in the list of requirements my plugin has to meet.

 If your plugin has any unusual installation or configuration options, you may also want to include a readme.txt file in this folder that explains this. This README file will be useful both as a reminder to you and as an instructional document to others who may use your plugin in the future. If you plan to submit your plugin to the WordPress plugin directory, you will be required to create a README file. To get the template for such a file, visit https://wordpress.org/plugins/developers/.

As mentioned earlier, your plugin has to start with a special comment that tells WordPress how to describe the plugin to users on the plugins page. Now that I've got my folder and a blank PHP file created, I'll insert the special comment. It has to be structured like the following. This really is fundamental (explained at https://codex.wordpress.org/File_ Header):

```php
<?php
/*
Plugin Name: Add Document Type Styles New
Plugin URI: http://newinternetorder.com/plugins
Description: Detects URLs in your posts and pages and displays nice
document type icons next to them. Includes support for PDF, DOC, MP3, and
ZIP.
Version: 1.1
Author: Karol K
```

```
Author URI: http://karol.cc/
Text Domain: add_doctype_styles_new
License: GNU General Public License v2 or later
*/
```

Another good piece of information to have in your plugin is about licensing. Most plugins use the **GNU General Public License** (**GPL**). This license essentially means that anyone can use, copy, and enhance your code and that they are not allowed to prevent anyone else from redistributing it. I've also added a note about the GPL to my plugin's PHP file. Remember that all PHP code you encounter in any WordPress plugin is GPL by default. However, graphic files, CSS, JavaScript, and other elements might have a different license, so be careful when copying other people's work and making it part of your own. You can read more about the license at https://www.gnu.org/copyleft/gpl.html.

That's all about the introductory code. Now, we can add the meat.

Writing the plugin's core functions

The core of any plugin is the unique PHP code that you bring to the table. This is the part of the plugin that makes it what it is. Since this plugin is so simple, it only has a few lines of code in the middle.

The *second* requirement the plugin has to meet is *have a PHP function that identifies links to documents and adds a special class to them*. The following function does just that. Note that in keeping with my efforts to ensure that my code is unique, I've prefixed both of my functions with doctype_styles_new:

```
function doctype_styles_new_regex($text) {
    $text = preg_replace('/href=([\'|"][[:alnum:]|
        [:punct:]]*)\.(pdf|doc|mp3|zip)([\'|"])/', 'href=\\1.\\2\\3
        class="link \\2"', $text);
    return $text;
}
```

When the function is given some $text, it will perform a search for any HTML anchor tag linking to a PDF, DOC, MP3, or ZIP file, and replace it with a class to that anchor. Then, the function returns the altered $text.

The *third* requirement the plugin has to meet is *have a style sheet that creates classes for displaying the icons*. The following function fetches our style sheet:

```
function doctype_styles_new_styles() {
  wp_register_style('doctypes_styles', plugins_url
      ('doctype_styles_new.css', __FILE__));
  wp_enqueue_style('doctypes_styles');
}
```

As you can see, this function uses the same enqueue mechanism that we used in `Chapter 8`, *Developing Your Own Theme*, when registering the style sheets for our custom theme. Here's the CSS file the preceding function fetches (inside `doctype_styles_new.css`):

```
.link {
  background-repeat: no-repeat;
  background-position: left center;
  padding: 0 0 0 18px;
}
.pdf { background-image: url(icon-pdf.png); }
.doc { background-image: url(icon-doc.png); }
.mp3 { background-image: url(icon-mp3.png); }
.zip { background-image: url(icon-zip.png); }
```

Indeed, a very simple file, containing just a handful of styles and icons to distinguish our document links!

Adding hooks to the plugin

We get our code to actually run when it is supposed to, by making use of WordPress **hooks**. The way in which plugin hooks work is as follows: at various times while WordPress is running, they check to see whether any plugins have registered functions to run at that time. If there are, the functions are executed. These functions modify the default behavior of WordPress.

There are two kinds of hooks:

- **Actions**: Actions are the hooks that the WordPress core launches at specific points during execution, or when specific events occur. Your plugin can specify that one or more of its PHP functions are executed at these points, using the `Action` API.
- **Filters**: Filters are the hooks that WordPress launches to modify the text of various types before adding it to the database or sending it to the browser screen. Your plugin can specify that one or more of its PHP functions is executed to modify specific types of text at these times, using the `Filter` API.

This means that you can tell WordPress to run your plugin's functions at the same time, when it runs any of its built-in functions. In our case, we want our plugin's first function, `doctype_styles_new_regex()`, to run as a filter along with WordPress' `the_content()` (this is the *fourth* requirement a plugin has to meet).

Now, add the following code to the bottom of the plugin:

```
add_filter('the_content', 'doctype_styles_new_regex');
```

This uses the `add_filter` hook that tells WordPress to register a function named `doctype_styles_new_regex()` when it is running the function called `the_content()`. By the way, if you have more than one function that you want to add as a filter to the content, you can add a third argument to the `add_filter()` function. This third argument would be a number representing the load priority (the default value is 10, the highest priority is 1, and there are no particular limits for the lowest priority--you can even assign values such as 100 or 999), and WordPress would run your functions in the ascending order.

All that's left in our list of requirements that a plugin has to meet is the *fifth* requirement: tell WordPress to include the new styles in the <head> tag. This is actually done the same way it's been done for themes, which is through the following hook using `add_action()` with the `wp_enqueue_scripts` handle:

```
add_action('wp_enqueue_scripts', 'doctype_styles_new_styles');
```

Here is the complete plugin PHP file:

```php
<?php
/*
Plugin Name: Add Document Type Styles New
Plugin URI: http://newinternetorder.com/plugins
Description: Detects URLs in your posts and pages
and displays nice document type icons next to them.
Includes support for PDF, DOC, MP3 and ZIP.
Version: 1.1
Author: Karol K
Author URI: http://karol.cc/
Text Domain: add_doctype_styles_new
License: GNU General Public License v2 or later
*/

// this function does the magic
function doctype_styles_new_regex($text) {
  $text = preg_replace('/href=([\'|"][[:alnum:]|
    [:punct:]]*)\.(pdf|doc|mp3|zip)([\'|"])/',
    'href=\\1.\\2\\3 class="link \\2"', $text);
```

```
    return $text;
}

// this functions adds the stylesheet to the head
function doctype_styles_new_styles() {
    wp_register_style('doctypes_styles',
    plugins_url('doctype_styles_new.css', __FILE__));
    wp_enqueue_style('doctypes_styles');
}

// HOOKS =============

add_filter('the_content', 'doctype_styles_new_regex', 9);
add_action('wp_enqueue_scripts', 'doctype_styles_new_styles');
```

 Make sure that there are no blank spaces before `<?php`. If there are any spaces, the PHP code will break, complaining that headers have already been sent. This is quite a common mistake developers stumble into during their initial attempts with WordPress plugins. It's also a generally good idea to not use the PHP closing tags (`?>`) at the end of your PHP files. It saves you from some of the most unfortunate execution errors.

Make sure you save and close this PHP file. You can now do one of two things:

- Using your FTP client, upload `add_doctype_styles_new/` to your `wp-content/plugins/` folder
- Zip up your folder into `add_doctype_styles_new.zip` and use the plugin uploader in wp-admin to add this plugin to your WordPress installation

 This version of the plugin is available in the code bundle for this chapter, inside a subfolder labeled `phase 1`. Our plugin files will go through a couple of phases before we have the final version.

Once the plugin is installed, it will show up on the plugins page:

☐	Plugin	Description
☐	**Add Document Type Styles New** Activate | Edit | Delete	Detects URLs in your posts and pages and displays nice document type icons next to them. Includes support for: PDF, DOC, MP3 and ZIP. Version 1.0 | By Karol K | Visit plugin site

Now, you can activate it and test it out.

Trying out the plugin

If you look at the podcast post we created in an earlier chapter, you'll notice that an MP3 icon has been added to it:

You can also try adding a new post with links to PDF, ZIP, or DOC files. This can be done by uploading the files through the Media Manager and clicking on **Insert into Post**. Then, when you view the post, you'll see that even more icons have been added to it by the plugin.

Now that you've learned about a basic plugin that uses hooks to piggyback on the existing WordPress functionality, let's enhance this plugin by giving the user some controls.

Adding an admin page

Some plugins add a page to wp-admin where you or the user can edit plugin options. We've seen this with W3 Total Cache, Yoast SEO, and others. Now, let's modify our plugin to give the user some control over which document types are supported. The following is what the new management page will look like when we are done:

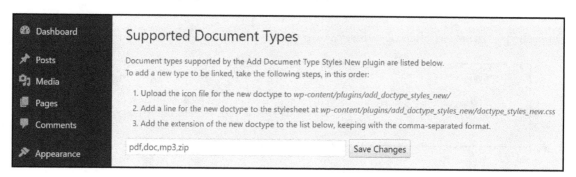

First, deactivate the plugin we just wrote. We'll make changes to it and then reactivate it. Following are the steps we'll carry out to modify the plugin in order to make this new page possible:

1. Add functions that create an admin page and save the user's input in a new option.
2. Modify the `doctype_styles_new_regex()` function so that it retrieves the user's input.
3. Add hooks for the admin page functions.

Let's get started!

Adding management page functions

The management page that we will create is going to add an option to wp-admin. This uses the existing space in the WordPress `options` table in the database, so no database modifications are required. The name of the new option has to be unique. I'm going to call the new option `doctype_styles_new_supportedtypes`.

There are six functions we need to add to the plugin so that an admin page can be added to wp-admin. Let's take a look at the first two:

1. The *first* function adds the new option `doctype_styles_new_supportedtypes` when the plugin is activated and sets the default value:

   ```
   function set_supportedtypes_options() {
       add_option("doctype_styles_new_supportedtypes",
           "pdf,doc,mp3,zip");
   }
   ```

2. The *second* function removes the new option when the plugin is deactivated:

   ```
   function unset_supportedtypes_options () {
     delete_option("doctype_styles_new_supportedtypes");
   }
   ```

3. Let's look at the new *third* function:

   ```
   function modify_menu_for_supportedtypes() {
     add_submenu_page(
     'options-general.php',      //The new options page will be added as
                                 //a submenu to the Settings menu.
     'Document Type Styles',     //Page <title>
     'Document Type Styles',     //Menu title
   ```

```
    'manage_options',          //Capability
    'add_doctype_styles_new',  //Slug
    'supportedtypes_options'   //Function to call
    );
}
```

This function adds a new item to the **Settings** menu in wp-admin using the `add_submenu_page()` function call. This takes six arguments, namely: where the options page should be placed, page title, menu link text, the user at the maximum level who can access the link, what file to open (none, in this case), and the function to call, `supportedtypes_options()`.

4. The `supportedtypes_options()` function is, in fact, the *fourth* new function we are adding:

```
function supportedtypes_options() {
  echo '<div class="wrap"><h2>Supported Document
    Types</h2>';
  if (isset($_POST['submit'])) {
    update_supportedtypes_options();
  }
  print_supportedtypes_form();
  echo '</div>';
}
```

This function actually displays our new page. It prints a title, checks to see if someone has clicked on the submit button; if the submit button has been clicked on, the `supportedtypes_options()` function updates the options and then prints the form.

5. The new *fifth* function we have to add is responsible for updating options, if the submit button has been clicked on:

```
function update_supportedtypes_options() {
  $updated = false;
  if ($_POST['doctype_styles_new_supportedtypes']) {
    $safe_val = addslashes(strip_tags($_POST
      ['doctype_styles_new_supportedtypes']));
      update_option('doctype_styles_new_supportedtypes',
      $safe_val);
    $updated = true;
  }

  if ($updated) {
    echo '<div id="message" class="updated fade">';
    echo '<p>Supported types successfully updated!</p>';
```

```
        echo '</div>';
    } else {
        echo '<div id="message" class="error fade">';
        echo '<p>Unable to update supported types!</p>';
        echo '</div>';
    }
}
```

6. The last function we need to add, the new *sixth* function, prints the form that the users will see. Make sure to have no spaces before or after the closing tag (EOF;):

```
function print_supportedtypes_form() {
    $val_doctype_styles_new_supportedtypes =
        stripslashes(get_option('
        doctype_styles_new_supportedtypes'));
    echo <<<EOF
<p>Document types supported by the Add Document Type Styles New
plugin are listed below.<br />To add a new type to be linked, take
the following steps, in this order:
<ol>
    <li>Upload the icon file for the new doctype to <i>wp-
        content/plugins/add_doctype_styles_new/</i></li>
    <li>Add a line for the new doctype to the stylesheet at
        <i>wp-content/plugins/add_doctype_styles_new/
        doctype_styles_new.css</i></li>
    <li>Add the extension of the new doctype to the list
        below, keeping with the comma-separated format.</li>
</ol>
</p>
<form method="post">
    <input type="text" name=
        "doctype_styles_new_supportedtypes" size="50"
        value="$val_doctype_styles_new_supportedtypes" />
        <input type="submit" name="submit" value="Save Changes"
        />
</form>
EOF;
}
```

These six functions together take care of adding a link in the menu, adding the management page for this link, and updating the new option.

Modifying the doctype_styles_new_regex() function

Now that the users are able to edit the list of supported document types by appending the document types they want, we should have a way of telling the `doctype_styles_new_regex()` function to use the user's list instead of the built-in list. To do so, we need to use `get_option('doctype_styles_new_supportedtypes')` in our `doctype_styles_new_regex()` function. The `get_option()` function will retrieve the value that the user has saved in the new option we just created. Modify your `doctype_styles_new_regex()` function so that it looks like this:

```
function ahs_doctypes_regex($text) {
    $types = get_option('doctype_styles_new_supportedtypes');
    $types = preg_replace('/,\s*/', '|', $types);

    $text = preg_replace('/href=([\'|"][[:alnum:]|
        [:punct:]]*)\.('.$types.')([\'|"])/i', 'href=\\1.\\2\\3
        class="link \\2"', $text);

    return $text;
}
```

Adding hooks

We have added our management page functions, but now we have to tell WordPress to use them. To do so, we just need to add the following three new hooks:

```
add_action('admin_menu', 'modify_menu_for_supportedtypes');
register_activation_hook(__FILE__, "set_supportedtypes_options");
register_deactivation_hook(__FILE__,
    "unset_supportedtypes_options");
```

The first hook tells WordPress to add our link to the menu when it creates the menu with `admin_menu()`. The next two hooks tell WordPress to call the activation and deactivation functions when the plugin is activated or deactivated.

 This version of the plugin is available in the code bundle for this chapter-- inside a subfolder labeled `final`. It is the final version of our plugin.

Trying out the plugin

We have added all of the new functions. Now it's time to save the file and see what happens. You can go ahead and reactivate the plugin. Now, when you look at the **Settings** menu, you will see that the new link has been added:

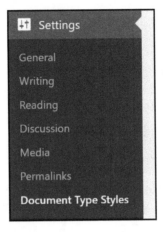

Click on it to see the management page:

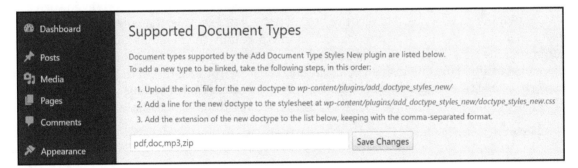

If you follow the three steps here on the management page (upload the file icon, add a new style to the style sheet, and add the extension to the option), then that new document type will be supported.

There are already a number of ways in which this plugin could be improved. Some of them are as follows:

- Instead of making the user upload his or her new icon using FTP, the plugin could allow the user to upload the new icon directly via the new management page
- The plugin could display the icons for the supported document types on the management page so that the users see what they look like
- The plugin could check to make sure that for every document type in the option field there is an existing icon, else it displays an error to the user

Perhaps, you'd like to try to make these changes yourself!

Testing your plugins

Just a minute ago, we've tried out our new plugin, so it's probably a good moment to say a word or two about testing your plugins and making sure that they don't cause any problems for regular users in general.

Our particular plugin is a very simple one; the only thing it does is process each link it finds inside any post's or page's content and adds a custom icon next to it. However, even such a simple plugin can be a possible security breach point. For example, the only place where the user can input anything is the plugins section in wp-admin (the field handling the supported file types). Now, there is a possibility that someone might use this field to input a piece of specific PHP code instead of a standard file type, for instance, code that is meant to perform a specific action on the server side, which could result in a serious security breach. That is why our `update_supportedtypes_options()` function has these two lines:

```
$safe_val = addslashes(strip_tags($_POST
    ['doctype_styles_new_supportedtypes']));
update_option('doctype_styles_new_supportedtypes', $safe_val);
```

Thanks to them, everything that the user inputs will have all PHP and HTML tags stripped by `strip_tags()`, and then every character that needs to be quoted in database queries will be handled by `addslashes()`. Using such functions is a just-in-case practice, but it tends to be something that eventually pays off.

Apart from testing our work against some of the common hacking practices such as code injection and SQL injection, we also need to handle all kinds of unconventional uses we can think of. For instance, would anything bad happen if someone put a value that's not a standard file type? Or what if the CSS file goes missing all of a sudden? These are just some of the questions a good testing session should answer.

One more good way of testing plugins is to hand them over to a handful of trusted users and ask for feedback. Someone who's entirely new to your plugin will usually do a way better job at testing it than you--the author.

Of course, this short section here only scratches the surface of plugin testing and code testing in general, so I encourage you to give it a closer look on your own. There are many great resources on the internet and in the nearest bookstore.

A plugin with database access - capturing searched words

We're going to leave the document types plugin behind now, and create a new one--featuring the active use of the database. Let's create a simple plugin that stores all the words that visitors search for (when using the blog's search feature).

Overall, this plugin is very basic and doesn't require its own folder like the previous plugin that we worked on. That's why this whole plugin will be done inside one file--`capture_searches_new.php`. I'm calling the plugin `Capture Searched Words New`.

The database table structure for this plugin will be as follows. The table name is `wp_searchedwords`:

Field	Type	Null	Key	Default	Extra
Id	INT	NOT NULL	PRI	-	auto_increment
Word	VARCHAR(255)	-	-	NULL	-
created	DATETIME	NOT NULL	-	Today 00:00:01	-

Now, let's write the plugin code.

 Even though I say that the table is named `wp_searchedwords`, it won't always be the case. It's all based on the table prefix that's set for your site (the default one is indeed `wp_`). Here, I'm going to refer to the table as `wp_searchedwords` anyway, for convenience.

Getting the plugin to talk to the database

The first part of this plugin has to be run only when the plugin is activated. This will be the initialization function. One of its tasks is to create or update the database table (the table will be created only if it hasn't been created before):

```
function searchedwords_init($content) {
    global $wpdb;
    $sw_table_name = $wpdb->prefix.'searchedwords';

    //creating the table (if it doesn't exist) or updating it if
    // necessary
    if(isset($_GET['activate']) && 'true' == $_GET['activate']) {
        $sql = 'CREATE TABLE `'.$sw_table_name.'` (
            id INT NOT NULL AUTO_INCREMENT,
            word VARCHAR(255),
            created DATETIME NOT NULL DEFAULT \''.date('Y-m-d').'
                00:00:01\',
            PRIMARY KEY  (id)
        )';

        require_once(ABSPATH.'wp-admin/includes/upgrade.php');
        dbDelta($sql);
    }

    // in case a search has just been performed, store the searched
    // word
    if (!empty($_GET['s'])) {
        $current_searched_words = explode(" ",urldecode($_GET['s']));
        foreach ($current_searched_words as $word) {
            $wpdb->query($wpdb->prepare("INSERT into `$sw_table_name`
                VALUES(null,'%s','".date('Y-m-d H:i:s')."')", $word));
        }
    }
}
```

This function connects to the database using various function calls like dbDelta(), $wpdb->query(), and $wpdb->prepare(). The dbDelta() function takes care of creating the table or updating it (whatever is needed at the time; find out more at https://codex. wordpress.org/Creating_Tables_with_Plugins). Apart from this, when dealing with the WordPress database, you can utilize any database-related PHP function in existence. Or, you can use the WordPress' class member function $wpdb->get_results(). The function we're using here also stores the searched word in the database table if a search has just been performed. This is done through the $wpdb->query() and $wpdb->prepare() functions.

Adding management page functions

We now need a familiar-looking function that adds a management page to the **Admin** menu. In this case, we use `add_management_page()` instead of `add_submenu_page()` because this plugin is more of a tool than something that needs settings:

```
function modify_menu_for_searchedwords() {
  $page = add_management_page(
    "Capture Searched Words",
    "Capture Searched Words",
    'manage_options',
    'capture_searches_new',
    'searchedwords_page'
  );
}
```

For this plugin, we're not going to load any custom styling or CSS files. The topic here is to just showcase how database connection can be done, so we're going to keep everything else ultra-simple and minimal. Therefore, the only thing we have to do at this point is to write a function that retrieves the information from the database and displays it on the new management page (again, everything is done through the `$wpdb` object - it's a class defined by WordPress that contains a set of functions you can use to interact with the database):

```
function searchedwords_page() {
  global $wpdb;
  $sw_table_name = $wpdb->prefix.'searchedwords';

$searched_words = $wpdb->get_results("SELECT COUNT(word) AS
    occurrence, word FROM `$sw_table_name` GROUP BY word ORDER BY
    occurrence DESC");
  ?>
<div class="wrap" style="max-width: 600px;">
<h2>Searched Words</h2>
<table class="wp-list-table widefat">
<thead>
  <tr>
    <th scope="col">Search Words</th>
    <th scope="col"># of Searches</th>
  </tr>
</thead>
<tbody>
  <?php
  if($searched_words !== NULL) {
    foreach($searched_words as $searched_word) {
      echo '<tr valign="top"><td>'.$searched_word-
          >word.'</td><td>'.$searched_word->occurrence.'</td></tr>';
    }
```

```
        $searched_perfomed = true;
      }
      else {
        echo '<tr valign="top"><td colspan="2"><strong>No searches
          have been performed yet</strong></td></tr>';
      }
      ?>
  </tbody>
  </table>
  </div>
    <?php
  }
```

That's it. The previous plugin had more functions because data was being captured from the user and then saved. Here, that's not necessary.

Lastly, we just need to add two hooks:

```
add_filter('init', 'searchedwords_init');
add_action('admin_menu', 'modify_menu_for_searchedwords');
```

The first hook tells WordPress to run the initialization function when the plugin is activated, or when a search is performed. The second hook modifies the admin menu to add a link to the new management page.

 This version of the plugin is available in the code bundle for this chapter-- inside a subfolder labeled `final`. It is the first and final version of the plugin.

Trying out the plugin

As with the last plugin, you can now either upload your plugin using FTP to wp-content/plugins or turn it into a ZIP file and add it using the uploader to wp-admin.

Once you've installed it, activate it. Then, look at the menu under **Tools** and you'll see a link to the new management page:

When you click on **Capture Searched Words**, you'll see a new page that the plugin created:

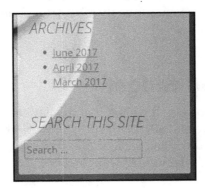

As you can see, I did perform some searches beforehand just to have something to show on this new page. You can do the same by placing a search field widget in your sidebar (the next screenshot) and then experimenting with different search words and phrases. The plugin will pick them all up and display the most searched ones in its section in wp-admin:

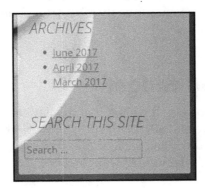

Learning more

There are hundreds of hooks available in WordPress--way too many to cover in this book. You can learn more about them by going online. Start out at these online reference sites:

- The *Plugin API* article contains very thorough information about writing plugins and using hooks (`https://codex.wordpress.org/Plugin_API`).
- For a complete list of action hooks, visit `https://codex.wordpress.org/Plugin_API/Action_Reference`.
- For a complete list of filter hooks, visit `https://codex.wordpress.org/Plugin_API/Filter_Reference`.
- You may also want to take a step back and look at the general *Plugin Resources* page in the WordPress Codex at `https://codex.wordpress.org/Plugin_Resources`.
- Another page that you might find very helpful is the new *Code Reference* for developers: `https://developer.wordpress.org/reference/`.
- If you want to submit your plugin to the WordPress plugin repository, you'll have to take steps similar to those you took when preparing a theme, and you'll also have to get hooked up to the WordPress SVN repository. Learn more about how to submit a plugin to the WordPress plugin repository at `https://developer.wordpress.org/plugins/wordpress-org/`.

Widgets

Writing a widget bears some similarities to writing a plugin, but in some ways, it's easier because there is a widget class that you can leverage for some of the functionalities. In other ways, it's also a bit more time-consuming as there's a lot of mandatory code that every widget has to feature.

Custom tag cloud widget

In this section, we'll see how to write a widget that displays a custom tag cloud that we can then place in the sidebar. There will also be the possibility to change the title of the widget, and although this is a tag cloud widget, we'll be able to switch tags to categories and display them using a tag-cloud-like style as well. In its final form, the widget will look like this:

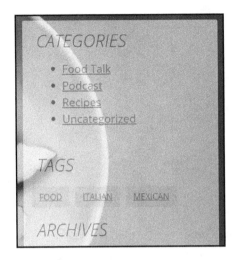

Just as a comparison, here's what the standard tag cloud widget (the native one in WordPress) looks like:

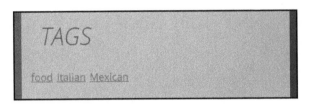

Let's get started!

Naming our widget

In this case, we're going to create the widget as a standalone plugin. So, just like any other plugin, it needs a unique name and a unique appearance in the `wp-content/plugins` folder.

 I encourage you to search the web whenever you're creating a new widget or plugin just to make sure that there's nothing out there going by the same name. On top of that, use "namespace" as a prefix with every file name (and function name) that you're creating. For example, mine is `kk_`.

I'll name the new plugin file (which holds the widget) `kk_tag_cloud_widget.php` and put it in its own `kk_tag_cloud_widget` folder inside `wp-content/plugins`.

This main PHP file starts just like any other plugin, with this declaration:

```php
<?php
/*
Plugin Name: Karol K's Tag Cloud Widget
Description: Displays a nice tag cloud.
Plugin URI: http://newinternetorder.com/plugins
Version: 1.1
Author: Karol K
Author URI: http://karol.cc/
License: GNU General Public License v2 or later
*/
```

The widget structure

When you are building a widget using the widget class, your widget needs to have the following structure:

```php
class UNIQUE_WIDGET_NAME extends WP_Widget {

  public function __construct() {
    $widget_ops = array();
    $control_ops = array();
    parent::__construct('base id', 'name', $widget_ops,
      $control_ops);
  }

  public function widget($args, $instance) {
    // used when the sidebar calls the widget
  }

  public function form($instance) {
    // prints the form on the widgets page
  }

  public function update($new_instance, $old_instance) {
    // used when the user saves his/her widget options
  }
}

// initiate the widget

// register the widget
```

My unique widget name for this project is `KK_Widget_Tag_Cloud`. Now, let's go over each of the preceding functions one by one and understand what's going on.

The widget initiation function

Let's start with the widget initiation function. Blank, it looks like this:

```
public function __construct() {
  $widget_ops = array();
  $control_ops = array();
  parent::__construct('base-id', 'name', $widget_ops,
    $control_ops);
}
```

In this function, which is the constructor of the class, we initialize various things that the `WP_Widget` class is expecting. The first two variables, to which you can give any name you want, are just a handy way to set the two array variables expected by the third line of code.

Let's take a look at these three lines of code:

- The `$widget_ops` variable is where you can set the class name, which is given to the `div` widget itself, and the description, which is shown in wp-admin on the widgets page.
- The `$control_ops` variable is where you can set options for the control box in wp-admin on the widget page, like the width and height of the widget and the ID prefix used for the names and IDs of the items inside. For my basic widget, I'm not going to use this variable (it's optional).
- When you call the parent class's constructor, `WP_Widget()`, you'll tell it the widget's unique ID, the widget's display title, and pass along the two arrays you created.

For this widget, my code now looks like this:

```
public function __construct() {
  parent::__construct(
    'kk-tag-cloud',
    'KK Tag Cloud',
    array(
      'description' => 'Your most used tags in cloud format; same
        height; custom background'
    )
  );
}
```

The widget form function

The widget form function has to be named `form()`. You may not rename it if you want the widget class to know what its purpose is. You also need to have an argument in there, which I'm calling `$instance`, which the class also expects. This is where the current widget settings are stored. This function needs to have all of the functionalities to create the form that users will see when adding the widget to a sidebar. Let's look at some abbreviated code and then explore what it's doing:

```php
public function form($instance) {
    $instance = wp_parse_args((array) $instance,
    array('template' => ''));
    $current_taxonomy = $this->_get_current_taxonomy($instance);
    ?>
    <p>
      <label for="<?php echo $this->get_field_id('title');
         ?>">Title</label>
      <input type="text" class="widefat" id="<?php echo $this-
         >get_field_id('title'); ?>" name="<?php echo $this-
         >get_field_name('title'); ?>" value="<?php if
         (isset($instance['title']))
         {echo esc_attr($instance['title']);}
      ?>" />
    </p>
    <p>
      <label for="<?php echo $this->get_field_id('taxonomy');
         ?>">Taxonomy</label>
      <select class="widefat" id="<?php echo $this-
         >get_field_id('taxonomy'); ?>" name="<?php echo $this-
         >get_field_name('taxonomy'); ?>">
      <?php foreach(get_object_taxonomies('post') as $taxonomy) :
        $tax = get_taxonomy($taxonomy);
        if(!$tax->show_tagcloud || empty($tax->labels->name))
          continue;
        ?>
        <option value="<?php echo esc_attr($taxonomy) ?>"
        <?php selected($taxonomy, $current_taxonomy); ?>>
        <?php echo $tax- >labels->name; ?></option>
      <?php endforeach; ?>
      </select>
    </p>
    <?php
}
```

First, you use a WordPress function named `wp_parse_args()`, which creates an `$instance` array that your form will use. What's in it depends on what defaults you've set and what settings the user has already saved. Then, you create form fields. Note that for each form field, I make use of the built-in functions that will create unique names and IDs and input the existing values:

- `$this->get-field_id()` creates a unique ID based on the widget instance (remember, you can create more than one instance of this widget)
- `$this->get_field_name()` creates a unique name based on the widget instance
- The `$instance` array is where you will find the current values for the widget, whether they are defaults or user-saved data

All the other code in there is just regular PHP and HTML. Note that if you give the user the ability to set a title, name that field `title`, WordPress will show it on the widget form when it's minimized. The widget form this will create will look like this:

The widget save function

When a user clicks on the **Save** button on the widget form, WordPress uses AJAX to run your save function. You need to be sure to save whatever the user types in, which is all we're doing in this case, but you can put other functionalities here if it's appropriate for your widget (for example, database interactions, conversions, calculations, and so on). The final code for this function is as follows:

```
public function update($new_instance, $old_instance) {
    $instance['title'] = $new_instance['title'];
    $instance['taxonomy'] = stripslashes($new_instance['taxonomy']);
    return $instance;
}
```

Be sure this function is named `update()` and is prepared to accept two instances, one with the old data and one with the just-submitted data. You can write your code to check `$new_instance` for problems, and thus, return `$old_instance` if the new one isn't valid. The `$instance` data you return will be what's shown in the update widget form.

The widget print function

The third main function in your widget class is the one that is called by the sidebar when it's time to actually show the widget to people visiting the website. It needs to retrieve any relevant saved user data and print out information for the website visitor. In this case, our final print function looks like this:

```
public function widget($args, $instance) {
  extract($args);
  $current_taxonomy = $this->_get_current_taxonomy($instance);
  if(!empty($instance['title'])) {
    $title = $instance['title'];
  }
  else {
    if('post_tag' == $current_taxonomy) {
      $title = 'Tags';
    }
    else {
      $tax = get_taxonomy($current_taxonomy);
      $title = $tax->labels->name;
    }
  }
  $title = apply_filters('widget_title', $title, $instance, $this-
    >id_base);
  $before_widget = '<div class="widget-container kk_widget_tag_cloud">';
  $after_widget = '</div>';
  $before_title = '<h1 class="widget-title">';
  $after_title = '</h1>';

  echo $before_widget;
  if ( $title )   echo $before_title . $title . $after_title;
  echo '<div class="kk_tagcloud">';
  wp_tag_cloud(apply_filters('widget_tag_cloud_args',
    array('taxonomy' => $current_taxonomy)));
  echo "</div>\n";
  echo $after_widget;
}
```

The preceding function calls one more helper function responsible for fetching the current taxonomy. A very simple one, though:

```
function _get_current_taxonomy($instance) {
    if ( !empty($instance['taxonomy']) &&
        taxonomy_exists($instance['taxonomy']) )
        return $instance['taxonomy'];
    return 'post_tag';
}
```

The first thing I do in the main function is extract the data in the instance, which has the information the website administrator had saved when filling out the widget form. Then, the widget takes a look into the selected taxonomy (tags or categories) and displays all individual items as a simple one-line list.

Custom widget styles

Our small widget has its own style sheet that needs to be included in the current theme's `head` section, like any other style sheet.

The file is named `kk_tag_cloud_widget.css` and contains the following:

```css
.kk_widget_tag_cloud .kk_tagcloud {
    line-height: 1.5em;
}

.kk_widget_tag_cloud .kk_tagcloud a {
    display: inline-block;
    margin: 3px 2px;
    padding: 0 11px;
    border-radius: 3px;
    -webkit-border-radius: 3px;
    background: #eee;
    color: #279090;
    font-size: 12px !important;
    line-height: 30px;
    text-transform: uppercase;
}

.kk_widget_tag_cloud .kk_tagcloud a:hover {
    color: #f2f2f2;
    background: #404040;
}
```

Nothing fancy, just a set of classes that will make sure that the widget looks great. The only thing we have to do with this style sheet is enqueued it through a standard WordPress hook. Place this in your plugin's main file:

```
function kk_tag_cloud_widget_styles_load() {
  wp_register_style('kk_tag_cloud_widget_styles',
      plugins_url('kk_tag_cloud_widget.css', __FILE__));
  wp_enqueue_style('kk_tag_cloud_widget_styles');
}
add_action('wp_enqueue_scripts',
    'kk_tag_cloud_widget_styles_load');
```

Initiating and hooking up the widget

That's it for widget functionality! Now, you just need to add a little piece of code that will hook the widget up to the rest of WordPress:

```
function KK_Widget_Tag_Cloud_Reg() {
  register_widget('KK_Widget_Tag_Cloud');
}
add_action('widgets_init', 'KK_Widget_Tag_Cloud_Reg');
```

This tells WordPress that when it initiates widgets, it should be sure to register our new widget.

 This version of the widget is available in the code bundle for this chapter-- inside a subfolder labeled `phase 1`. We'll still be adding one more feature before we can call it the final version.

Trying out the widget

Your widget is ready to go! Save all your changes, and upload your widget to the `wp-content/plugins` folder. Go to the **Installed Plugins** page, and you'll see your widget waiting to be activated, as usual. After you click on the **Activate** button, you can navigate to **Appearance | Widgets**. You'll see the widget waiting to be added to a sidebar:

KK Tag Cloud

Your most used tags in cloud format; same height; custom background

Drag the widget to a sidebar, and then click on the little down arrow to edit it. You'll see the options slide down, as shown in the following screenshot:

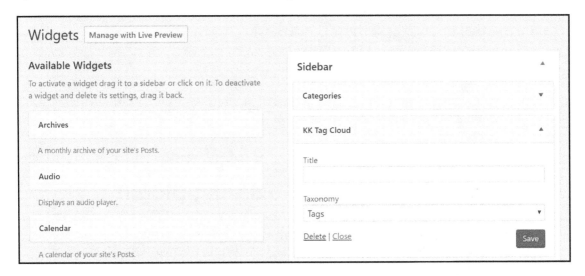

You can enter **Title** or leave it blank for the default, and choose **Taxonomy** to use. Then, click on **Save** as you would with any widget. When you return to the frontend of the site and reload, the new tag cloud will be right there:

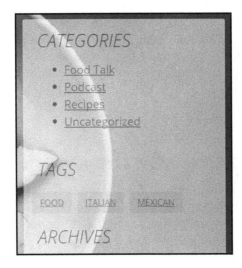

Learning more

You can browse the following online reference sites to learn more about widgets:

- The WordPress *Widgets API* is located at
  `https://codex.wordpress.org/Widgets_API`
- WordPress lists a number of widgets at
  `https://codex.wordpress.org/WordPress_Widgets`
- If you want to find more widgets to install on your website, visit the widgets section of the plugin repository at `https://wordpress.org/plugins/tags/widget`

Bundling a widget with an existing plugin

If you're writing a plugin and you'd like to make a widget available with it, you don't have to create a separate widget plugin. Just include all of the widget code, like what we created in the preceding section, in with your plugin's PHP file. When the user activates the plugin, the widget you created will automatically show up on the widgets page in wp-admin. No need for a separate file!

Shortcodes

Shortcodes are a handy way to let a nontechnical person, such as an editor of a website, include dynamic content within pages and posts, without having to actually use any PHP, complex HTML structures, or custom JavaScript. In other words, shortcodes are handy reusable pieces of code, yet they don't require any actual coding experience or knowledge on the end user's part.

Shortcodes and the way they work

The way a shortcode works is that you tell WordPress to look at the text within square brackets (`[]`) and evaluate it by running a PHP function. That PHP function can live in the `functions.php` file of your theme, or in a plugin file, or in a widget file. Let's create a simple shortcode and include it with our most recent widget.

Types of shortcodes

Shortcodes are a pretty simple concept by definition, but we can still distinguish three main types:

- **Single-tag shortcodes**: These shortcodes are executed with just a single tag, for example, `[my_first_shortcode/]`.
- **Double-tag shortcodes**: These shortcodes are executed with opening and closing tags, for example, `[my_2nd_shortcode]some text here[/my_2nd_shortcode]` (notice that the closing tag has an additional /). As you can see, there's also some content within the tags. This content can be processed by the shortcode function.
- **Shortcodes with attributes**: These shortcodes can have one or two tags and also a number of attributes we can use to customize the output, for example, `[my_3rd_shortcode name="Karol" twitter="carlosinho"]some text here[/my_3rd_shortcode]`.

Creating a simple shortcode

Let's create a simple shortcode that will make it possible to use our widget's output inside any given post or page. This is going to be a double-tag shortcode with one additional attribute, which we'll use to indicate whether the output should be formatted using our custom CSS or WordPress' native styling.

Let's start by creating a new function at the bottom of our `kk_tag_cloud_widget.php` file, and then, we'll go through each individual line:

```php
function kk_tag_cloud_handler($atts, $content=null) {
  extract(shortcode_atts(array(
    'use_css' => '1',
    'taxonomy' => 'post_tag'
  ), $atts));

  $tax = 'post_tag';
  if(taxonomy_exists($taxonomy)) $tax = $taxonomy;

  $result = '';

  if ('0' != $use_css) {
    $result .= '<div class="kk_widget_tag_cloud"><div
      class="kk_tagcloud">';
  }
  if (null != $content) {
```

```
        $result .= addslashes(strip_tags($content)).' ';
    }
    $result .= wp_tag_cloud(apply_filters(
        'widget_tag_cloud_args',
        array('taxonomy' => $tax, 'echo' => false)
        ));
    if ('0' != $use_css) {
        $result .= '</div></div>';
    }

    return $result;
}
```

First of all, note that this function does not *echo* or *print* anything. It just returns a string. If you let your function print, it won't look correct on the website.

Inside our function, the first line handles the custom attributes that the shortcode receives (in this case, just the use_css parameter for indicating whether the styles should be used or not, and the taxonomy parameter to indicate the taxonomy that should be shown in the shortcode). WordPress will hand off the $atts argument automatically, and we only have to use the extract() function to turn the attributes the user submits into variables available in the function. The values in the array passed to extract() set the defaults, in case the user chooses no options. In general, there is no limit to the number of options that you can make available to the shortcode users.

The next line extracts the taxonomy identifier and tries to turn it into a valid taxonomy. In case the user's input is not valid, the default post_tag taxonomy will be used. The final part of the function handles the display based on the state of the use_css attribute. Pretty basic at this point! There's also a possibility to include custom text as the main content of the shortcode. This can be useful in some situations.

What we have to do now is tell WordPress that this function is a shortcode, and we do so using a hook. Be sure to choose something unique. I've chosen kk_tag_cloud as the name for this shortcode, so the hook looks like this:

```
add_shortcode('kk_tag_cloud', 'kk_tag_cloud_handler');
```

To use this shortcode in our content, all we have to do is edit any given post or page and put a line like this in it:

```
[kk_tag_cloud taxonomy="category"] Select the category you'd like
    to read next:[/kk_tag_cloud]
```

Such usage will have the following effect:

Select the category you'd like to read next: FOOD TALK   PODCAST   RECIPES

UNCATEGORIZED

We can also use the shortcode like this:

```
[kk_tag_cloud use_css="0" taxonomy="category"]Select the category
    you'd like to read next:[/kk_tag_cloud]
```

This will disable the custom styles and produce this effect:

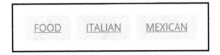

Select the category you'd like to read next: Food Talk Podcast Recipes

Uncategorized

To display the tag cloud in its default form (showing the tags and using the custom style sheet), all we have to do is execute the shortcode like this:

```
[kk_tag_cloud][/kk_tag_cloud]
```

The effect is shown in the following screenshot:

FOOD   ITALIAN   MEXICAN

There are very few limitations regarding what you *can* and *cannot* do with shortcodes. However, the most common uses are for embedding online videos from sites such as YouTube (using the `[youtube]` shortcode, for example), or for showing various social media boxes and activity streams.

This version of the widget is available in the code bundle for this chapter--inside a subfolder labeled `final`. It is the final version of our widget.

The WordPress REST API

The WordPress REST API is a relatively new addition to the WordPress platform. Before it was added to core, the REST API was available as a standalone mechanism via a separate plugin. You could get everything and also learn how to work with the package from the project's official website at `http://v2.wp-api.org/`.

However, starting from WordPress 4.7, REST API is now included in the core WordPress package, and you don't need any additional plugins or tools to make it work. Basically, as long as you're on the most recent version of WordPress, you have REST API installed and enabled by default. Which is great news! But let's get a bit deeper.

What REST API is

Under the hood, REST API--officially called *WordPress REST API*--is just another layer of technology that allows you to interact with your WordPress site, as well as sites of other people. Chiefly, REST API allows you to separate the presentation layer of a WordPress site from the mechanism of how WordPress operates in the background. In other words, with specific REST API calls, you can perform actions on the contents of a WordPress site without having to enter wp-admin of that site or even visit it via a web browser at all.

Why use WordPress REST API?

The introduction of REST API opens up a lot of new possibilities as to *what you can do* with a WordPress site and *what you can use it for*. For instance, via REST API, you can interact with WordPress content remotely, add new content, erase content, or perform any other operation. Just to name one major possibility, this makes it easy to create a mobile app for your website, and have the app communicate with the website via REST API. In other words, if you want to communicate with a WordPress site via any other way than by visiting the site directly, then you can do that with the REST API.

How to get started with REST API

We're only scratching the surface here, and the description provided in this chapter is by no means exhaustive. REST API is a rather advanced piece of technology that lets you do a multitude of things, sometimes via rather complex code structures. So the only thing we want to achieve here is help you get started--give you a foundation that you can then explore further as you're learning about REST API elsewhere. A great place to get started if you want to truly master REST API is the official developer manual at `https://developer.wordpress.org/rest-api/`. With that being said, what follows are the basics of how to begin with REST API.

REST API allows you to interact with any WordPress site via the means of sending *requests* and receiving *responses* through the WordPress HTTP API. To make a valid request, you need to reference the following: the *base URL path* of REST API, *route*, and *endpoint*.

The base URL path is similar for all WordPress websites:

```
http://YOURWEBSITE.com/wp-json/wp/v2/
```

The route defines the exact part of the website's content that you want to communicate with. For example, you can use `posts/` in order to communicate with the site's posts. In that case, the full URL would be `http://YOURWEBSITE.com/wp-json/wp/v2/posts/`.

Endpoints are specific functions available through REST API. For example, if you expand the route to target a specific post by ID, such as `http://YOURWEBSITE.com/wp-json/wp/v2/posts/123` then this allows you to call one of three endpoints:

- `GET`: Returns the post data
- `PUT`: Updates the post data and returns that updated post data
- `DELETE`: Deletes the post and returns the now-deleted post data

Apart from the default endpoints, you can also create your own, depending on what you want to be able to do with your content through the REST API. This, however, is perhaps a topic for a more in-depth REST API manual. For the purpose of this book, let's just do a simple demonstration and create a plugin that will communicate with an external WordPress website via REST API.

Creating a plugin that uses REST API

You've already learned how to create basic WordPress plugins in this very chapter, so now, let's combine this knowledge with the new addition of REST API. The plugin we're building is going to simply display a list of posts from another blog based on a shortcode.

Let's have a look at the full code of this plugin--all within a single file named `kk_rest_demo.php`:

```php
function kk_rest_handler($atts, $content=null) {
  extract(shortcode_atts(array(
    'website_domain' => 'newinternetorder.com',
    'how_many' => '3'
  ), $atts));
  $response = wp_remote_get( 'http://' . $website_domain . '/wp-
  json/wp/v2/posts/' );

  if( is_wp_error( $response ) ) {
    $error_string = $response->get_error_message();
    return 'Error occurred: <em>' . $error_string . '</em>';
  }
  $posts = json_decode( wp_remote_retrieve_body( $response ) );
  if( empty( $posts ) ) { return 'No posts found'; }
  else {
    $result = '<ul>';
    $post_count = 0;
    foreach( $posts as $post ) {
      $post_count++;
      if ($post_count <= $how_many) {
        $result .= '<li><a href="' . $post->link. '">'
        . $post->title->rendered . '</a></li>';
      }
    }
    $result .= '</ul>';
    return $result;
  }
}
add_shortcode('kk_rest', 'kk_rest_handler');
```

The first function call, `extract()`, is something we know from the previous shortcode plugin/widget. It extracts the attributes given to the shortcode. In our case, the shortcode works with two optional attributes:

- `website_domain`: Indicates the domain name of the WordPress site that the plugin should communicate with (defaults to `newinternetorder.com`)
- `how_many`: Indicates how many posts should be fetched (defaults to 3)

The next function call is where the main REST API communication happens. This call references a given route and fetches blog posts using the GET endpoint (by default):

```
$response = wp_remote_get( 'http://' . $website_domain . '/wp-
json/wp/v2/posts/' );
```

After that, we just need to check if there weren't any errors, and if so, halt the function. The next function call decodes the response and allows us to reference individual posts one by one later on:

```
$posts = json_decode( wp_remote_retrieve_body( $response ) );
```

The final `foreach` loop and `if` clause go through each post and retrieve its title and URL, which then get added to a standard HTML unordered list and returned by the shortcode. At this point, and once I activate this plugin on my test site, I can create a new post and add this shortcode to it:

```
[kk_rest website_domain="newinternetorder.com" how_many="2"]
[/kk_rest]
```

This tells the plugin to communicate with `newinternetorder.com` and fetch the two most recent posts. Here's the result of that as visible on the frontend:

Of course, the plugin we've built here is very simple, and it does not do anything in terms of making sure that the domain provided is valid, or anything else security-related. However, the purpose of this demo is only to show you the simplest way of working with REST API, and nothing else. Once again, I strongly encourage you to visit some of the official resources, such as the *REST API Handbook* at `https://developer.wordpress.org/rest-api/`.

This version of the plugin is available in the code bundle for this chapter-- inside a subfolder labeled `final`.

Summary

In this chapter, you learned everything you need to know about creating basic plugins and widgets. Now you know how to structure the PHP file, where to put your functions, and how to use hooks. You also learned about adding management pages, enabling plugins and widgets to have database access, and how to create shortcodes--a powerful tool that lets you make dynamic functionalities available to all WordPress users.

On top of all this, you learned how to work with REST API and perform basic communication with other WordPress websites. With your existing knowledge of PHP and HTML, you now have the tools to get started with writing every plugin and widget your heart may desire.

The next chapter will be all about community blogging--running multi-user blogs, and other aspects of turning your site into a serious online magazine.

11
Community Blogging

So far in this book, we've focused on working with a personal website: one that belongs to and is used by just one person. However, many blogs are used in a different way--there may be a single blog or website with a variety of writers, editors, and administrators. This makes the site more like a community project or even an online magazine.

Furthermore, it's by no means uncommon for bigger online publishers to use WordPress as the base of their websites. In which case, the site has a number of authors, editors, reviewers, and overall contributors with varying responsibilities. Not to mention the technical staff or designers.

In this chapter, we'll discuss allowing a blog to have multiple authors with differing levels of control over the blog's administration and content. We'll explore user management for multiple users on one blog, as well as other aspects of blogging as a member of a community. We'll also take a look at using a non-blog website with multiple users.

Concerns for a multi-author blog

A multi-author blog is useful when a group of people with similar interests want to collaborate and share space to publish their writing or if an organization or company wants to have an online magazine. If that group wants to publish news on a particular topic, or on many topics in a broad sense, then they'll each need to be able to log in and post their content, update their profile, and so on. For example, I can decide that I want every member of my family to be able to contribute to my *daily cooking* blog. Each of my sisters, brothers, cousins, aunts, and uncles can add their recipes and discoveries regarding food, which has the potential to make my food blog a richer and more exciting place for visitors.

However, content moderation is also essential to a multi-author blog. The best way to keep a blog clean and relevant to the topic is using a moderation flow that restricts the display of content until it travels through an approval process. Such practice is sometimes called **workflow**. A workflow makes working in large groups much easier and more manageable.

User roles and abilities

WordPress includes the ability to have an unlimited number of users. Each user can be assigned one of five different roles. Let's look at these roles one at a time, starting with the most powerful one.

Administrator

When you installed WordPress, it created a user with administrative powers for you. This role is called *administrator*, and every WordPress site must have at least one admin (you will not be allowed to delete them all). As you have already seen in the earlier chapters, administrators can do everything.

> The administrator's primary purpose is to manage everything about a website.

In general, you don't want to have a lot of administrators on a single blog or website. It is best to keep just one administrator for a blog with 10 to 20 authors and editors, or perhaps up to three administrators for a blog with dozens of users.

Some examples of the actions that only a user with the administrator role can take are as follows:

- Switch blog theme
- Add, edit, activate, or deactivate plugins
- Add, edit, or delete users
- Manage general blog options and settings

When creating more administrator accounts (or managing the main one), make sure to use only complex passwords that are hard to break using any sort of brute-force methods. In a nutshell, use as many numbers, special characters, combinations of uppercase and lowercase letters as you can. A lot of hacking attempts revolve around password guessing, so the more complex your password is, the tougher it will be to break.

Editor

After the administrator, the *editor* has the most powerful role. This role is for the users who need to manage everything about the content of a website, but don't need to be able to change the basic structure, design, or functionality of the blog itself (that's for administrators).

 The editor's primary purpose is to manage the content of a blog.

To get an idea of what the screen looks like when a user logs in as an editor, let's take a look at the editor's menu (to the right) in comparison to the administrator's menu (to the left):

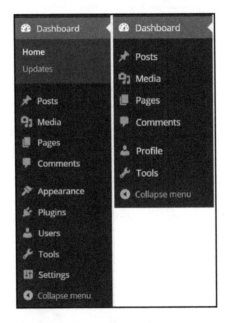

As you can see, the top section is unchanged (apart from the **Updates** link). However, nearly the entire bottom menu, with **Appearance**, **Plugins**, **Users** (which is replaced with **Profile**), and **Settings**, has disappeared. We can see that the editor is left with only the ability to edit his or her own profile, and access to the **Tools** section, which includes any plugin pages that allow editor-level users.

Examples of actions that a user with the editor role can take are as follows:

- Manage all posts
- Create and edit pages
- Moderate comments
- Manage categories, tags, and links
- Edit other users' content

There's one very useful aspect of the editor's role. If you take a closer look, you'll see that it has all the credentials that one would need to publish any piece of content on a given WordPress site. This makes it perfect for everyday use, even for single-author blogs/sites. Therefore, what I actually encourage you to do is set up a separate editor account for yourself, and use it for posting and editing content, instead of working with the default administrator account. This setup is a lot safer, particularly if someone tries to hijack your password, or in case of any other mishap to your account, the site itself won't get harmed (considering the fact that editors can't install new plugins or delete any existing ones).

For multi-author blogs/sites, the editor role is meant to be assigned to users who are in charge of the content published on the site. Essentially, like the name itself indicates, the "editor" role is perfect for editors.

Author

Authors have much less access than editors. Authors can add and edit their own posts and manage the posts made by their subordinates. However, they can neither edit posts made by other authors, nor manage comments on posts that don't belong to them.

 The author's primary purpose is to manage his or her own content.

To get an idea of the experience of a user with the *author* role, let's take a look at the author's menu (to the right) in comparison to the editor's menu (to the left):

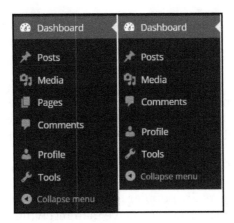

As you can see in the preceding screenshot, the **Pages** section has disappeared. Additionally, if the author looks at the complete list of posts, they will only have the ability to view, and not edit, quick edit, or delete posts that he or she did not author (highlighted):

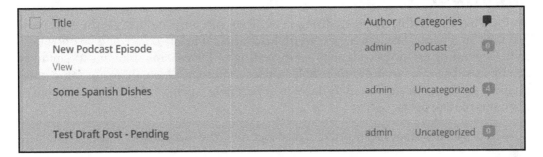

As you would imagine, the author role is perfect for, well ... authors--users who are actively involved in creating content for your site. Authors can, for example, do the following:

- Submit and publish their posts
- Manage their posts after the publication
- Moderate the comments under their posts

Contributor

Contributors are only able to write posts and submit them for review. These posts will be in **Pending Review** status until an editor or administrator agrees to publish them. Contributors cannot upload images or other files, view the media library, add categories, edit comments, or any of the other tasks available to more advanced users.

The contributor's primary purpose is to submit content for consideration.

One important thing worth mentioning is that although contributors can create and submit their work for review, once the article is published, they no longer have the ability to edit it in any way. However, they do get access to the comments section (for moderation).

When it comes to the real-world application of this role, it's most commonly used when working with guest bloggers or any other regular contributors who are not part of your in-house team. Guest blogging is really popular nowadays, and handling it through contributor accounts is much less labor-intensive than receiving articles via email and then having to copy and paste them into WordPress.

Subscriber

Subscribers have no ability to do anything at all. They can only log in and edit their profile (adjust their first name, last name, password, biographical information, and so on), and that's it. Depending on the permissions set in **Settings | Discussion**, blog visitors may have to sign up as subscribers in order to be able to post comments. Also, there are some plugins that handle sending informational updates to subscribers, such as newsletters or email notifications of new posts.

 A subscriber has no editorial power over the website.

Most of the time, this role is used as a placeholder. Take, for example, a specific author who had been contributing to your site regularly in the past, but hasn't submitted anything for months. Instead of deleting their account completely, you can simply change their role to that of a *subscriber*.

Managing users

To manage users, log in (as an administrator, of course) and navigate to **Users**. You'll see a list of your existing users, as seen in the following screenshot:

When we installed WordPress, it created only our first user (which is how we've been logging in all this time). So let's create a new user and assign that user the next most powerful role--*editor*. To do this, navigate to **Users** | **Add New**. You'll see the **Add New User** form as shown in the next screenshot:

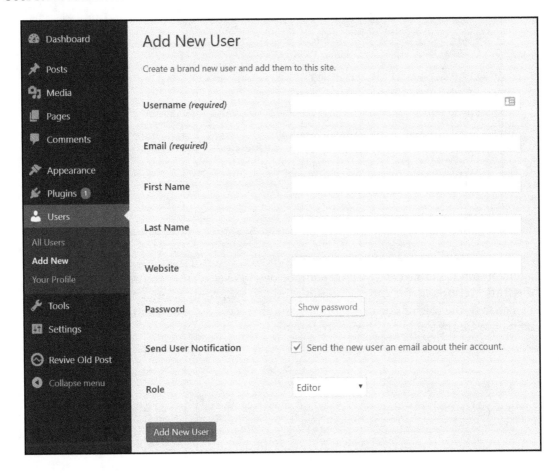

In this form, only the **Username** and **Email** fields are required. The **Password** field is handled automatically. WordPress will generate a safe password on its own and then send it to the new user once it's done. You can also change **Role** from the default (**Subscriber**) to one of the other roles. In this case, I've selected **Editor**. Then, I clicked on the **Add New User** button. Apart from the required fields, it's also a good practice to fill in **First Name** and **Last Name**. This can make the task of further managing the user accounts much clearer.

I can repeat this process to add an author, a contributor, and a subscriber. When I'm done, the **Users** page (where the users can be managed) will look like the next screenshot:

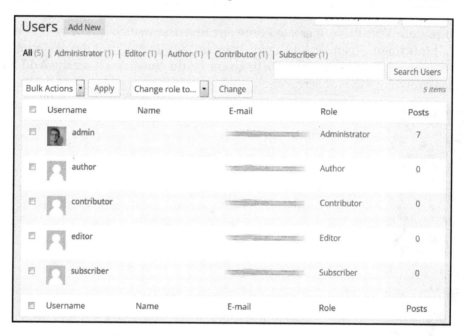

As with any other management list in wp-admin, you can roll over a row to see the management links. In this case, you can edit or delete users. You can use the checkboxes and the **Bulk Actions** menu, or use the filter links to view only users with particular roles. You can change the role of one or more users on this page by checking the box (or boxes) and using the **Change role to...** drop-down menu.

Enabling users to self-register

Adding users by yourself is not the only way to add users to your WordPress website. You can also give your users the ability to register themselves. First, navigate to **Settings** | **General** and make sure you've checked **Anyone can register** next to **Membership**:

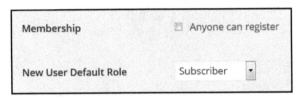

I strongly recommend leaving **New User Default Role** as **Subscriber**, though **Contributor** would also be fine if the purpose of your blog requires it. However, allowing new users to automatically be assigned a role with more power than that is just asking for trouble.

Next, add a link somewhere on your blog that links the users to the login and registration pages. The easiest way to do this is to use the widget named **META**, which comes with your WordPress installation. It will add a box to your sidebar with a few useful links, including **Log in** and **Register**:

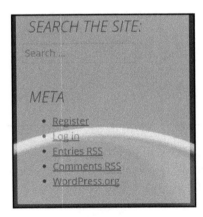

Of course, if this is not exactly the collection of links that you want, you can create your own widget. Users clicking on **Register** will be taken to the following basic registration page that asks for only **Username** and **Email**, as seen in the following screenshot:

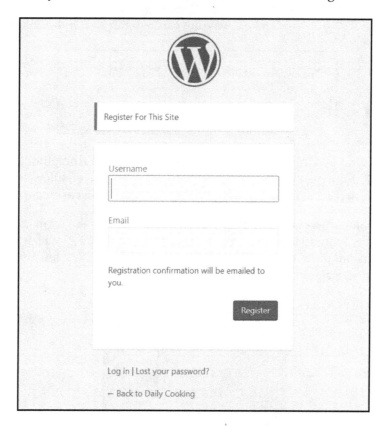

After submitting this form, the user will be emailed a password, and the main site administrator will be sent an email notification of the new registration. The user can now log in and edit his/her profile, or do more if an administrator changes their role.

Learning more

You can learn more about the built-in WordPress roles and capabilities at `https://codex.wordpress.org/Roles_and_Capabilities`.

User management plugins

At the time of writing, there are hundreds of plugins tagged with `users` in the WordPress `plugin` directory (`https://wordpress.org/plugins/tags/users`). We can actually divide those plugins into many groups as the functionality offered is exceptionally wide. For example, there are plugins for the following:

- Dealing with various author accounts, co-authoring posts, and multi-author sites
- Constructing membership sites around WordPress where members can get access to premium packages of content based on their subscription model
- Building a classic e-commerce store where everybody can make a purchase from the available directory of "things"
- Building an online forum based on WordPress
- Building an email newsletter sent to a given site's users directly from within WordPress, instead of using external services
- Launching a social network on WordPress
- Managing user profiles for registered users

As you can see, the number of possibilities is really striking. If we want to, we can do essentially anything with a WordPress site and its users. Only our imagination is the limit.

Finally, let's not forget about one of the more popular areas in modern website launches-- social networks (like Facebook). As it turns out, you don't need a huge budget at your disposal in order to launch such a network. A plugin like **BuddyPress** (`https://buddypress.org/`) has all the functionality you'd need and, best of all, it's free. We'll actually give BuddyPress a closer look in the next chapters where we'll focus on building non-blog websites, but I just wanted to mention it here to keep the message complete.

Summary

In this chapter, you learned how to manage a group of users working on a single blog, which is a community of users. Community blogging can play an important role in a user group or a news website. You also learned how to manage the different levels of privileges for users in a community.

In the next chapter, we'll walk through the process of creating a complete non-blog website from scratch.

12
Creating a Non-Blog Website Part One - The Basics

As you have seen while reading this book, WordPress comes fully equipped to power a blog with all its particular requirements of post handling, categorization, chronological display, and so on. However, powering blogs is not WordPress' only purpose. Not anymore. In fact, there are millions of websites out there right now running WordPress, where blogging is not the primary focus of the website. I myself have built a number of such sites.

Just to give you a general idea of what's possible, here's a list of some popular non-blog type websites that you can build and launch using WordPress (we will cover some of them in more detail later in this and the next chapter):

- **Static websites**: Featuring just a handful of static subpages that are not meant to be updated very often; also, the main content is not organized chronologically like blog posts.
- **Corporate or business websites**: Similar to the previous type, but usually a bit bigger in size and in the number of subpages; additionally, for most business sites, their design appears very official and toned down.
- **One-page websites**: Websites that only have a single page of content; used mostly as a business card type site, or used by businesses that don't have a lot of content to showcase on their site. Even though the whole site is comprised of just a page, the designs are usually attractive with a lot of dynamic transition effects and parallax scrolling backgrounds.
- **E-commerce stores**: Websites where anyone can browse through a number of products and then use a shopping cart to make a purchase. Apart from the shopping cart functionality, there's also online payment integration and often a backend inventory management system.

- **Membership websites**: A kind of site where some of the content is available only to those users who have signed up for a membership and (often) paid a small fee for the privilege; such members-only areas can contain any type of content that the site owner finds suitable--WordPress doesn't limit this in any way.
- **Video blogs**: Just like a standard blog; only instead of text-based posts, the blogger publishes video posts.
- **Photo blogs**: Just like video blogs, only revolving around photos; a very common type of blog for photographers, graphic designers, and other people of similar professions.
- **Product websites**: In short, it's a type of site very similar to an e-commerce store, only this time, we're usually dealing with just a single product on sale. It's a very popular type of website for all kinds of web apps, iOS, or Android apps.
- **Social networks**: Just like Facebook, only run on WordPress.
- **Niche business websites**: Some examples of such sites are local restaurant websites, hotel websites, coffee shop websites, personal portfolio websites, art gallery websites, and so on.

Again, if I were to explain, in brief, what a general non-blog website is, I'd say that it's any kind of website where the blog is not the main functionality used by the website owner. And of course, non-blog websites make up the majority of the internet as a whole. However, since we're discussing WordPress here, which many still believe to be a blog system only, I just want to assure you that it's no longer the case. These days, WordPress can be used for virtually anything.

In this chapter and the next, we will go through some of the types of websites just mentioned and present an effective way of building them with WordPress. We'll also use the knowledge that we've acquired in the previous chapters, so it's best that you get familiar with everything that's been going on so far before consuming the information in the following pages.

Here are the types of websites we're going to cover in depth:

- Static websites
- Corporate or business websites
- One-page websites
- E-commerce stores
- Video blogs and photo blogs
- Social networks

Also, there are a number of new pieces of functionality that we have not explored in the previous chapters, and this is what we will be focusing on. These include the following:

- Designating a standard page to be the front page of the website
- Creating a custom post type with a custom taxonomy
- Altering the custom post type display in the wp-admin

Let's get started!

The must-do tasks

Even though there are many different types of sites that one can build with WordPress, there are some steps that are mandatory for all of them.

For instance, no matter what type of website you want to launch, you always have to start by installing WordPress properly. This is exactly what we talked about in Chapter 2, *Getting Started with WordPress*. Virtually, nothing is different at this point. The installation process is the same, all the steps are the same, and the final result is the same too--you end up with a clean, blank WordPress installation. Also, whenever installing specific themes and plugins, make sure to follow the same guidelines that we discussed in Chapter 5, *Plugins - What They Are and Why You Need Them*, and Chapter 6, *Choosing and Installing Themes*.

Last but not least, to ensure that your site is secure and has a good user management structure, you have to keep in mind all the best practices revolving around user accounts, and editorial workflow (publishing new content).

Basically, the only element that's different when building a non-blog website is the process of picking the theme and selecting the plugins for the site. Additionally, if you want to take it to the next level, you'll have to look into implementing various functionalities by hand or getting a custom solution made for you by a professional.

Luckily though, the process itself is not much more difficult than working with a standard blog. So once you have some experience with WordPress under your belt, you'll be able to get it done just as quickly.

Static websites

Let's start with static websites, as they are the simplest type of non-blog websites and, also, the easiest ones to create (which shouldn't be surprising).

The best part about static websites is that building them doesn't require any specific themes or plugins. The secret is your mindset as the developer. In essence, to pull this off effectively, the only things you need to do are the following:

1. Utilize the page's functionality in WordPress.
2. Tune up the default home page to create a more static experience.

The process

Firstly, let's tackle one common misconception. The point of a static website isn't to make the content hard-coded into the HTML or PHP files at all. The actual point is to abandon the standard chronological organization of content (to abandon the blog functionality) and to focus on building a site where pages exist on their own, independently of one another. So, in the end, we can still edit everything pretty easily through the wp-admin, and the only difference is that we're not using the standard WordPress posts for anything. Instead, we're focusing on the WordPress pages.

During the setup process of a good static page, you'll have to do the following:

1. Pick a WordPress theme that fits your goals and one that looks attractive for your particular project (something we talked about in `Chapter 6`, *Choosing and Installing Themes*); this is a mandatory step for all types of non-blog websites. Quite simply, not every theme will fit every type of website. So whenever picking a specific one, keep in mind what you want to use the website for--this is going to make your work easier as a developer and make the website better for future visitors once the site is launched.
2. Create a list of all static pages that you want to make a part of your website. For instance, for a local pet grooming service, the pages could be: gallery, offer and pricing, testimonials, contact, and map.
3. Create each page in the wp-admin (through **Pages** | **Add New**).

4. Create one more page, call it **HOME** and tweak it to provide a good home page experience. For instance, start by focusing on the elements that a first-time visitor would consider useful on your home page. A good home page should answer the question of "what is this site about?"

5. Create easy-to-grasp menus to make navigation a breeze.

Steps 1 to 3 are pretty straightforward, so let's just focus on the last two.

Building your home page

By default, WordPress takes the main blog listing (the chronological list of posts) and uses it as the home page. This is not the desired situation in our case since there will be no posts. What we'll do instead is create a custom page and then use it as a static front page (home page).

We'll start by doing something very familiar to us by this point--go to **Pages** | **Add New** and create a new page titled **HOME**. What you'll place on this page is up to you. Essentially, a home page should be a great starting page for anyone who visits a given site for the first time. For instance, I've decided to go with a short introductory message, a list of some popular articles on the site, a contact form provided by the **Contact Form 7** plugin, and an interactive map by *Google Maps*.

Once you have your page ready, the only thing you have to do is assign it as the *front page*. Navigate to **Settings** | **Reading**, click on the radio button next to **A static page (select below)** and select your new page as the **Front page**, like this:

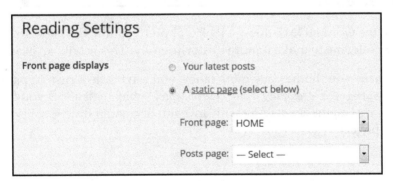

[337]

The other setting--**Posts page** is not important at this stage, as posts are not the focus of this particular project. When I go to my main website now, the home page no longer presents the standard listing. Now, I can see this:

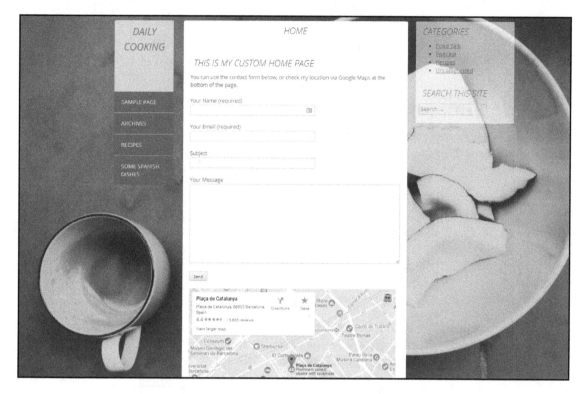

I have to admit, the word **HOME** doesn't look that pretty, but it's possible to change it to something like **Welcome** to make it more visitor-friendly. This is only an example.

If you want to make your home page more fancy, you can create a custom page template (described in Chapter 8, *Developing Your Own Theme*), which will allow you to include any design elements you might need along with a wealth of custom functionality. Again, it all depends on the project.

Creating easy-to-grasp menus

The last element of this static-website puzzle is a proper menu (or proper menus). Because our home page is just like any other page one can create in WordPress, it will appear in the default pages menu (pages widget), which isn't the most optimized situation.

Therefore, whenever working with static websites, make sure to use only custom menus created in **Appearance | Menus**. This gives you full control over what gets displayed either in the header, the sidebar, or anywhere else on the site.

Corporate or business websites

When we look at the main purpose of corporate or business websites, it becomes apparent that their construction is very similar to static websites. The only difference is that they are much bigger (more pages and more content), and their design seems much more official. Also, most businesses like to publish some occasional announcements, so a blog-like functionality is required too (but it still won't be the main element on the site).

In essence, creating a quality corporate site with WordPress is all about picking (or building) the right theme. If you do a quick bit of research on the web, you'll see that most corporate sites (at least the good ones) feature hardly any design. The thing that makes them stand out is their very subtle branding (through a certain color scheme or clever use of logos) and stellar navigation layout.

What this means is that the easiest way to build a great corporate site with WordPress is to do the following:

- Pick a clean theme with good content organization and featuring almost none of the design bells and whistles
- Include specific branding elements and pick the right color scheme
- Build a nice user-friendly navigation structure through custom menus
- Construct a custom home page
- Add one visual element in the form of a home page slider to make the site seem more alive (optional)

Let's go through this list one by one.

Picking a clean theme

This is something we talked about in the previous chapters, so let me just point you towards some of the top places where you can get WordPress themes real quick. They are: the official directory (`https://wordpress.org/themes/`), ThemeIsle (`https://themeisle.com/`), Elegant Themes (`https://www.elegantthemes.com/`), and ThemeForest (`https://themeforest.net/category/wordpress`). The thing to keep in mind is to go straight to the business-related part of the theme directory you're browsing. For example, at ThemeForest, go straight to `https://themeforest.net/category/wordpress/corporate`. This will make the selection process a lot quicker.

 Keep in mind that if it's a free theme you're after, you should always get it from the official directory (we discussed this in `Chapter 6`, *Choosing and Installing Themes*).

The features to look for in a quality corporate theme are as follows:

- Minimal design that lets you include your branding elements
- Easy way of adding a logo and other graphics
- Custom header functionality
- Favicon support
- Responsive layout (meaning that it'll be equally as attractive on a desktop computer as on a mobile phone)
- Widget areas
- Breadcrumbs
- Customizable sidebars
- Customizable layouts (for example, full-width, 1-sidebar, 2-sidebar, and so on)
- Multi-author support (there's usually a number of people taking care of a corporate site simultaneously)
- Built-in color schemes to choose from
- SEO compatible
- Custom page templates for home page, contact page, FAQ, offer, gallery, team, testimonials, 404 errors, portfolio, and so on
- Cross-browser compatible

Your theme doesn't have to do all of these things, but this list should be a good benchmark in determining how suitable the theme you're about to pick is when it comes to running a corporate site.

Branding elements

From a business point of view, branding is the most important parameter of a recognizable site. Therefore, make sure that the logo and the corporate identity of the company both match the color scheme of the theme. Also, as I mentioned in the previous section, a good theme should allow you to pick the color scheme from one of the predefined ones.

Finally, turn the logo into a favicon and upload it to the site too (this can be done through your theme's built-in favicon functionality or via a plugin like **All In One Favicon** available at `https://wordpress.org/plugins/all-in-one-favicon/`). This will give the site some additional visibility in the bookmarks menu (should the visitor bookmark it).

Good navigation

This is probably the toughest part of the job when building a corporate site, mainly because we can never be sure how much content the site is eventually going to feature. There's always the danger that our navigation will either be too much for a handful of pages of content or too little for hundreds of pages. There are, however, some good practices that you can follow:

- Focus on providing an extensive menu in the footer. This will make sure that every visitor will be able to find what they're looking for once they scroll down to the bottom of the page. This is easily doable with footer widget areas, which every good corporate theme should provide you with. Here's an example by Samsung:

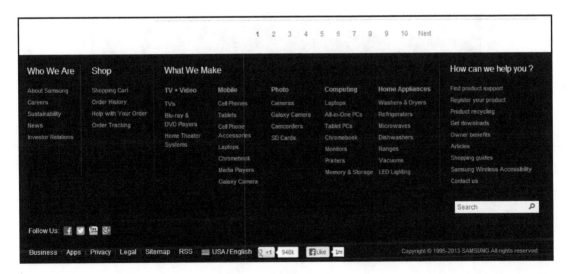

- Create a top menu with only a couple of the most essential pages. Sometimes, news and about will be enough:

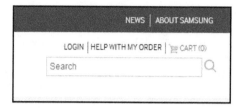

- Create a sidebar menu linking to the important areas of the site, like specific categories, products, announcements, or other things the average visitor might find interesting.
- Use breadcrumbs. Breadcrumbs are small links that present the path of the visitor in relation to the home page. Most themes provide this functionality by default. It's best to place them just below the header. That way, the reader can easily go back to a more general page. Here's an example (highlighted):

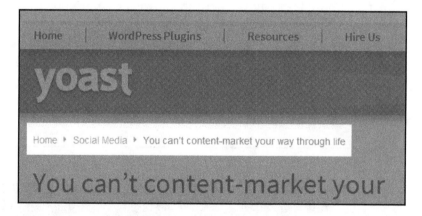

- Display a visible search field. A large number of visitors coming to a corporate site are after a specific piece of information, so they naturally start looking for a search field right away. Therefore, making their life easier is a very good idea. A good placement for a search field is in the header and in the main sidebar (sidebar menu) for good visibility.

Custom home page

Just as with static websites, the default blog listing rarely makes a good home page for a corporate site either. Going with a custom home page is always a better strategy and gives us a more optimized way of presenting the company, its goals, and its field of expertise. To create such a home page, you can safely follow the instructions given earlier in this chapter, when we were discussing static websites.

Now, like I said, showing the default blog listing as the home page is not a good approach here. We should provide at least some integration with the blog part of the website. The two most sensible solutions are to either link to a blog listing page in a visible place on the home page or include a simplified listing as a widget in one of the available widget areas on the home page itself.

The latter can be done by the **Recent Posts** widget that's available in WordPress by default (we covered widgets and how to use them in Chapter 5, *Plugins - What They Are and Why You Need Them*). The former can be done as follows:

1. Create a new page (**Pages** | **Add New**) and call it **NEWS**. The page doesn't have to feature any content. It only needs to exist with a unique name. I'm suggesting **NEWS** because it gives a clear indication of what's going on.
2. Navigate to **Settings** | **Reading** and set your new page as the default **Posts page**, like this:

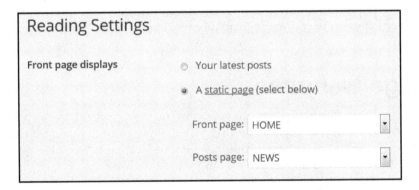

3. As you can see, there's also the old **HOME** page that's currently set as the **Front page**; we're going to leave it like that.

4. Place the link to the new blog section (**NEWS**) in the top menu (preferably). You can do it in **Appearance | Menus**.

5. Now, if you navigate to your new **NEWS** page (something like `http://yoursite.com/news`), you will see the default blog listing, which the company, the owner of the website, can use to publish various announcements or whatever else they see fit.

Slider (optional)

The last element worth discussing here is a home page slider. Although most corporate websites are not about the graphics, this single visual element is often added. Animated sliders make any website seem more alive and attractive to the visitor. For a corporate site, the slider can present photos from events, individual announcements, product offers, contact details, and a number of other things.

Some themes will come with a slider functionality built in right from the get-go. If they don't, you can always get a plugin to handle the job. The only downside is that most slider plugins are not free. Among those that are free, I can point out these two:

- **Master Slider**: `https://wordpress.org/plugins/master-slider/`
- **Huge-IT Slider**: `https://wordpress.org/plugins/slider-image/`

In general, sliders are not a mandatory thing for corporate websites, but they might improve the user experience, so they're probably worth a try.

One-page websites

One-page websites are a relatively new invention in the online world. A couple of years ago, webmasters were not that keen on having just a single page to make up their entire websites. It simply seemed like not working hard enough on your website's presence. These days, however, things have changed. It's no longer looked down on. In fact, single-page websites are the new trend.

In some way, a one-page or a single-page website is similar to a static website. You mostly get to work with WordPress pages rather than its blog functionality and after you set that page in place, it will likely stay that way for a longer period of time--it will remain static. On one-page websites, though, you simply get to work with only one page as opposed to having a number of them.

Just to give you a general overview of what a one-page site looks like, visit `http://karol.cc/`. It's my personal website, which I use to market my freelance writing services:

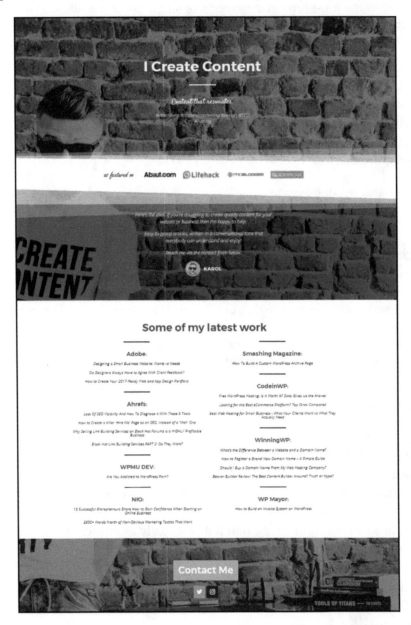

As you can see, the website is built up of just a single page--the home page. However, each block on that page is visually separated from the previous and the next one. This visual separation is one of the most important aspects of single-page websites. So as with many types of websites, creating a truly great-looking one-page site is about picking the right theme--something that your target audience will enjoy and appreciate. The easiest way to build a great one-page site with WordPress is to do the following:

- Pick a theme that's marketed explicitly as a one-page theme and has a clean design, with good-looking content blocks on the main page
- Include specific branding elements and pick the right color scheme
- Make sure to prepare a number of high-quality images, which you can use in the background

Let's go through this list one by one.

Picking a one-page theme

Just as with most other categories, one-page themes are now highly popular in most theme stores on the web. The best places to go include: again, the official directory (`https://wordpress.org/themes/`), ThemeIsle (`https://themeisle.com/`), and ThemeForest (`https://themeforest.net/category/wordpress`). Not all of them, however, feature specialized categories for one-page themes, so you might have to use the search option to find something interesting. Searching for terms like *single page* or *one page* should give you great results.

The features to look for in a quality one-page theme are as follows:

- Minimal design that lets you include your branding elements
- Easy way of adding a logo and other graphics
- Custom header functionality
- Parallax scrolling option (where the background images move by the camera slower than the foreground)
- Responsive layout (meaning that it'll be equally as attractive on a desktop computer as on a mobile phone)
- Widget areas
- Built-in color schemes to choose from
- SEO compatible
- Cross-browser compatible

The more of the preceding features your theme includes, the better. If anything is missing, you can always find a plugin that will fill the void. After all, there's a plugin for everything, remember?

Branding elements

Branding elements are particularly important with one-page sites because, by definition, you don't get much online real estate to work with, so to speak. If there's just one page on the site, you need to make sure that it's as in tune with your brand and identity as possible. Therefore, a good theme should allow you to place elements like your own logo, social media links, and custom graphics in places like the header, footer, and the background. Luckily, those sorts of features are considered the standard among modern WordPress themes, so you probably won't have to worry about this part at all.

High-quality images

One of the main flaws with one-page themes is that they often rely heavily on good visuals and high-quality images. The designs are often simple and very minimalist, and their attractive appearance is based on the images used in the background of the site. Unfortunately, finding such images is entirely up to you. Themes rarely come with unique images that you would be able to use on your site.

How to get those images? You can buy them in places such as `http://www.istockphoto.com/`, that's one solution. But, you can also get a lot of great images for free in places such as `https://unsplash.com/` or `http://mystock.photos/`. The last solution is, of course, to take your own photos and use them on your site.

As an example, I will get one of the most popular one-page themes in the WordPress directory right now--**Zerif Lite** (available at `https://wordpress.org/themes/zerif-lite`) and do some basic tuning up around it to show you how one-page themes work.

Right after downloading and activating the theme (standard procedure; see `Chapter 6`, *Choosing and Installing Themes*, for the how-to), you can go straight to the WordPress Customizer at **Appearance | Customize**. You'll see a large customization panel there. With it, I can change the main headline on the site, the following buttons, the appearance of individual blocks, and also the background image of the whole site:

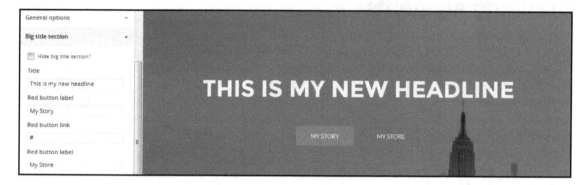

After a handful of tweaks, I end up with a great-looking one-page site. You can see what my final header looks like in the next screenshot:

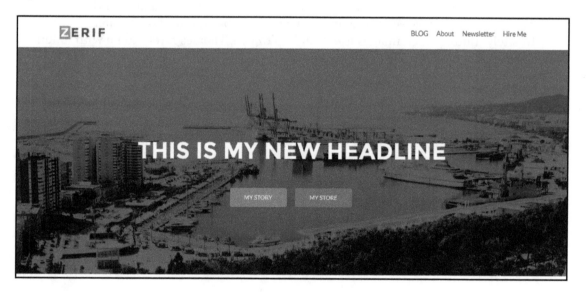

That's pretty much it when it comes to launching a nice one-page website with WordPress. The most remarkable thing here is how easy it is to actually do this. Just imagine how much time it would take to create something like this (considering the nice transitions and background-foreground interactions) from the ground up, or the cost required to set it up. The possibilities that WordPress delivers these days are really incredible.

Summary

We covered a lot of excellent material in this chapter. We started by listing some of the popular types of non-blog websites that you can build successfully with WordPress. Then, we went through some of those types individually and discussed the specific elements to focus on, in order to guarantee a quality final product.

The next chapter is part two of our guide to create a non-blog website. In it, we'll go through some of the more user-centered types of websites, such as e-commerce stores, photo and video blogs, and finally, building your own social network.

13
Creating a Non-Blog Website Part Two - E-Commerce Websites and Custom Content Elements

Let's get straight down to business here. In the previous chapter, you saw different types of non-blog websites. This chapter is a continuation of that topic, so let's do two things. First, let's go through some of the more trendy uses of WordPress and focus on a step-by-step process of reaching a great final result. Then, let's discuss some of the custom content elements you can create in WordPress, such as custom post types, custom taxonomies, and the process of customizing the admin display slightly.

E-commerce stores

E-commerce stores, in general, are websites where anyone can browse through a number of products and then use a shopping cart to make a purchase. Also, most e-commerce stores offer some kind of online payment integration, which allows every visitor to make and complete a purchase quickly. Additionally, sometimes there's even a backend inventory management system (an online warehouse of sorts) to make backend business management easier and integrated with the website.

Is WordPress a good platform for an e-commerce store?

The best thing about e-commerce is that you can actually launch a fully functional online store with WordPress. This, in my opinion, is simply incredible. As a former website developer, I actually remember how expensive and time consuming it was to build such a store from the ground up. And now, you can just install WordPress, get a proper theme, download a specialized e-commerce plugin, and you're good to go. This is a prime example of how technology meets the expectations of running a business the modern way.

Okay, enough with the intro. Now, let's focus on the actual process of building a quality e-commerce store. First of all, the thing with e-commerce stores on WordPress is that they are extremely plugin-driven, so to speak. What I actually mean is that if you want to launch such a website, you will need to get one main e-commerce plugin that's going to be responsible for the complete set of operations available in your store. In short, this plugin will run your store. For that reason, choosing the right plugin is extremely important, which is something I'm sure you understand.

Getting a good e-commerce plugin

There are numerous premium plugins on the market. They offer a ton of features and integrate with almost any online payment processing method possible. But, what's actually quite surprising is the fact that the most popular plugin of them all is 100% free. It's called *WooCommerce*, and it has become the *de facto* standard for running an e-commerce store on WordPress.

WooCommerce (available either at `https://woocommerce.com/` or `https://wordpress.org/plugins/woocommerce/`) is beautifully designed and offers a truly exceptional range of features, which I will get into in a minute. The main reason why I like the WooCommerce plugin so much is because it can be integrated with any theme. And I really do mean *any*. However, for a real-life business website (not just a test website, like the one we're going to build in a minute), I still think that you should use an optimized e-commerce theme. Again, feel free to visit one of the popular theme stores to get something of top quality. I listed a number of them in `Chapter 6`, *Choosing and Installing Themes*.

In short, a good e-commerce theme should:

- Have a clear design
- Present the center content block in an attention-grabbing way (this is where the products are going to be displayed)

- Allow you to tune the number of sidebars you want to display
- Be responsive (viewable on any device)
- Have a good navigation structure that's ready to house hundreds, if not thousands of subpages (product pages)
- Handle multilingual content
- Provide some level of social media integration (sharing product links on Twitter or Facebook)

Just to summarize this introduction, to set yourself up for a head start to run an e-commerce store on WordPress, you need to pair the WooCommerce plugin with a good-looking WordPress theme that's optimized to work on an e-commerce website.

Plugin installation and initial setup

To get WooCommerce, you can either go to `https://wordpress.org/plugins/` `woocommerce/` or install it straight from the wp-admin when you go to **Plugins** | **Add New**. Just input `WooCommerce` into the main search field. Most likely, the first plugin on the list is the one you're looking for. Click on **Install Now** and when the process finishes, activate the plugin. This is what you'll see afterward:

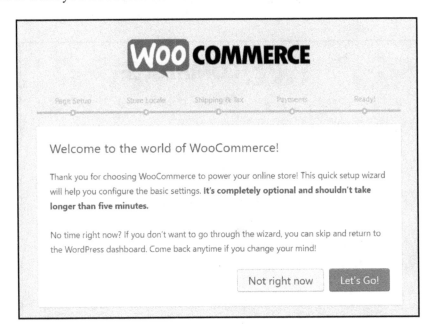

WooCommerce shows you the main page of the onscreen setup wizard. The best thing about it is that you're being guided through the whole process step by step:

Setting up the main store pages

Among the first things that you need to do is create some of the mandatory pages that allow your website to transform into a fully fledged e-commerce store. Luckily, WooCommerce takes care of this for you--all you have to do is click on the **Continue** button. Here are the pages you get:

- **Shop**: Your main shop page--this is where your products are going to appear
- **Cart**: The shopping cart area of the store
- **Checkout**: The area where your customers can finalize their orders
- **My Account**: Profile pages for your registered customers

Your store location

The next step is setting up your store location. This is quite simple, since you only need to select where your store is based and which currency it will use. Additionally, if you're going to be charging sales tax, you can set that up there too.

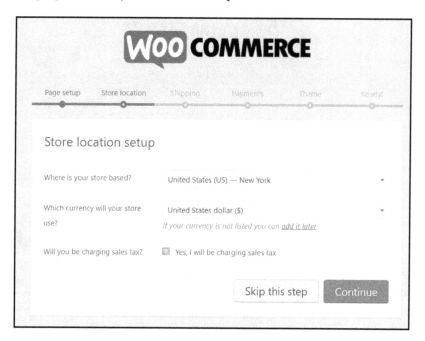

Shipping and payments

The next screen in the WooCommerce wizard is about setting up your shipping details, along with weight and dimension units. After that, you get to set the payment methods that your store will use. What you select there depends on the type of your store and the kinds of goods that you're going to be selling. Here's what's available:

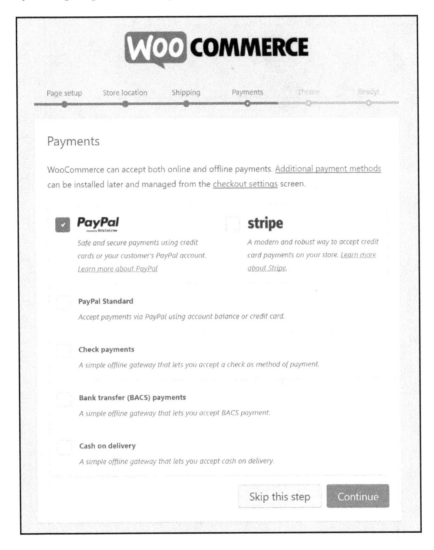

Usually, you will want to enable PayPal at the very least.

Adjusting your store design

The next step in the process, a very important step, is picking a design for your store. One of the best ways to get started here is to go with the official WooCommerce theme, called **Storefront**. This theme can be installed with a click on the right from the WooCommerce wizard, as follows:

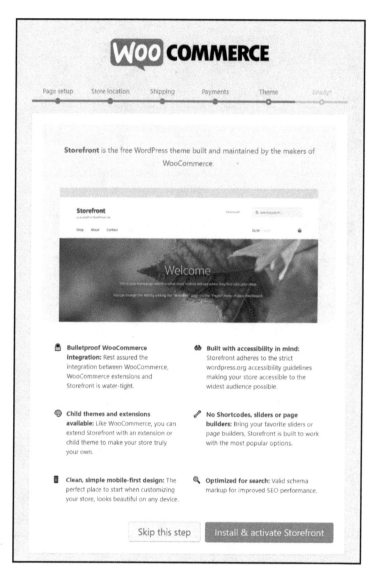

Once you get **Storefront** installed, the setup process is done and the store is fully operational, as in, you can begin adding your first products.

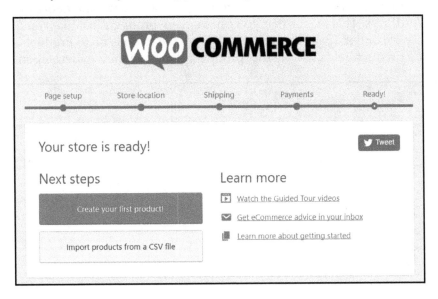

Adding products

When it comes to products, WooCommerce follows the standard content organization method in WordPress. This means that you can manage products just like you'd manage any other piece of content (pages or posts). All you have to do is go to **Products** | **Add New** and fill out the product fields. Notice that products also have their own categories and tags:

Once you have a handful of products added, this is what the **Products** | **All Products** section of your wp-admin is going to look like:

This is the main page of the store with all the products available to your customers:

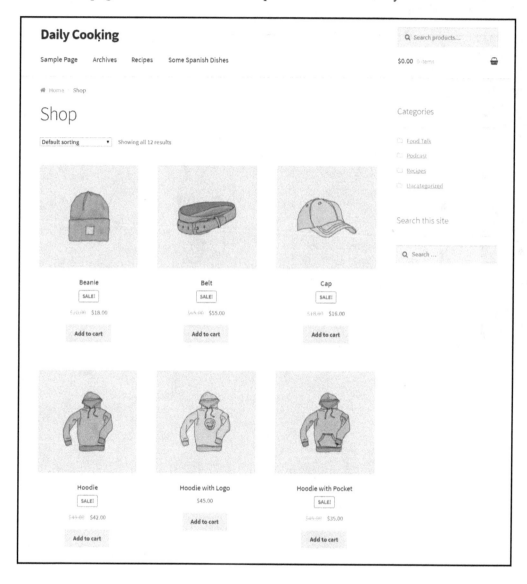

Each individual product also looks quite nice when you view it. Here's an example:

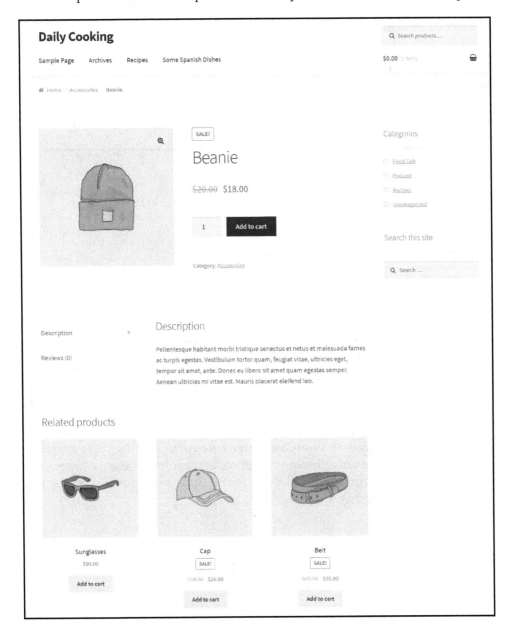

Stats – orders, coupons, and reports

The last element of the plugin worth discussing here for a minute is the management backend--the orders, coupons, and reports.

Orders can be found in **WooCommerce | Orders**. You can manage them just like any other piece of WordPress content. There are a number of additional fields and parameters, though, so there might be a slight learning curve. But still, a very friendly and easy to use environment. Here's an example of what orders look like:

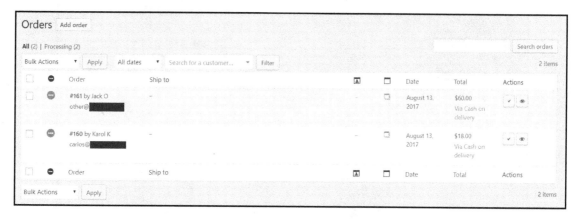

To view and create new coupon codes, navigate to **WooCommerce | Coupons**. Coupons are a great way to bring new people to your store. Everyone loves a bargain, don't they? Or, you can make your coupon codes publicly available on the internet as a promotional method.

Lastly, to view reports, navigate to **WooCommerce | Reports**. There's a nice graphical representation of what's been going on in your store. You can view sales, coupons used, customer activity, and your current stock. Right now, I don't have much going on in my store, so the graph looks like this:

To learn more about managing orders and coupons, look at these official pages in the WooCommerce docs:

- `https://docs.woocommerce.com/document/managing-orders/`
- `https://docs.woocommerce.com/document/coupon-management/`

That's pretty much it on the topic of using the plugin and launching a nice e-commerce store on WordPress. The most remarkable thing here is how easy it is to actually do it. Just imagine how much time it would take to create something with similar functionality from the ground up. Or, better yet, the cost required to set it up. The possibilities that WordPress and various plugins deliver these days are really incredible. I'm sure that a couple of years ago, no one would even believe that launching a quality e-commerce store could be done this easily.

One last thing, WooCommerce is not entirely free all the time. If you want to install additional features, the official extensions are anything between $29 and $99. So for some specific, real-world applications, investments might be required. Additionally, neither WordPress nor WooCommerce are optimized to work with multilingual content (including products in your store), so if you want to operate internationally and cater to customers speaking different languages, you might experience some difficulties with that.

We've only touched the surface here, and there's a lot more that WooCommerce can do. It is a truly impressive piece of software and it's absolutely exceptional when it comes to giving you reliable e-commerce functionality that turns your otherwise standard WordPress website into a professional e-commerce store. If you want to learn more about building a store with WooCommerce from scratch, probably the best place to get your information from is the official docs section at `woocommerce.com`. Specifically, `https://docs.woocommerce.com/documentation/plugins/woocommerce/getting-started/`.

Video blogs and photo blogs

Let's cover these two types of WordPress sites together because the individual goals for each are often very similar (although their designs may still be a bit different). In short, a video blog is one where the author mainly publishes videos, instead of traditional text-based posts. A photo blog, on the other hand, is essentially the same thing, the only difference being it revolves around photos.

Now, why would you even bother with a customized setup for a video blog or a photo blog in the first place when you can just use a standard WordPress installation with a traditional blogging-optimized theme? Well, to be honest here, you can indeed go with a standard setup, and your video/photo blog will be just about *fine*. But with some additional work (not much) put into building something that's tailor-made for multimedia blogs, your site can gain a big advantage over your competition, mostly in terms of usability and content presentation.

For instance, let's focus on some of the interesting features you can add to a video blog:

- Main blog listing built as a grid layout with big thumbnails, so every visitor can see the snapshots of the videos right away
- Videos in the main listing presented as concise blocks containing the thumbnail and a small amount of text to convince people to click on the video
- Wide main blog listing with just a narrow sidebar on the left (or right)
- Integrated social media features (including YouTube subscription buttons)

- Social media comments fetched from the platform where the video was originally hosted
- Custom backend to host the videos on the blog (or on an external server)
- Shareable embed code, so your visitors can embed the videos easily
- Custom player to replace the native YouTube or Vimeo players

And for a photo blog, some interesting features are:

- Custom home page featuring one main photo ("photo of the day")
- Automatic photo slider on the home page
- Lightbox functionality for viewing the photos in full size
- Wide main blog listing
- Integrated social media features
- Social media comments
- Custom backend to host photos
- Shareable embed code
- Custom photo controls (such as save, view full size, share, and so on)

As you can see, most of these features can work equally well on both video blogs and photo blogs. As usual with WordPress, you can get most of them either by obtaining a quality theme or using some third-party plugins. Let's cover both of these approaches.

Exploring themes for video and photo sites

Being quite popular kinds of blogs, both video and photo blogs have a very wide range of themes available on the internet. But, be careful! Searching for a theme on Google can get you in trouble. Well, maybe not in trouble per se, but if you end up downloading a theme from a random site, you have no guarantee that it's a secure solution and that there's no malicious or encrypted code inside. A much better method is to either go to the official directory or to some of the recognized theme stores.

For starters, let's check what's available out there:

- **Shapely** available at `https://wordpress.org/themes/shapely/`
- **TheMotion Lite** available at `https://wordpress.org/themes/themotion-lite/`
- **RokoPhoto** Lite available at `https://wordpress.org/themes/rokophoto-lite/`
- **Activello** available at `https://wordpress.org/themes/activello/`

The above are all free, but you can also get a premium theme. However, this will require an investment, so do it only if you're devoted to creating a really high-quality multimedia blog.

Getting plugins for video and photo sites

As I said, apart from video and photo optimized themes, you can also get a number of plugins that will make your site more functional. The good news is that we're only going to focus on free plugins:

- **WP Smush** (https://wordpress.org/plugins/wp-smushit/): This plugin doesn't present any particular output on the frontend of your site because what it actually does is automatically optimize your images in the background. This is a great plugin for saving your bandwidth, especially if you're publishing a lot of images. The installation process is quite standard. Once the plugin is activated, it starts working in the background with no supervision required.

- **Lightbox** (https://wordpress.org/plugins/lightbox/): This plugin delivers a really good-looking lightbox functionality. The best thing about this plugin is that it's ultra easy to use. All you have to do is activate it and it will immediately start taking care of the images you're displaying on your blog. The plugin will intercept image clicks and show the image file in a nice lightbox instead of loading them individually (on a blank page).

- **Envira Gallery** (https://wordpress.org/plugins/envira-gallery-lite/): This is one of the most popular gallery plugins for WordPress. It allows you to create responsive (optimized for desktop and mobile) photo and video galleries. The great thing about it is that you can build your galleries with drag and drop.

- **Instagram Feed WD** (https://wordpress.org/plugins/wd-instagram-feed/): Instagram is now a crucial part of any photographer's and/or videographer's presence on the web. This plugin offers you quick integration with everyone's favorite photo platform. Use it to showcase your Instagram feed as a widget.

Just to sum up the topic of multimedia blogs, I have to point out that this is a very crowded area among both theme and plugin developers. The plugins mentioned here will give you a good start, but having your finger on the pulse and paying attention to what's new on the market (cool new plugins and themes) is actually the best way to keep your photo or video blog on top of its game. That being said, getting and testing every new plugin out there is not the recommended approach. However, from time to time, you can find a true gem that's going to help you take your blog to the next level.

Social networks

Finally, it's time to discuss one of the most surprising topics in relation to building various types of websites with WordPress. As it turns out, the platform can be very well used to run a fully functional social network. In other words, you can have your own Facebook if you'd like to... at least when it comes to functionality.

And speaking of functionality, in short, a social network built with WordPress can offer the following features:

- Support for any number of user accounts
- Facebook-like publishing method for users (a "Wall" or an activity stream)
- Forums
- Blogs and microblogs
- Friends
- Groups
- Private messages
- Comments
- Photo and video content
- Much, much more

That being said, building and then running a well-constructed social network utilizing all of the available features will require some serious work. This is way beyond the scope of this book. So, here we're only going to focus on the basic setup process and getting started. If you're planning to launch an actual social network and make it available to the world, you should probably get more info, either by going to the official online documentation or obtaining some more publications on the topic.

Essentially, social networking on WordPress works through one specific plugin--**BuddyPress,** although calling it just a plugin is a massive understatement. BuddyPress is actually a whole online publishing environment on its own that integrates with WordPress. Unlike other plugins, it doesn't just display some custom content here and there. It actually changes the whole appearance (structure) of your WordPress site to make it look and operate like a social network.

Let's take the topic step by step, starting with installation.

Installing a social network

There's nothing fancy here, but all you have to do is either go to
`https://buddypress.org/`, download the main plugin and then upload it to your
WordPress site, or search for the plugin from within the wp-admin (**Plugins | Add New**)
using the name `BuddyPress`. The installation process of the plugin itself is quite standard,
meaning that after getting it on your server, you only have to click on the **Activate** button.
Right after doing so, you will see the following welcome screen:

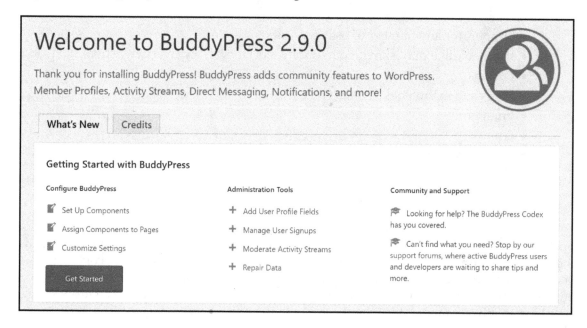

It's actually advisable to go through the information in this to get a basic understanding of
the platform and the things it has to offer.

Next, visit the settings section under **Settings | BuddyPress**. First, pick the components
you'd like to use in your new social network. For testing purposes, I just enabled all of
them:

Component	Description
✓ 🖼 Extended Profiles	Customize your community with fully editable profile fields that allow your users to describe themselves.
✓ 🗂 Account Settings	Allow your users to modify their account and notification settings directly from within their profiles.
✓ ⫴ Friend Connections	Let your users make connections so they can track the activity of others and focus on the people they care about the most.
✓ 💬 Private Messaging	Allow your users to talk to each other directly and in private. Not just limited to one-on-one discussions, messages can be sent between any number of members.
✓ 🐾 Activity Streams	Global, personal, and group activity streams with threaded commenting, direct posting, favoriting, and @mentions, all with full RSS feed and email notification support.
✓ 💡 Notifications	Notify members of relevant activity with a toolbar bubble and/or via email, and allow them to customize their notification settings.
✓ 🌸 User Groups	Groups allow your users to organize themselves into specific public, private or hidden sections with separate activity streams and member listings.
✓ Ⓦ Site Tracking	Record activity for new posts and comments from your site.
✓ 🅑 BuddyPress Core	It's what makes ~~time travel~~ BuddyPress possible!
✓ 👥 Community Members	Everything in a BuddyPress community revolves around its members.

The second tab on this settings page, titled **Pages**, lets you assign the pages that will house some standard areas of your social network such as the activity stream, user groups, member profiles, and so on. You can create new pages here or use the ones that BuddyPress has already created during installation.

Finally, there's the last tab, **Settings**, where you can adjust some of the other standard settings such as the presence of the top toolbar, various profile settings, and group settings. That's all about the main settings area. As you can see, the plugin is designed in a way that makes using it as easy as possible.

Designing your social network

In its current form, BuddyPress can work with any WordPress theme. That's right, you don't have to have an optimized social networking design if you don't want to. BuddyPress will manage to display its contents inside either the main content block of your current theme or the widget areas you have available.

However, as usual, if you want to make your social network look more professional, then you should probably look around and get something that's specially optimized for social networks. The best rule of thumb when you're searching for such themes, in my opinion, is to compare them against the biggest social network of them all--Facebook. Although some people don't enjoy the design that Facebook offers, it is still the most successful social network around, so they are clearly doing something right. Treating it as a benchmark of sorts is, therefore, a very good idea.

If you want to find a nice list of BuddyPress-compatible themes, the WordPress directory comes to the rescue yet again. When you go to `https://wordpress.org/themes/search/buddypress/`, you'll find a filtered list of themes that have been tested with BuddyPress and are optimized to work as a social network.

Once you've found yourself a nice-looking theme, you can go straight to working with your new social network without focusing any more on the setup. However, if you really want to get to know the platform and the way it's built, I advise you to go to the official documentation, which is one of the best BuddyPress resources available (`https://codex.buddypress.org/`). It's also where you can learn all the ins and outs of BuddyPress development, creating your own themes or even BuddyPress extension plugins.

Extending the functionality

BuddyPress is constructed in a way that provides the basic social networking functionality and site organization. If you want to extend your social media site and give it some new features, you can install a number of BuddyPress plugins. You can find them at `https://wordpress.org/plugins/search/buddypress/`. Basically, they are just like other WordPress plugins (the installation process is the same), but instead of delivering some new functionality to WordPress, they focus more on BuddyPress.

There is a lot more waiting for you inside BuddyPress, and I actually encourage you to do some researching and learning on your own, especially if you're planning to launch a social network at some point. But for now, I think that we've got the topic covered at least when it comes to giving you an introduction to social networking with WordPress and getting started with the best social networking plugin available--BuddyPress.

Introducing custom post types

While building some of the sites described in the current and the previous chapters, you may stumble upon what's called custom post types. Or you may even decide to create them yourself for the purpose of your individual projects. But let's take it from the top. The most commonly known types of content in WordPress are posts and pages. However, if we feel that the situation/project calls for it, we can create any number of new post types by taking advantage of the custom post type functionality and its wide versatility.

The need for custom post types can appear in many scenarios. For instance, when a writer is building a personal portfolio site, they might need a custom post type named **book** to present their publications in an attractive way instead of just using standard posts. This is exactly what we're about to do in this section of the chapter. So, gear up to learn how custom post types work by building a new one.

For this purpose, we'll go back to our main cooking blog theme--*Daily Cooking Custom*. In its default form, it doesn't feature any custom post types, and that's a good thing as we've got a blank canvas to work on. To specify that you'd like to have a custom post type in your theme, you can add some code to your theme's `functions.php` file. This is what we'll be doing. However, keep in mind that you can also attach the custom post type to a plugin or a widget if you don't want it to be tied to a particular theme.

Registering a new post type

To register a new post type, all you have to do is add some simple code to your theme's `functions.php` file. It's good practice to tie the creation of the new type to the `init` function of the theme so that it gets called at the right moment in the booting process. The initial, blank, custom post type code looks like this:

```
function book_init() {
  register_post_type('book');
}
add_action('init', 'book_init');
```

The `register_post_type()` function takes an array as its second parameter, and in that array, you can specify whether the object is public or should be involved in rewriting the URL, what elements it supports on its editing page, and so on. Let's set up an array of all the arguments and then pass it to the function. Now, our code looks like this:

```
function book_init() {
  $args = array(
    'description' => 'A custom post type that holds my books',
    'public' => true,
    'rewrite' => array('slug' => 'books'),
    'has_archive' => true,
    'supports' => array('title', 'editor', 'author', 'excerpt',
    'custom-fields', 'thumbnail')
  );
  register_post_type('book', $args);
  flush_rewrite_rules();
}
add_action('init', 'book_init');
```

I've chosen each of these parameters, because they make sense for the `book` custom post type. Let's take a look at them:

- `description`: This one's pretty self-explanatory.
- `public`: This means that the post type is available publicly, like how posts and pages, in fact, are, rather than being hidden behind the scenes. It'll get a user interface and can be shown in navigation menus, and so on.
- `rewrite`: This specifies that the post type can be used in the rewrite rules for pretty permalinks.
- `has_archive`: This enables post type archives (a classic index page like we can see for our standard posts).
- `supports`: This is an array of the capabilities which users see when they're creating or editing an item. For books, we're including six items.

The final function call, `flush_rewrite_rules()`, will allow us to show a standard archive listing of the books later on (just like a standard post listing but for our custom post type).

 These are just some of the arguments you can pass. Read about the others in the codex at `https://codex.wordpress.org/Function_Reference/register_post_type`.

Now that we've got the basic post type set up, let's add some labels.

Adding labels

You can add labels to your custom post type so that WordPress knows what to say when talking about it. First, let's simply create an array of all the labels. Put this as the first thing inside the `book_init()` function:

```
$labels = array(
    'name' => 'Books',
    'singular_name' => 'Book',
    'add_new' => 'Add New',
    'add_new_item' => 'Add New Book',
    'edit_item' => 'Edit Book',
    'new_item' => 'New Book',
    'view_item' => 'View Book',
    'search_items' => 'Search Books',
    'not_found' =>  'No books found',
    'not_found_in_trash' => 'No books found in Trash'
);
```

Then, add a single line of code to the `$args` array telling it to use the labels, as shown in the following snippet:

```
$args = array(
    'labels' => $labels,
    'description' => 'A custom post type that holds my books',
/* the rest of the function remains the same */
```

The next step is to add messages, which is what WordPress tells the user when they are doing stuff with books.

Adding messages

Whenever a user updates, previews, or does anything with a book, you'll want them to see an accurate message. All we need to do is create an array of messages and then hook them to WordPress. Here's the code for doing that:

```
function book_updated_messages( $messages ) {
    $messages['book'] = array(
        '', /* Unused. Messages start at index 1. */
        sprintf('Book updated. <a href="%s">View book</a>',
        esc_url(get_permalink($post_ID))),
        'Custom field updated.',
        'Custom field deleted.',
        'Book updated.',
        (isset($_GET['revision']) ?
        sprintf('Book restored to revision from %s',
```

```
          wp_post_revision_title((int)$_GET['revision'], false)) : false),
          print('Book published. <a href="%s">View book</a>',
          esc_url(get_permalink($post_ID))),
          'Book saved.',
          sprintf('Book submitted. <a target="_blank" href="%s">
          Preview book</a>',
          esc_url(add_query_arg('preview', 'true',
          get_permalink($post_ID)))),
          sprintf('Book scheduled for: <strong>%1$s</strong>.
          <a target="_blank"
          href="%2$s">Preview book</a>',
          date_i18n('M j, Y @ G:i', strtotime($post-
          >post_date)), esc_url(get_permalink($post_ID))),
          sprintf('Book draft updated. <a target="_blank" href="%s">
          Preview book</a>',
          esc_url(add_query_arg('preview', 'true', get_permalink($post_ID))))
      );
    return $messages;
  }
  add_filter('post_updated_messages', 'book_updated_messages');
```

This code creates a function named `book_updated_messages()`, which sets up an array of messages and returns it. We call this using the filter for `post_updated_messages`.

Now, our custom post type is ready to use! Go to your wp-admin and reload it. You'll see that a new menu has appeared under **Comments**. It's called **Books**. Let's add a book:

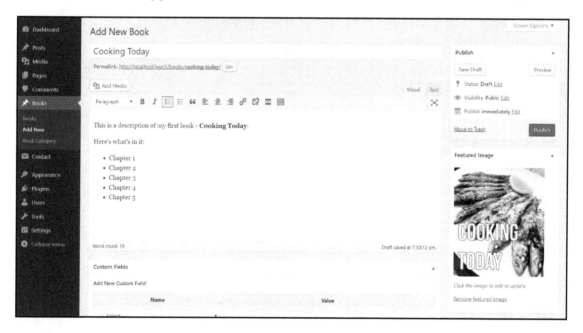

Note that I gave it a custom field named `book_author`, I also uploaded a featured image for the book cover. Now, when you go to the main **Books** page, you'll see the book listed. If you click on the **View** link under the book's title, you'll see the book displayed using the `single.php` theme template, which won't be the most reader-friendly experience. Therefore, let's make some new template files to display our books.

Creating book template files

WordPress needs to know how to display your new post type. You have to create a template for a single book and one for the listing of books.

First, we'll make a book version of `single.php`. It must be named `single-POST_TYPE_NAME.php`, which in our case is `single-book.php`. Using `page.php` as our starting point (as it's already the closest to what we'd like our book page to look like), we're going to add the display of the custom field `book_author` and the featured image. So, let's start by taking our `page.php` file, making a copy of it, and renaming it `single-book.php`. Also, let's make a copy of `content-page.php` and call it `content-book.php`. Next, it's time to include all the elements.

Here's what the two files look like. First, `single-book.php` looks like this:

```php
<?php
/**
 * The template for displaying a single book.
 *
 * @package Daily Cooking Custom
 */
?><?php get_header(); ?>

<div id="primary" class="content-area">
  <main id="main" class="site-main" role="main">
    <?php while (have_posts()) : the_post(); ?>

      <?php get_template_part('content', 'book'); ?>

      <?php endwhile; // end of the loop. ?>

  </main><!-- #main -->
</div><!-- #primary -->

<?php get_sidebar(); ?>
<?php get_footer(); ?>
```

The only change that's been made to this file is the `get_template_part()` function call. Next, the `content-book.php` file looks like this:

```php
<?php
/**
 * The template used for displaying book content
 *
 * @package Daily Cooking Custom
 */
?>

<article id="post-<?php the_ID(); ?>" <?php post_class(); ?>>
  <header class="entry-header">
    <?php the_title('<h1 class="entry-title">', '</h1>'); ?>
  </header>

  <div class="entry-content">
    <?php if(has_post_thumbnail()) : ?>
      <div class="post-image alignleft">
      <?php echo get_the_post_thumbnail($post->ID, 'medium',
      array('style' => 'border: 1px solid black;')); ?></div>
    <?php endif; ?>
    <?php echo '<p><em>by '.get_post_meta($post->ID, 'book_author', true).
    '</em></p>'; ?>
    <?php the_content(); ?>
  </div>

  <footer class="entry-footer">
  </footer>
</article><!-- #post-## -->
```

Now, let's take our custom field, `book_author`, and display it right below the featured image. We can do this by adding one new line of code in between the featured image code and the main content code, as shown in the following code snippet:

```php
<?php if(has_post_thumbnail()) : ?>
  <div class="post-image alignleft">
  <?php echo get_the_post_thumbnail($post->ID, 'medium',
  array('style' => 'border: 1px solid black;')); ?></div>
<?php endif; ?>
<?php echo '<p><em>by '.get_post_meta($post->ID, 'book_author', true).
'</em></p>'; ?>
<?php the_content(); ?>
```

At this point, when you visit a single book page, the author's name is displayed and the book cover shows up automatically:

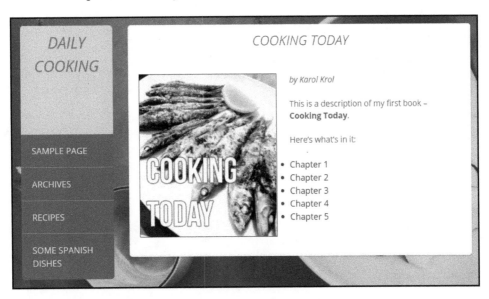

Our next task is a page that will show a listing of the books like what `index.php` does for the posts. By default, WordPress uses the `archive.php` file to show the listing of every new custom post type. We can customize this by creating a new template file and calling it `archive-book.php`. To be more exact, every template file controlling the archive for any new custom post type has to be named `archive-POST_TYPE.php`. The easiest way to create such file is by making a copy of the standard `archive.php` file or the `index.php` file and renaming it to `archive-book.php`. Then, we can take it from there and modify the file to fit our requirements. So what I'm going to do here is use my `index.php` as the template and do some tuning up around it.

Right now, my new `archive-book.php` file doesn't offer any custom way of displaying my books. Here's what it looks like:

```php
<?php
/**
 * The listing of books.
 *
 * @package Daily Cooking Custom
 */
?><?php get_header(); ?>

    <div id="primary" class="content-area">
```

```php
        <main id="main" class="site-main" role="main">

        <?php if (have_posts()) : ?>

          <?php /* Start the Loop */ ?>
          <?php while (have_posts()) : the_post(); ?>
          <?php get_template_part('listing', 'book'); ?>
          <?php endwhile; ?>

          <?php daily_cooking_custom_paging_nav(); ?>

        <?php else : ?>

          <?php get_template_part('content', 'none'); ?>

        <?php endif; ?>

        </main><!-- #main -->
      </div><!-- #primary -->

  <?php get_sidebar(); ?>
  <?php get_footer(); ?>
```

As you can see, the actual display is done by the `get_template_part('listing', 'book')` function call. In order to make this line work, we have to create the listing file itself. The simplest way of doing this is by making a copy of `content.php` and modifying it slightly. First, rename it to `listing-book.php`.

Right away, I'm going to erase some of the unnecessary sections and leave only those that can be used to make our books listing look great. Next, I will also include a thumbnail display. Quite frankly, I don't have to do this, but I believe that the book listing will look better with smaller thumbnails. Finally, I will also display the author of each book. The finished file will look like this:

```php
<?php
/**
 * @package Daily Cooking Custom
 */
?>
<article id="post-<?php the_ID(); ?>" <?php post_class(); ?>>
  <header class="entry-header">
    <?php the_title(sprintf('<h1 class="entry-title"><a href="%s"
    rel="bookmark">', esc_url(get_permalink())), '</a></h1>'); ?>
  </header>

  <div class="entry-content">
    <?php if(has_post_thumbnail()) : ?>
```

```
    <div class="post-image alignleft">
      <?php echo '<a href="'.esc_url(get_permalink()).'"
      >'.get_the_post_thumbnail($post->ID, 'thumbnail').'</a>'; ?>
    </div>
  <?php endif; ?>

  <div class="entry clearfix">
    <p><em>by <?php echo get_post_meta($post->ID,
    'book_author', true); ?>
    </em></p>
    <?php the_content(sprintf(__('Continue reading %s
    <span class="meta-nav">&rarr;</span>', 'daily-cooking-custom'),
    the_title('<span class="screen-reader-text">"',
    '"</span>', false)));
    ?>
  </div>
</div>

<footer class="entry-footer">
</footer>
</article><!-- #post-## -->
```

And here's the final effect (I've added one more book just for demonstration purposes):

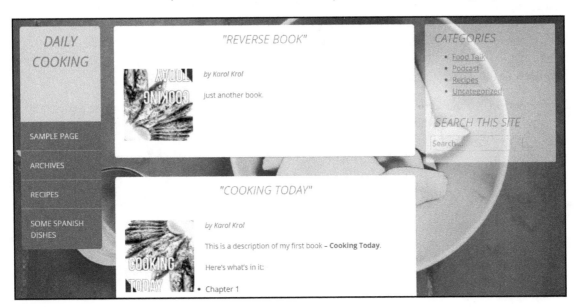

Registering and using a custom taxonomy

Just to follow the example given a while ago with our custom post type for books, let's now create a custom taxonomy. Essentially, you might not want to mix book categories and post categories, so we are going to create a custom taxonomy named **Book Categories**. Add the following code to your `functions.php` file:

```
function build_taxonomies() {
  register_taxonomy(
    'book_category',
    'book',
    array(
      'hierarchical' => true,
      'label' => 'Book Category',
      'query_var' => true,
      'rewrite' => array('slug' => 'available-books')
    )
  );
}
add_action('init', 'build_taxonomies', 0);
```

Like the `register_post_type()` function, the `register_taxonomy()` function allows you to register a new taxonomy within WordPress. You can read up on the details of all of the parameters you can add in the codex (https://codex.wordpress.org/Function_Reference/register_taxonomy). For now, you can see that we're calling it `book_category`; it belongs to the object type `book` and is hierarchical, and you can query it too. It needs to be included in the rewrite of URLs with a custom slug `available-books`.

Next, we need to make this taxonomy available to books. Simply find the `$args` array we used while registering the book post type (the `book_init()` function) and add the `taxonomies` item to the array:

```
$args = array(
  'labels' => $labels,
  'description' => 'A custom post type that holds my books',
  'public' => true,
  'rewrite' => array('slug' => 'books'),
  'has_archive' => true,
  'taxonomies' => array('book_category'),
  'supports' => array('title', 'editor', 'author', 'excerpt',
  'custom-fields', 'thumbnail')
);
```

When you return to the wp-admin and edit a book, you'll see that the book categories have appeared on the right, and they are also in the main navigation on the left:

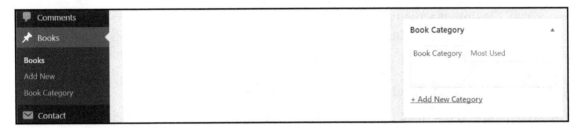

After you've added some categories and assigned them to the books, let's take a look at displaying those categories on the front of the website. First, we'll add them to the single book display. Open content-book.php and add this code in an appropriate place within the loop; for example, you can add it right after the the_content() function call:

```
<div class="entry-content">
  <?php if(has_post_thumbnail()) : ?>
    <div class="post-image alignleft">
    <?php echo get_the_post_thumbnail($post->ID, 'medium',
    array('style' => 'border: 1px solid black;')); ?></div>
  <?php endif; ?>
  <?php echo '<p><em>by '.get_post_meta($post->ID,
  'book_author', true).
  '</em></p>'; ?>
  <?php the_content(); ?>
  <?php echo get_the_term_list($post->ID, 'book_category',
  '<em>Categories: ', ', ', '</em>'); ?>
</div>
```

You're using the function get_the_term_list(), which takes the following arguments:

- ID of the post ($post->ID)
- Name of the taxonomy (book_category)
- Print before the list (Categories:)
- Separate items in the list with (,)
- Print after the list ()

Also, now that you have categories, you can visit **Appearance** | **Menus** and add links to those categories to your header menu, and you can also create a custom menu with all the categories and add it to one of the sidebars.

If you get a 404 error from WordPress at any point during the creation of your custom post type and custom taxonomy when you don't think you should, then navigate to **Settings | Permalinks** and just save the changes without actually changing anything. Sometimes WordPress needs to refresh the permalinks to make the new links work correctly.

Customizing the admin display

The final thing you can do to realize your new book custom post type fully is to change its display in the wp-admin. You don't need to know the WordPress user who created a given book, but you do want to see the book categories and the thumbnail. Let's go back to `functions.php`. First, we'll change the columns that are displayed:

```
function ahskk_custom_columns($defaults) {
  global $wp_query, $pagenow;
  if ($pagenow == 'edit.php') {
    unset($defaults['author']);
    unset($defaults['categories']);
    unset($defaults['date']);
    $defaults['book_category'] = 'Categories';
    $defaults['thumbnail'] = 'Image';
  }
  return $defaults;
}
add_filter('manage_book_posts_columns', 'ahskk_custom_columns');
function ahskk_show_columns($name) {
  global $post;
  switch ($name) {
    case 'book_category':
      echo get_the_term_list($post->ID, 'book_category', '', ', ', '');
      break;
    case 'thumbnail':
      if (has_post_thumbnail($post->ID))
        echo get_the_post_thumbnail($post->ID, array('40', '40'));
      break;
  }
}
Add_action('manage_book_posts_custom_column', 'ahskk_show_columns');
```

The first function says, *"don't show author, date, and categories, but do show book categories and thumbnail,"* and the second function says, *"for the book categories column, print the list of categories, and for the thumbnail column, print the* get_post_thumbnail() *function."*

Revisit the **Books** page in the wp-admin, and it now looks like the following screenshot:

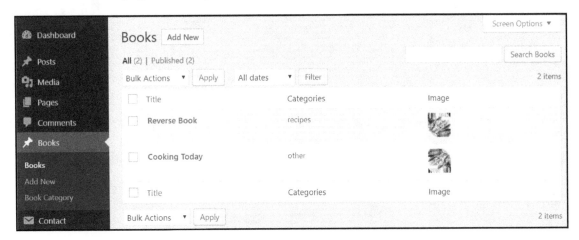

Summary

This chapter was part two of our non-blog website journey with WordPress. I hope you enjoyed the material. Here, you went through the process of setting up video blogs, photo blogs, e-commerce sites, and social networks. Along the way, you took a closer look at some interesting plugins and their functionalities, just to make your life easier as a WordPress developer. Finally, you created a custom post type and a corresponding custom taxonomy.

I believe that, at this point, you are well-equipped to work with WordPress and use it to build your next great website! WordPress is a top-notch CMS that has matured tremendously over the years. The WordPress admin panel is designed to be user-friendly and is continuously being improved. The code that underlies WordPress is robust and is the creation of a large community of dedicated developers. Additionally, WordPress functionality can be extended through the use of plugins and themes.

I hope you enjoyed this book and got off on the right footing by learning the process of administering and using WordPress for your own website, whatever that may be. Be sure to stay connected to the WordPress open source community! Thank you for reading; you rock!

Index

CPSIA information can be obtained
at www.ICGtesting.com
Printed in the USA
FSHW022337061219
64686FS